A Common Purpose

A Common Purpose

The Story of the Upington 25

A N D R E A   D U R B A C H

Continuum

NEW YORK · LONDON

2002

The Continuum International Publishing Group Inc
370 Lexington Avenue, New York, NY 10017

The Continuum International Publishing Group Ltd
The Tower Building, 11 York Road, London SE1 7NX

First published in 1999
Allen & Unwin

Library of Congress Cataloging-in-Publication Data

Durbach, Andrea, 1957–
[Upington]
A common purpose / Andrea Durbach.
p. cm.
Originally published: Upington. St. Leonards, N.S.W.: Allen & Unwin, 1999.
ISBN 0-8264-1330-7 (hardback)
1. Murder—South Africa—Upington—Case studies. 2. Trials (Murder)—South Africa—
Upington. 3. Upington (South Africa)—Race relations. I. Title.
HV6535.S73 U653 2002
364.15'23'09687—dc21
2002005340

Contents

For Max and Renee

I start with a disclaimer, as is the way of my profession. I have written this book with great reliance on memory. Some memories were more recent than others. Many had been pushed down and required excavation. Some took on new life and came back through interpretation. Others, failed to return at all.

While I have used diaries, letters, conversations, photographs, newspaper clippings and court transcripts and documents to resurrect the memories which fill this book, I have no doubt omitted reference to people and events which should feature and embellished facts without warranty. My apologies for any indiscretions on either count.

Preface

It has been a hard thing to do, this book. It came from a desire to tell a story about an extraordinary linkage of people whose course through life changed my own. And that was the difficult part. In telling their story, I unbundled my history and the events which brought me to them. With that unravelling came the exposure of the self, not confined to diaries or journals, but to be released in open print, where no self-conscious soul would think to tread. The story of loss of life, the loss of country eventually became too big to carry and the holding in stood in the way of my moving on. To admit pain, to declare loss, is perhaps the only way to shift. But it was all in my head, locked up, held like a fever determined to break. Writing the book became a way out of that impasse, stamping experience with an authenticity. I came to a reality with the writing, crossing a rickety bridge between head and heart.

Acknowledgments

My thanks to Anne McDermid who got me started a decade ago and to Sophie Cunningham who recharged the writing and kept me at it with enthusiasm and generous patience. To my production editor, Rebecca Kaiser, who softened the blows with warm insights and great care. For hunting down material and sending over essential supplies, my thanks go to my old firm, Bernadt, Vukic and Potash in Cape Town and especially to the late Allan Potash, and to Wayne Field and Fiona Zerbst. I am grateful also to Andre Odendaal and staff at the Mayibuye Centre at the University of the Western Cape for sifting through the archives and to my colleagues at the Public Interest Advocacy Centre (PIAC) who gave me time out to write.

To all the lawyers, experts and academics, diplomats, human rights workers, journalists and friends of the Upington 25 around the world, for maintaining excellence and pressure.

And to Anton, for bringing me to Upington.

Characters

THE DECEASED

Lucas 'Jetta' Sethwala murdered on 13 November 1985 in Paballelo, a black township in the town of Upington, Northern Cape, South Africa

THE ACCUSED

Accused No 1 Kenneth Pinkie Khumalo
Accused No 2 Eric Tros Gubula
Accused No 3 Abel Kutu
Accused No 4 David Lekhanyane
Accused No 5 Myner Gudlani Bovu
Accused No 6 Zuko Xabendlini
Accused No 7 Enoch Nompondwana
Accused No 8 Andrew Lekhanyane
Accused No 9 Elisha Matshoba
Accused No 10 Justice Bekebeke
Accused No 11 Zonga Mokhatle
Accused No 12 Ronnie Masiza
Accused No 13 Wellington Masiza
Accused No 14 Barry Bekebeke

Accused No 15 Boy Jafta
Accused No 16 Xoliswa Dube
Accused No 17 Elizabeth Bostaander
Accused No 18 Evelina de Bruin
Accused No 19 Gideon Madlongolwane
Accused No 20 Xolile Yona
Accused No 21 Albert Tywilli
Accused No 22 Jeffrey Sekiya
Accused No 23 Sarel Jacobs
Accused No 24 Roy Swartbooi
Accused No 25 Neville Witbooi
Accused No 26 Ivan Kazi

In April 1988, after a two-year trial, twenty-five of the accused were convicted of the murder of Lucas Sethwala on the basis of the common purpose doctrine. Under South African law at the time, a conviction of murder carried the sentence of death unless the court determined that extenuating circumstances were present. It is for this reason that the accused became known as the Upington 25.

The twenty-sixth accused, Accused No 7, Enoch Nompondwana, was charged with murder and convicted of attempted murder. His conviction did not carry a potential sentence of death.

THE UPINGTON SUPREME COURT

The Honourable Mr Justice Jan Basson with Mr R Kurland and Mr TJ Obbes (as assessors). Mr TJ Obbes died in July 1987 before the conclusion of the trial. The judge sat with one assessor, Mr Kurland, until the trial on conviction ended in 1988.

THE LEGAL TEAM FOR THE STATE FOR THE TRIAL ON EXTENUATION AND ON APPEAL

Advocate Terence van Rensburg
Advocate Jaap Schreuder

THE LEGAL TEAM FOR THE DEFENCE FOR THE TRIAL ON EXTENUATION

Advocate Ian Farlam SC

Advocate Anton Lubowski

Advocate Andre Landman (also counsel for the twenty-five during the trial on conviction)

Andrea Durbach (attorney)

Colin Kahanovitz (attorney)

Advocate Eben Boshoff appeared as *pro deo* counsel for Accused No 7, Enoch Nompondwana

EXPERT WITNESSES FOR THE DEFENCE

Professor Graham Tyson, social psychologist, head of the Division of Experimental Psychology, University of Witwatersrand, Johannesburg

Professor Martin West, Professor of Social Anthropology, University of Cape Town and Acting Head, University of Cape Town School of Social Work

Dr Herman Raath, clinical psychologist in private practice in Windhoek, Namibia

Professor Dirk van Zyl Smit, Director, Institute of Criminology, University of Cape Town

Professor Peter Folb, Professor of Pharmacology at the University of Cape Town and Chairman of the South African Medicines Control Council

EXPERT WITNESSES FOR THE STATE

Dr Johan Fourie, psychiatrist, in private practice in Bloemfontein, South Africa

Dr CP de Kock, sociologist, South African Human Sciences Research Council (HSRC)

THE LEGAL TEAM FOR THE DEFENCE ON APPEAL

Advocate Ian Farlam SC
Advocate John Whitehead
Advocate Les Rose-Innes
Andrea Durbach (attorney)
Stefan Raubenheimer (attorney)

THE APPELLATE DIVISION BENCH

The Honourable Mr Justice EM Grosskopf
The Honourable Mr Justice Smalberger
The Honourable Mr Justice Nienaber

Chronology of the trial

13 November 1985   Lucas Sethwala killed, Paballelo, Upington

13 October 1986   Murder trial of 26 accused commences in Upington Supreme Court before Mr Justice Jan Basson

27 April 1988   Upington Supreme Court convicts twenty-five accused of murder

The twenty-sixth accused, Accused No 7 Enoch Nompondwana, is convicted of attempted murder

Mr Justice Jan Basson orders trial on extenuation to commence on 2 May 1988

2 May 1988   Upington Supreme Court grants defence lawyers postponement to prepare for trial on extenuation to 1 June 1988

1 June 1988   Upington Supreme Court grants further postponement of trial on extenuation to 6 February 1989

6 February 1989   Trial on extenuation commences in Upington Supreme Court

23–25 May 1989   Judgment on extenuation

26 May 1989   Upington Supreme Court sentences fourteen of the twenty-five to death

1 June 1989   Evidence in mitigation of sentence for remaining eleven commences

2 June 1989 Upington Supreme Court sentences remaining eleven accused to jail terms or community service

26 June 1989 Application for leave to appeal convictions and sentences argued in the Kimberley Supreme Court before Mr Justice Basson

27 June 1989 Mr Justice Basson refuses leave to appeal

17 July 1989 Defence lawyers lodge a 3000-page petition to Chief Justice of Appellate Division for leave to appeal

5 September 1989 Chief Justice grants conditional leave to appeal to twenty-five accused

23 October 1989 Bail application made on behalf of five accused sentenced to imprisonment and death-row prisoner, Evelina de Bruin

Mr Justice Jan Basson grants bail to four of the five serving jail terms

30 November 1989 Record of appeal lodged with the Appellate Division

6 May 1991 Appeal hearing commences before Appellate Division in Bloemfontein

8 May 1991 Appeal hearing concludes

29 May 1991 Appellate Division delivers judgment

1

———————— • ————————

In the place
of my past

I was angry for weeks when I landed in Australia. Angry at the ordinariness, the lightness and the freedom from fear. It's only now, years later, that I can interpret and name the reasons for my miserable rage. Some years ago, however, in November 1989, I clung to a world that had shaped my apparent reason for being in it and, fearing release, heaved its baggage around with me. The top layer, tightly packed together in my African chest, held raw memories of twenty-five clients convicted of the murder of a policeman, fourteen of them sentenced to death and awaiting a reprieve or execution, and one of their counsel, and my treasured friend, assassinated. My way of approaching Australia in the initial years of my migration was to grind my small history deep into its landscape. What I had not anticipated was that I would knock rock each time.

It is true that I arrived from South Africa still wedded to a script in which I had a part. I knew the lines, the nuances, the set. I could read my audience and, if necessary, play into its hands. But as I began my life in Australia, so began my struggle to accept that my shift of location could not easily accommodate the story-line or characters of the text. I learned over time that what was required was a flexibility to view these two worlds as complementary rather than at odds with one another. In some sense, the resolution of the tension between South Africa, the land of my birth, and Australia, the country of my regeneration, mirrored the interior battle that I was to wage between the grand pull of the politics of a nation and the fundamental challenge of my own discovery.

I had grown up in South Africa with an abundant need to change its ways. This desire had no doubt stemmed from family and friends, from a cultural spirit which accompanied my own growth and from an anger with the obvious inhumanity of apartheid. In many ways, and maybe without my even knowing, I had cast my aim too high, disappointed when it finally moored out of reach. The fight for change, the urgent, saturated focus on the exterior world and its heady forces eventually caught up with me and pulled me back reluctantly, to face an unexplored and unattended self.

I was born in the Mother City, Cape Town, an exquisite, poignant place on earth that exerted an enormous influence upon my nature. I learnt about a life cast by shadows of deep-blue mountains—Table Mountain, Devils Peak, Signal Hill, Lions Head, the Twelve Apostles—and captured by the warmth of the Indian Ocean on the east and the cool Atlantic on the west. The open interaction of the colours of the landscape stood apart from the closed segregation of the colours of the people. We shaped our lives in a particular way to deal with that insanity.

Ours was a crisp white suburb. I grew up in a house called 'Good Morning' and went to an all-white, all-girls school. I came home to purple plum trees in blossom pruned by our coloured gardener, George, and a steamy kitchen and tea with Elizabeth Siboma, our live-in maid whose home was a thousand kilometres north in a Black *bantustan* called Transkei. Elizabeth was my confidante and my critic. She knew what was best for me without even saying. A simple look of distaste that squared off her face or one firm sound from her slow full voice would often lead to a change of friends or clothing. It was Elizabeth to whom I talked while she cooked rhubarb and lemon pudding or paired washed socks into flat balls of colour, before I told my parents of plans too bold for rash announcement. And when I discovered the pull of politics, I went to rallies and funerals with the proud comfort of being able to sing all the verses of the African national anthem, '*Nkosi Sikelel' i-Afrika*', written down and learnt phonetically, trained by Elizabeth Siboma who was available for instruction on ironing days.

My father was in timber and steel. He worked hard for a multinational, with offices in the Far East, as he called it, and on Saturdays he played golf religiously. He loved his garden and Dinkey, our favourite dog, with whom he walked in Newlands Forest. My mother was an artist of sorts, a doodler of unusual talent. She filled telephone message pads and the backs of envelopes with sketches of women's faces with long earrings and coiffured hair. Or high-heeled shoes, images reminiscent of pen and ink cigarette ads for sophisticated living. She worked initially in advertising, moving from drawing to writing copy and then wrote more seriously as a journalist. She had an old black typewriter with keys on bent steel stalks which clacked late at night while I read before sleep. As a writer, she did a bit of PR work, often for black artists and musicians who came to be interviewed and perform on our crowded *stoep*. I loved the drama of their arrival and how our house became the setting for a most exciting event, as if something hidden and precious was to unfold.

Neil, older than me by three years, gave me a hard time as brothers do. He drew in charcoal and oils and the walls of his bedroom were filled with life-sized drawings of Bob Dylan and Albert Einstein and numberplates from abandoned cars. He listened to Françoise Hardy and Alice Cooper and when the north winds blew, Neil and Tom Davies would wax their heavy boards and drag them into prime surf at Muizenberg Beach. That's where he wanted to be, even when I thought, in my politically precocious way, he should rather come to the airport when our cousin Bill, banned for political activities, was forced to leave the country on an exit permit.

From age six, I attended Greenfield Girls' Primary School. The school was housed in a small white building on an old estate with wide lawns and tended gardens and well-established trees. The Old House, which was the original estate property and first school-house, was where I liked to spend my time. It had a fireplace, a library, a projection room for film shows and a tuckshop, super-vised by Maggie, a pretty coloured woman identified on the school staff photograph as 'Mrs M. Windvogel (school maid)'. Our moth-ers ran the library and the thrift club, the lunch club and the lift club. I was nine years old and in the back of Mrs Krop's Volks-wagen when news of the assassination of our Prime Minister, Hendrik Verwoerd, came over the car radio. It was 6 September 1966. Mrs Krop stopped at the side of the road and we sat in silence and listened to the broadcast. A white parliamentary mes-senger, Dimitri Tsafendas, had stabbed Verwoerd in the House of Assembly. A leader knifed in the House, his sanctuary from the citizenry. I wondered how it could have happened and worried that it did.

The traffic slowed and there was a strange silence, as if the country had bowed its head in sorrow. I hated the apartheid which Verwoerd had refined. I hated the fact that he had hurt people whom he had classified as non-whites and non-South Africans. But I feared the brutal, desperate act of assassination and how it made me feel. Unsettled, exposed, unprotected from whim. I remembered the source of those feelings, how my mother and I had stood close to our grand radio in the dining room of Angelina Avenue when John F Kennedy had been killed three years earlier. We crouched next to the long polished wooden cabinet with doors and dials inside and a big square of white plaited wire from which came sound. I remember more the photographs in the *Cape Times* of John-John and Caroline. They were my height in their button-down coats and we were children with parents and I cried with them in their grief. I knew that Verwoerd's death would not bring change but only angry heels digging in. I wanted to talk but at that moment I sensed that Mrs Krop and my three friends from Standard Two may not have been the right company with which to explore hope for a new direction in our land.

Behind the school we played tennisette and netball on tarred navy courts. At half-time, we sucked on slices of orange and at close of play we had tea from silver urns with zoo biscuits or ginger snaps. I wore a school uniform, a green dress with a belt in summer and a shirt and tunic in winter. The Greenfield uniform was never an issue, but I loathed the panama (summer) and felt (winter) hats which completed the school costume. My hair curled and grew upward and outward—I would explain to curious schoolmates that my hair grew tall and fat, rather than down and long—and my school hat perched on my head, some distance above my crown. For this reason, my hat was often carried in hand. For bringing the school into disrepute by being hatless in public, I was sent to detention after school to write idiotic lines of repetition. 'I must wear my hat in public. I must wear my hat in public.'

High school followed a similar tradition. An all-girl, all-white, government school. But it was here, at Sans Souci Girls' High, that the sentiments expressed at home took some shape. Despite the intrusion of the hallmarks of apartheid at home and at school and its mad features which masqueraded as the norm, I was lucky enough to be punched by the meanness and vile brutality of the system. Along with this collision came the comfort of knowing that difference should be embraced and dissent declared. I made friends with girls who slowly revealed a similar unease with white privilege and a curiosity about how our nation had developed so out of step with the post-war world. I learnt to question, to speak with passion and savour the thrill of modelling an argument which could win. I felt the whirr in my stomach and then the subsequent delight when we dared to talk out loud about things that were wrong and unfair, taking a risk against keeping quiet. And I discovered failure and disappointment when I felt the mood of classmates sweep against me and I lost friends whose parents thought me trouble.

The process of learning created opportunity. I was in Standard Seven, year two of high school, and my friend Laura, two years ahead of me, smuggled me into her history lesson to watch a film on Mussolini. A brief study of fascism. The similarities with modern-day South Africa are amazing, Laura instructed. I hid beneath a table and sat glued, watching a good segment of the film undetected. When all were quiet with concentration, Mrs Murphy, my singing teacher, opened the door and asked if I was present. I squirmed out from behind a table leg to looks of indignation from older girls and dragged myself to singing class, hanging my head when I was told to lead 'Summer is a-coming in' in the round. I qualified as a comrade from then on and Laura invited me to Saturday-afternoon meetings at the flat of a schoolteacher from a neighbouring school. I met girls and boys from other schools and we read poetry and wrote prose and planned film evenings to raise money for black schoolchildren. Black schoolchildren, unlike their white counterparts at government schools, had to pay for their schoolbooks. From this group, National Youth Action (NYA) was established, a multiracial organisation of schoolchildren who would raise money for stationery and uniforms and books for children at black schools. NYA grew in size and had office-bearers and a news-sheet and I made friends from its ranks for life. I had joined a small movement, become a member of a collective at the age of fourteen and I loved the intensity with which we worked and played and the firm belief in our purpose.

In 1976, the year after I matriculated from high school, I travelled to America as a Rotary exchange student. I had never been overseas before, beyond the borders of the pure white way, of Afrikaner Calvinism and Christian national education. I lived on Long Island and watched television for the first time. (In 1971, the South African government had sanctioned the introduction of a television service and advised that operations would begin in 1976, with separate channels for whites and 'non-whites'. My father bought a small portable black-and-white set which stayed the family set for years, a symbol perhaps of the faith my parents had in those who controlled the service to lift the country from its insular life.) I attended school on the Island and found that a tough initiation. I was a white South African and 1976, the year of the Soweto riots and large-scale police shootings, was a year when the savagery of apartheid was writ large across television screens and newspapers throughout America. It took time for many in my school to feel comfortable with me around, to look a white South African in the eye. It took much longer for me to shed the responsibility I harboured for those who ruled my country.

I travelled the Long Island railroad into New York and rolled about in the city's thick layers, amassing books which we couldn't read at home and 'hanging' in the Village and listening to black musicians play their jazz. Bolstered by fresh experience, I let go of the clamp of self-censorship and spoke my mind before a group of ninth-graders at Eastport High School and a visiting journalist from the Long Island daily, *Newsday*. I forgot about this simple dalliance with freedom of speech until, soon after my return to South Africa, just before I was to start my law degree at the University of Cape Town, I was visited by two men from the South African Security Police. They came to warn me, a failed ambassador for my country, about the dangers of what I had said. They produced a copy of the short article with my offending quotes. What irked them were a few short sentences: 'I went to an all-girls school by choice, and an all-white school by law...Apartheid is a ludicrous system that suppresses 80 per cent of the population which is black. It is an absurd situation and I have always been opposed to it.' These words, they growled, had placed the chances of prospective exchange students and my future as a lawyer in considerable jeopardy. After the police left, I remember feeling confused by my own response. I was stung by the impact of intimidation, opting for safety and attempting a show of remorse, then prodded by a strong belief in simple truth. If nothing else, the visit marked my introduction to the reaches of the state.

•

There are few incidents which happen early in one's life that remain in sharp focus for years to come and perhaps even fewer that mould the choices we make for our middle life. Many images of cruelty and hurt of white against black filled my formative years but one event opened my mind to the possibility of living beyond the hatred, of fashioning the spaces for the new South Africa.

I was eight or nine and adored my cousin Bill. He was a professor of medicine at the University of Cape Town and lived in a house at the top of a hill, filled with laughter on hot New Year's Eve nights with sparklers and catherine-wheels and people who talked of politics and foreign lands. Bill spoke out against the government once too often, he took the Minister of Justice to court and then one morning we were told he'd been banned and placed under house arrest. Suddenly this man of generous spirit, with a love for humanity and a harmless irreverence, was shut down. From then on, an unmarked white Volkswagen beetle circled his house each day to watch that visitors and family saw Bill one by one, in accordance with his banning order. I was a child who yearned to see him, to hear his voice and laugh, but time was precious and visits rare and kept for those who talked the language of covert plans to flee.

The day Bill left the country on an exit permit, a stuffy *berg* wind blew, lifting the quiet heat from the mountains as we drove in silence past the townships to the airport. Crowds lined the tarmac at the start of the runway, and high above the airport building, leaning over observation railings, hundreds with black armbands swayed in song. 'We shall overcome.' I stood close to Bill and his family, my family, and watched him say goodbye with grace as policemen and their muzzled dogs barked at people to make way. Beads of sweat trickled down Bill's face and he smiled as if to make it better. I turned to my father and saw a policeman in khaki uniform and cap approach. He greeted my father and I froze as he began to speak: 'It will be good when we get this bastard out [of] the country.' My father stared ahead. I felt his rage bubble as he took my hand and said, 'I'm sure, so that you can get back to bashing heads'. It seemed an odd retort from my father, almost childlike, and I felt afraid at what it might elicit from the bully in khaki. The policeman glared at us and moved on.

'This bastard.' This man who fought for simple justice, who loved his country with deep affection and resisted those who harmed its citizens because of the colour of their skin. 'This bastard' who was silenced for reminding us of the evil that men do. I think Bill, the bastard, was the reason I studied law.

•

The University of Cape Town was built into the nape of Table Mountain. A beautiful, sweeping campus steeped in classical architectural tradition, it felt special but incongruous, out of place. Turning on to campus from De Waal Drive, the freeway into town, often felt like arriving on an elaborate set for a long-running play. And so it was. Contained by avenues and mountain backdrops, we stepped inside and created our own theatre amidst the teachings that were on offer. We understood and accepted that politics was central to our lives of learning and we balanced courses like Roman Law with intense extramural activity. We read banned books and journals and produced newspapers and posters declared unlawful by the government's Director of Publications. We joined Students for Social Democracy and sat in smoky meeting rooms watching for the spy. We argued and read through the night and marched and stood in protest, shouting out our anger at police with gasmasks and batons who stalked our moves, waiting for their signal to cross the line. We watched friends dragged by their hair into yellow police vans, others beaten across their breasts and we boycotted products and sent letters to the editors of daily newspapers.

In the winter months, we walked to the tearoom behind the campus, along mountain slopes of blue and silver trees and damp brown pine needles, away from lecture halls and Latin. We ordered hot chocolate and sat close to a small log fire packed with crackling pine cones and talked things out. We climbed stairs to the giant stone piazza of Rhodes Memorial, with its temple-like columns and bronze lions on terraced steps, dedicated to Cecil John and his vision for a civilised South Africa. Above the sprawling peninsula, we stood on top of the world and watched the city breathe. Dragged back by the clock, we'd run down the hill and slide into hours of translation from Pliny and Ovid and readings from Afrikaans literary history and try to fit the teachings of Roman–Dutch law to an African land. As we learnt about the law and its practice in South Africa, the principles and essentially liberal ideals for which it stood and for which we fought seemed frequently diminished by legislative enactments of government and the interpretation of that law by our courts.

In the Law Faculty Common Room we would question whether the practice of law in South Africa would retard rather than advance progress towards social justice. We would worry about earning our keep from working with laws which propped up the system of apartheid. Was working within the system not tantamount to our justification of it? Friend and law lecturer, Dennis Davis, reminded us of cases where sound legal principles had been approved by the courts and government action and unjust laws reversed. He exhorted and inspired us to use the law creatively, to exploit loopholes and ambiguities in legislation and occasion opportunities for justice. And so we moved between a loathing for the law and a belief in its potential to wedge open cracks in the fortress of apartheid which hinted at its demise.

Some years later, Dennis and I went to see the movie of Andre Brink's *A Dry White Season*. Marlon Brando played the liberal white lawyer representing a black woman at the inquest of her husband—an alleged suicide in a cell at John Vorster Square Police Station, Johannesburg. At the beginning of the inquest, Brando warns his client, 'Justice and law are distant cousins and here in South Africa they are not even on speaking terms'. I had been in practice as a lawyer for seven years, working with trade unionists, students, journalists and anti-apartheid activists. We had achieved some victories in the courts and the application of harsh laws and conduct may have been restrained as a result. Often legal remedies, however, remained symbolic, having little chance of enforcement. The overriding scale of hardship and harm and the enormity of damaged lives endured barely dented. After the movie, I remembered Brando's line and added that I thought it was still applicable despite witnessing the use of law in effecting change. Although I did see politics mould the law and insinuate social change, and I believed in the value of the use of law to effect transition, sometimes fatigue set in and undid the optimism of triumph so that I sided with Brando's character and doubted any familial ties at all between justice and the law.

•

One midyear varsity holiday, I came into direct contact with the law and its threatening application. I had driven with friends to the small neighbouring kingdom of Lesotho where we were to stay with some Peace Corps associates. We had planned to meet with law students at Roma University outside the capital city, Maseru. Amongst our luggage, we had packed boxes of our student newspapers and other material for the meeting. At the border post, South African police searched our car and found copies of what they declared to be illegal publications. Banned, they told us, for possession and distribution in terms of the Internal Security Act. Later, at the court case, no conviction followed. The vigilant police had overlooked a small technicality: the banning of the publication had been declared in the *Government Gazette* on the day after the police had laid the charge. No charge could arise before gazettal. Without this knowledge at the time, our sojourn in Lesotho was filled with anxiety about our impending court case and fears of criminal convictions and records. Despite this initial confrontation with the law, we continued to take risks, swept along by some imperative to exact political mileage from each new meeting and experience.

Lesotho was an odd country, a compact independent nation landlocked by South Africa, with a liberal air sufficient to offer shelter to anti-apartheid workers, exiles and Dutch Reform sinners who crossed the border to gamble and slink into blue-movie screenings illegal in South Africa. We met with students from the banned African National Congress (ANC) and attended a rally at a church hall filled with anti-apartheid refugees and activists and openly raised our fists in salutes to the people and freedom. We bought books by Mandela and Lenin which were banned in South Africa, copies of *Marxism for Beginners* and collections of speeches by Che Guevara and Martin Luther King. One afternoon we spent hours wrapping them in brown paper and addressing the packages to dead relatives and unknown people with Afrikaner names at our Cape Town addresses. Despite our elaborate efforts at camouflage, the packages, which looked awkward at best, were intercepted and never arrived.

It was a holiday that lived on for many months. Two of our party, who travelled separately, were caught at the South African border with potato sacks of *dagga* in the boot of their car, a present from friends on a farm in the Basotho hills. Next came our victorious trial regarding the illegal possession of a publication not yet banned and deemed unlawful. And a few weeks later, we all received visits from the security police about our meetings and purpose in Lesotho. The *boere* who visited me sat in the lounge of my parent's home, charming and firm. One of them was dressed in a baby-blue safari suit, the kind with long pants. Both carried swinging, weightless black attaché cases which they placed on a table near where I was sitting, an obvious signal that tape recorders formed their contents. They knew a fair amount about our movements in Lesotho, at times more than I could remember. Fifteen minutes into the interview, Elizabeth Siboma, who had hovered with my mother just beyond the door to the lounge, came in to the room with a tray of tea and biscuits. She pushed an attaché case to one side of the table, out of hearing range, to make room for the tray and stared long and hard at our guests. My mother, slightly hysterical from the stress of the morning visit, skipped in to be helpful and pour the tea. She glided over to the man in blue to offer milk and sugar. Captain Vermeulen held out his cup and my mother, determined to hold eye contact with the captain, gently poured the milk on to the top of his thigh, emptying the jug a tiny distance from his teacup. As he sat, a dark-blue stain began to emerge along his inner thigh. As interrogations went, it was probably one of Vermeulen's least favourite.

2

•

Coming to the law

Contrary to an earlier expression of will that I could never practice law in South Africa, I joined the Cape Town law firm Frank, Bernadt and Joffe (later renamed Bernadt Vukic and Potash) as an articled clerk in 1984. The firm's history was attractive and I knew some of its younger attorneys from our days of student politics. My parents had often spoken of their friends, Jean and Hymie Bernadt, Mr Bernadt being one of the firm's founders. I knew that in the firm's early days, the 1950s and 60s, Mr Bernadt had taken on work primarily for anti-apartheid activists and organisations and, despite the firm's growing commercial practice, it still carried an impressive reputation as being one of the few white firms in the Cape committed to doing political work. When I joined the firm, Mr Bernadt had been in practice for close to forty years, and his links with the progressive trade union movement, with anti-apartheid groups and individuals and overseas agencies which funded political trial work were well established.

It was in Mr Bernadt's office, as an articled clerk, that I learnt about the rich tradition of political trial lawyers in South Africa and those who had left as exiles. His office was filled with bulging files—on the floor—piled high on filing cabinets—with names across the top written in his hand, names from a clandestine past

which would stand tall in the future. For as long as I worked at
the firm, each month Mr Bernadt would visit Nelson Mandela at
Pollsmoor Prison, where he had been transferred from Robben
Island. It was unimaginable then that any of us would come to
know of Mandela outside of prison walls and I looked forward to
Mr Bernadt's post-visit tales. He would comment on Mandela's
extraordinary range of discussion, on law and books of fiction, on
current world events and political tides and leadership. One image
which stayed in mind and one which Mr Bernadt would relate
with remarkable consistency was the elegance of this prisoner and,
in particular, the ever-present crease in the trousers of his prison
uniform, as if steam-pressed for each visit.

Throughout my six extraordinary years at the firm, and particularly in the latter time when I was working on the trial of the
Upington 25, I would seek Mr Bernadt's counsel on the complex
interplay of legal rules, trial strategy and ethical standards thrown
up by political trial work. By that time he was close to eighty and
had become a consultant to the firm, but his wisdom and insights
and his tough-minded approach to ensuring that justice emerge
from legal pursuit, were crystal clear and fortifying.

My mandatory two-year period of articles with the firm started
as most did. Uncontested divorces, debt collection, brief appearances in magistrate courts, stamp duty calculations and drafting
of wills and simple pleadings. My initial trial work involved haphazard representation of men and women who had sought work
and family reunion in urban centres in breach of the Pass Laws
which relegated black people to impoverished homelands. Against
clear principle, but not yet able to chose work on that basis, my
earliest achievement was securing the reclassification of a 'coloured'
client to her preferred race, 'white'. This was a complicated procedure permitted under the Population Registration Act at great
emotional and financial cost to the applicant. With extreme seriousness of approach, I collected references from her school
headmistress, her white friends who were able to testify that she
'behaved like a white person', and from her employers, who said,
'In all honesty, we thought she was a white'. Inspectors from the

Department of Home Affairs surveyed her in different environments, speaking to her co-workers and neighbours to gauge how well she fitted in with white society. Months later, my client was designated 'white'. Her elation was short-lived as she over-extended her quest for acceptance into racist society. She insisted that both her first and last names sounded 'too coloured' and she instructed us to apply for a change of name. The first name she took from an American soap opera, while the surname of Greek origin she remembered from a newspaper report some years earlier. It belonged to a leading criminal who had cleaned up across South Africa, a highly regarded swindler, but he was white and that was all that mattered.

I quickly discovered my lack of interest in matters commercial and found dull the collation of balance sheets and prospectuses and the dreary analysis of contracts and annexures stored in airless boxrooms of city buildings. Rather, I revelled in litigation which involved the behaviour of people and their engagement with life. Ultimately, it was the political context for behaviour and the combination of forces that compelled people to act in certain ways which drew me towards the use of law to negotiate power and balance rights. I was lucky that my interests and the work that came my way coalesced. With the backing and commitment of senior partners in the firm, I was able to work almost entirely for clients who faced prosecution for political activity, for those who challenged government decrees and for workers or trade unions in their fight for labour rights. There is no doubt that initially the commercial wing of the firm, which had a strong and growing reputation, sustained our human rights work to a great degree. This work, however, could not have been maintained without the defiant dedication of anti-apartheid overseas funders and aid agencies which financed a 'human rights industry' within the country.

During the early 1960s, legal assistance for the conduct of political trials was provided by the International Defence and Aid Fund for Southern Africa (IDAF), established in London as a humanitarian organisation dedicated to constructive opposition of injustices of apartheid. The objects of the fund included the defence of victims of unjust legislation and arbitrary procedures and support of their families and dependents. In 1966, the organisation was declared unlawful under the Suppression of Communism Act and banned by the South African government. With the strengthened resolve of the fund's initiators and the assistance of creative lawyers like the London-based South African lawyer, Bill Frankel, IDAF was resurrected in a different guise. An elaborate network of dummy trusts was created and a legal aid fund was subsequently administered from abroad with contributions from sources in Britain, North America and western Europe, including Sweden, Denmark, Germany and Holland.

The original objects of IDAF continued to determine how the the funds were utilised. Primarily, they were provided to cover the fees of attorneys and advocates who defended victims of apartheid laws and to ensure and enhance the welfare and educational needs of the victims and their families. The assistance to the families was provided using a pen-friend model: friends in various countries, approached by administrators and supporters of the fund, wrote to families in South Africa. The writers would express concern about news of a trial or imprisonment of a member of the South African family. They would offer moral and financial support, often enclosing banknotes or drafts in the letter, supplied to the writer from the IDAF trust. The pen-friend would continue to write letters and offer support for as long as the South African family required help. And for years after, friendships were maintained via Christmas cards and photographs and visits, where resources could be found. It was this magnanimity which underwrote much of our work for anti-apartheid activists and the casualties of white rule.

My work as a lawyer in 1980s South Africa was full and exhilarating. It was an exceptional period when the law was resurrected as a respectable political weapon and held a surprising credibility. I think we knew that the wave of legal activism during this time would inevitably recede. When this happened would depend on a combination of factors—the receptivity of certain judges to uphold the rule of law despite the intent of legislation and the ability of international and domestic forces to prolong political and economic pressure on a repressive state. But for the moment, we rode the wave until history took us on another course and a new cycle forced a change of approach and emphasis. It was work that I never imagined work could be, and it was all I ever wanted to do. I loved its dishevelled energy, its contradictions, its immediacy, and through it, I made an entry into a world largely kept at bay. Each day brought mysteries and challenges, some of them frightening, many of them defying the boundaries of my own experience. I walked into lives of deep inhumanity, of terror and broken spirits and I witnessed a parallel capacity for enthusiasm, humility and faith. It was my own initiation and it took me away from myself and tested the character of my soul. And with the heat of those experiences, came a toughening up and an insidious easing into a self-made suit of armour.

When you trace contemporary South African political history, almost every year can be described as tumultuous. As a new lawyer representing clients charged under rambling laws and regulations which shored up apartheid rule, 1985 seemed intensely dramatic, filled with a rapidly escalating chaos. Almost every month that year we were called onto the University of Cape Town campus during battles between students and police, tear-gas still spiking the air, or to various police stations to arrange bail applications for students who had attended demonstrations deemed illegal under the Internal Security Act. Journalists demonstrated against curbs on the media, police broke up peaceful gatherings and candlelight vigils and scuffles and violence led to compounded charges of assault. When a young coloured boy died while in police custody, white middle-class mothers padlocked themselves to the gates of Parliament and foreign television crews were arrested for filming police tearing the mothers from their chains. More and more, children became targets of police brutality, and their retaliatory stone-throwing or *klipgooi* gave rise to hundreds of charges of public violence.

I left in a hurry early one morning to travel to a country town almost two hours east of Cape Town to represent schoolchildren on public violence charges. If guilty of the offence, they faced up to twelve months in jail by a local magistrate who was apparently intent on cleaning up his *dorp*. In my rush, I had left my black court gown in my office. There was a firm of attorneys across the road from the magistrate's court. The one attorney present in the office that morning was a very helpful, gentle giant. I could borrow his gown but being over six feet tall, he warned it would be long. I was met at the court by close to fifty anxious parents and as many children waiting for my appearance on their behalf. I slipped my arms into the gown sleeves which fell way below my fingers and tried to balance its frame on my shoulders, the remainder falling in endless folds onto the ground. I sat behind the bar table and placed my files to one side. The magistrate, a crisp white man of middle years, asked, in an incredulous tone, if I was representing the accused. I rose from my chair to my full five feet and three inches to take him on, my best Afrikaans perched for my opening address. As I emerged from the envelopes of gown, I stepped back with strong purpose onto the overflow of black cloth. The gown pulled swiftly, tightly around my throat and I fell into my chair and toppled backwards, crashing onto the floor to horrified gasps from the accused and public gallery. My physical prowess in that case was matched by the ineptitude of the police and the laziness of the prosecution, who thankfully failed to present evidence beyond a reasonable doubt against my clients.

As the government tried to muzzle and contain political objection, so it increased, and when the police failed to halt protests, they resorted to beating, dogs, tear-gas, rubber bullets and open fire. This experience strengthened collective resistance and in turn provoked further retaliation. In March 1985, 4000 black people began to walk from Langa, a black township in the Eastern Cape, to a funeral near the town of Uitenhage. Unable to stop the procession, police opened fire, killing twenty people, and violence and consumer boycotts spread through the depressed towns of Port Elizabeth, Cradock and Uitenhage. The army moved in to control areas of unrest and the government threw a blanket ban across meetings of several listed organisations. In July, for the first time in twenty-five years, President PW Botha declared a state of emergency effective in over thirty cities and towns across South Africa, but excluding my province, the Western Cape. People were detained by the hundreds and in September, in the Eastern Cape, which held the country's record for detentions, I drove past special camps constructed in soccer stadiums, where detainees, unable to fit into bursting prisons, were housed. At night, after curfew time, giant floodlights set townships ablaze and residents hung coloured blankets over windows to shut out light to sleep. Streets were patrolled by police in vans, and yellow casspirs and army trucks ferried detainees to Algoa Park Police Station and St Alban's and North End jails. It was my first visit to a state of emergency.

I had arrived at Halton Cheadle's invitation. I came to know Halton when I was a student. He was based in Johannesburg at the Witwatersrand University's Centre for Applied Legal Studies and then started his own human rights and labour law firm. I had studied labour law in the early 1980s and Halton's writings and participation in devising a new labour dispensation for South African workers had an enormous influence on the design of my legal studies and the focus of my legal practice. It was due to Halton that I learnt the value and limits of litigation in asserting worker rights and began to work with trade unions, discovering a whole new energy of opposition. Halton had a 'large workers compensation claim' on the go and asked if I would fly to Port Elizabeth for a few days to be part of a team of lawyers assisting him with its preparation. At Port Elizabeth airport, I was briefed, given a dictaphone and sent to work.

A young doctor, working as a medical officer in the office of the district surgeon of Port Elizabeth (an office which had attracted criticism after the death in detention of Steve Biko in 1977) had been placed in charge of the treatment of detainees. Dr Wendy Orr, unable to contain the horror of the wounds she saw and the stories of torture told to her by hundreds of detainees, had confided in Halton. Her desire to stop these assaults led to Halton drawing together evidence for an urgent interdict restraining the South African Police from assaulting emergency detainees held in the Port Elizabeth or Uitenhage areas. Over a few long days we travelled from our hotel in Port Elizabeth to union offices in Uitenhage where we drafted affidavits from the stories of parents and relatives of detainees in support of the interdict application. Police trailed us and burst in on meetings with clients, but miraculously they never uncovered the nature of our task. The scale of suffering was unbearable in the accounts given by Dr Orr, the relatives of the detainees, and two clergymen who had also been detained in a Port Elizabeth prison. We were told of giant weals, bruising and swelling, blisters and lacerated lips and split skin. Of perforated eardrums, suffocation, forced drinking of petrol and 'the helicopter', where detainees' wrists were handcuffed behind their ankles. Then, suspended by a pole edged between their limbs, they were set spinning and assaulted.

I flew back to Cape Town on the morning the case was to be filed in the Port Elizabeth Supreme Court. In my Cape Town office, I waited for a call from Halton to advise the papers had been lodged before I felt it safe to tell my colleagues about the 'workers compensation claim'. The morning papers were filled with the news. The application was unopposed by the state and an order restraining the police was granted by the Supreme Court. It was remarkable that the evidence had reached a public forum without derailment by police given their expanded and unbridled powers under the state of emergency. What hit home however, was the editorial in the *Argus* which concluded that 'Dr Orr's evidence was not unique, or even unusual'.

Over the next few years, the state of emergency expanded in coverage. Student and other political organisations were outlawed, meetings banned, close to 8000 people detained and police-related deaths increased to an alarming degree. Millions of black workers staged boycotts, work stoppages and went out on strike. Military, trade and cultural sanctions were imposed by the European Community, the Commonwealth nations and, symbolically, by the United States. Although the government rescinded the state of emergency in March 1986, it was resurrected nationwide in June of that year in anticipation of the tenth anniversary of the Soweto riots. The security forces were endowed with sweeping powers, participation in school, rent and consumer boycotts was prohibited and news reports on 'unrest' and police action were subject to strict censorship regulations. The resultant national protests proclaimed that 'No news is bad news'. In May 1987, the white general election returned President Botha's National Party to power with an increased parliamentary majority. Botha had a mandate for enhanced security measures and in early 1988, using powers under the emergency declaration, the activities of leading anti-apartheid organisations and major trade union bodies were severely curtailed, effectively paralysing their daily administration.

During 1987 and 1988, much of our work contested the validity of emergency regulations or challenged the authority and motive of those who sought to enforce them. This period saw the rolling in of a new judicial wave where the courts took bold steps and quashed regulations, declaring them inimical to the freedom of the individual. Courts ordered the release of detainees from prisons around the country and overturned regulations banning political and labour organisations and their activities. For a while, it seemed as if justice had resurfaced and we were greedy for more. We would walk from courts with judgments still warm with victory, along corridors which echoed with songs of defiance. Clients and families, in clothes of ANC colours, strode ahead, clenched fists in the air, and filled us with an agitated happiness. Perhaps judges were beginning to see beyond the law and appreciate the impact of a savage state on ordinary lives. They showed courage and we felt a buoyed confidence in the rule of law. Then, in April 1988, Mr Justice Jan Basson of the Upington Supreme Court tipped the balance and convicted twenty-five black people of murder under the common purpose doctrine. And that's where the story really begins.

3

•

A new instruction

I met Anton Lubowski for the first time in early April 1988 over a drink at the Vineyard Hotel. We had been at a labour law conference at the University of Cape Town and Anton had been one of the speakers. I knew about Anton Lubowski. He was the first white man to join and publicly declare his membership of the South West African Peoples Organisation (SWAPO), an organisation dedicated to ending South Africa's illegal and oppressive occupation of his country, Namibia. I knew him to be an outspoken human rights lawyer who had handled several of Namibia's most important political trials and a passionate defender of an embattled Namibian trade union movement. Newspaper reports and colleagues and friends who knew Anton well revealed that he had suffered for his stand, for his unwavering commitment to justice and democracy in Namibia. He was the target of death threats and the full range of smears, branded a white *kaffir* or government spy for SWAPO, and his practice as an advocate at the Windhoek Bar buckled as colleagues snubbed him and instructing attorneys withdrew briefs from his charge. His punishment for betraying the white establishment, for leaving the *laager* was successive arrests on trumped-up charges, periods of detention without trial and solitary confinement.

In some circles Anton was a political folk hero, a contentious spirit from the north and I went to the conference intrigued to see what he looked like and hear what he had to say. He spoke in a hurried manner: punchy, frank, sometimes glib and confused. He had extraordinary presence and was unashamedly flamboyant. He struck me as someone with too much on his plate. After the conference, we drove down Woolsack Drive from the university campus to the Vineyard Hotel. Posters of the *Argus* evening head-lines tied to lampposts slowed our traffic. ANC lawyer in exile, Albie Sachs, had been critically injured by a car bomb in Maputo, Mozambique. An assassination attempt. Someone in the car bought a paper from a street vendor and read half-sentences from the main report. We drove in a frightened silence to the hotel and I remembered meeting Albie five years earlier. I was studying law and development as a one-year postgraduate course at Warwick University in England. Albie had been teaching law at the Eduardo Mondlane University in Maputo and I was hungry for ideas for a new legal system which could be implemented in a new South Africa. I had sat with Albie in a flat in North London. He was optimistically cautious about transformation in a liberated Mozam-bique and convinced that people could solve political and social disputes if they participated in devising the structures for resolu-tion. The attempt on his life was a shocking attack on Albie's belief in people's capacity to change.

The conference delegates and speakers, a boisterous group of lawyers, trade unionists and activists, were subdued as they entered the pub. We huddled together to read the newspaper report. There was a familiar period of hushed reflection, a reminder that bold-ness of spirit could so easily be undone. A photograph showed a body torn apart, an eye blown out and an arm dangling from a shoulder. Albie was in danger but he would live.

We sat on chintz couches at a large round table and I ordered a pot of tea. Anton Lubowski pulled up a chair next to me. We introduced ourselves. 'So, finally, I get to meet you. I thought you'd be bigger and taller somehow, much older,' he said grin-ning, a tiny glint in his eye. It was effective flattery. Even then, at our first meeting and with our mood low, he exuded a charisma, an attractive openness and compassion. We exchanged names of friends and acquaintances in common, a social ritual endemic to South Africans world over, and then he asked me how I knew Albie. My tea arrived and Anton walked over to the bar. He returned with two whiskys. 'I like tea, but I think this will ease the pain.' He handed me a whisky on the rocks and we clinked glasses and wished each other luck.

•

In retrospect, my first meeting with Anton Lubowski held no hint of future contact. I liked him and I was pleased we'd met, but I had no inkling that he would enter my life and change my personal itinerary mid-stream. I believed that I had a life plan and that I would live it in my country with its inevitable pull to the future, surrounded by those I loved and admired. I could never imagine practising law anywhere else. South Africa offered such a clear illustration of right and wrong and the ultimate setting, so I thought in my insular way, for using law to extricate some form of liberty. I knew the terrain well and perhaps I had become too comfortable with the battles that we fought and sometimes won. Unwittingly, my meeting with Anton would present a new direction, one which would take me on an irreversible journey through regions of the human condition not yet charted on my map.

A few days after our initial meeting, on a Monday evening late in April, Anton left an urgent message for me to call. He was still in Cape Town, consulting with labour law experts. He had invited them to work with the National Union of Namibian Workers on a draft code of labour law for an independent Namibia. I was predictably late for dinner with friends down from Johannesburg but I was curious, slightly intrigued and decided to call.

Anton sounded rushed and exasperated, then apologetic. 'I'm helluva sorry to hassle you Andy, but there's been a disaster. Do you know about this case in Upington? It's been running for over a year. A common purpose trial. Twenty-five or twenty-six people charged with the death of a policeman. It looks like another Sharpeville Six. It's unbelievable, man, what's going on up there. And no one seems to know about it. There's been no media. And the court's getting away with murder.' I had heard nothing about the trial. It seemed a huge number of people for such silence on the issue and I wondered whether Anton tended to exaggerate.

Earlier in the day, Anton had received a call from an Upington resident, Mr Alfred Gubula, requesting help. Upington was a small town in the north-west corner of South Africa, close to the Namibian border. Anton would have been known in the town, possibly with the same degree of admiration and loathing bestowed on him by most white South West Africans. He was an obvious person to call for help. The following morning the Upington Supreme Court, a circuit court of the Northern Cape Provincial Division, seemed likely to convict twenty-five black people for the murder of a black municipal policeman. Under South African law, once convicted of murder, the death sentence was mandatory punishment unless the existence of extenuating circumstances could be proved. The case was riddled with complexity and huge practical difficulties. The judge had indicated that the defence should be ready to commence its case on extenuating circumstances within four days. For most of the trial, the accused had been represented by a single advocate from Johannesburg, Andre Landman. He was likely to withdraw from the case at the prospect of having to prepare a case on extenuation for twenty-five clients in four short days. Anton had agreed to act as their advocate. Would I act as instructing attorney to the twenty-five and try to save them from the death penalty? If I agreed, Andre Landman or Mr Gubula would call me after court the following morning to give me further details.

I would help. It was a tentative response. I had never done a murder case for a single client, let alone for twenty-five. I knew little about the notion of extenuation and the requirements for repelling the imposition of the death penalty. I knew that I didn't like the common purpose doctrine, a prejudice that had been shaped by the wide criticism and notoriety it had attracted from its application in the case of the Sharpeville Six, heard by the South African Appellate division only months earlier. All these aspects I could come to understand and learn about over time. What was clear, however, was that time was not on our side. And what was worse was that the twenty-five accused were soon to be convicted of the murder of one man and I knew nothing about the details of the murder or the evidence that had led to their convictions.

Anton explained as much as he knew. The murder had occurred in 1985 in Paballelo, a black township tucked behind the town of Upington. There had been twenty-six accused and twenty-five had been represented by attorneys Krish Naidoo and Associates from Johannesburg who had briefed advocate, Andre Landman. The other accused had been separately represented by an advocate from the Kimberley Bar. Eight months into the trial, the instructing attorneys had withdrawn from the case due to lack of funds. The court had requested Andre Landman to continue representing the accused as *pro deo* counsel. Andre had agreed to represent the twenty-five accused without the support of instructing solicitors and for the privilege he would be paid from the coffers of the state. Committed to the fight and to his clients, Andre's sole representation of the accused over the following ten months had been formidable and courageous. Now, with enormous pressure to prepare for the next phase of the trial as all his clients faced the death sentence, Andre Landman, still without assistance, was contemplating withdrawal as counsel the following day. He felt he could not do his clients justice. The accused and their families were desperate to engage attorneys and senior counsel.

Receiving new instructions in a matter, particularly one involving a large number of people, always induced a sense of apprehension. Often, there were different stories to explain one event, conflicting interests and, in political trials, competing agendas. Some clients had an understanding of the law and the pace at which it worked, some were impatient and insisted that expeditious and positive resolution was possible. As most of my work was Cape Town based, the parameters of my legal practice and the procedures with which I worked were fairly well established.

I was well acquainted with the courts, the prosecutors, the police-men and I often knew my clients or the institutions or organisations to which they belonged. In most cases, I would have represented my clients from the outset. We would be together from the start: collating evidence, debating decisions and strate-gies, watching the process unfold. In the Upington case, a critical phase had already taken its course, an eighteen-month trial about to end in twenty-five convictions of murder. To take on the case at this stage would mean inheriting a legacy and representing twenty-five clients whose views of the law and its servants had no doubt been refined and eroded by their prosecution under it.

The following morning, Andre Landman called me from the Upington Supreme Court. His voice was sombre and his words slightly hesitant. The predicted convictions had been confirmed: all twenty-five of his clients had been convicted of murder. He explained that it was hard to call and that he had to talk quickly. Unlike members of the state legal team, he had no office of his own and had difficulty gaining access to the court telephone in the general office. Andre had told the court that were the case to continue in the time frame indicated by the judge, he had no option but to withdraw as counsel. A debate had ensued with the court insisting that the case on extenuation begin on the follow-ing Monday, less than a week away. Andre had withdrawn from the case at his clients' request. The convicted had asked for an expanded legal team to present their case against the death penalty. The judge wanted to know who would continue their represen-tation and expected to see the lawyers in his court on the Monday as planned.

The task of preparation was considerable. The record of the trial to date ran to some 11 000 pages, the transcript being pri-marily in Afrikaans. We would have to read the transcript, conduct detailed consultations with the accused and confirm that they wished us to act for them; a senior advocate would have to be found who was willing to step into the case at an advanced stage; we would need to secure extensive funding for the representation of twenty-five people in a town almost 1000 kilometres away. Were these not reasons which might persuade the judge to give us more time to prepare? Andre agreed to convey them to the court and call me back at the next adjournment. We had a series of short calls throughout the day as he dashed from court to telephone, calling me to report new developments and then return to take instructions from his clients. The judge seemed impatient, piqued by Andre's frequent absence from the court and his requests for short adjournments to speak to me and then consult with his clients. I could sense the intolerance and antagonism of the court even then.

We decided to start with practicalities while waiting for Andre's further instructions. There was a large map in my firm's library. We located Upington in the north-west corner of the country, in the magisterial district of Gordonia. Colin Kahanovitz, a smart young lawyer who had almost completed his articles of clerkship with the firm, would work with me on the case. Our travel agent advised that flights to Upington were infrequent and, for some reason, heavily booked. All she could do was to wait-list us for the Sunday-afternoon flight from Cape Town. The only multiracial hotel in the town, the Upington Protea, later to become our home, was full for the week. We would have to settle for the whites-only Oranje Hotel. By late afternoon we had organised a hire car, if nothing else. Flights, car hire, accommodation: our expenses had begun to accumulate and we hadn't even met our clients.

I tried to persuade funders over the phone of the immediate need for cover. Although sympathetic to the urgency of our needs, they required extensive details of the case before they would commit themselves. I detected an initial resistance. The nature of the crime, the vicious murder and the burning of the policeman's body, was not attractive. The magnitude of the convictions and the possibility that twenty-five people were facing the death sentence were, however, factors that would probably attract funding. The case was beginning to seem an impossibility, too hard. The preliminary aspects were practically defeating us, let alone getting to grips with the facts of the State v Kenneth Pinkie Khumalo and twenty-five others, appreciating the complexity of the law and the nature of the evidence required for extenuation. By late afternoon, I began to tire of working with constant speculation and the whole undertaking seemed foolish. Despite the backing of my partners and the support of the firm for the project, I was irritable and fast losing interest.

Andre's last call on the Tuesday afternoon was to report that the court was not persuaded by our arguments for a postponement. Apparently, the Honourable Mr Justice Basson had confidence in our ability to find a way to Upington, consult with twenty-five clients and properly prepare our evidence and argument within days. Court, declared the judge, was adjourned for three days, until 9.30am on Monday, 2 May 1988, when the case on extenuation would commence. The implications of the decision and the blind iniquity of Basson's thinking pulled me back to the task and from then on the momentum for our work was cast. I telephoned Anton to tell him the news. He was returning to Windhoek on the Friday. He would fly to Upington on the Monday morning and meet us at court. I suggested that we meet with Andre for a short briefing in preparation for our first appearance in the Upington Supreme Court. We settled on Thursday morning. Meanwhile, I would start my search for a senior advocate to lead our team's initial quest for extra time before an intransigent judge.

On the Wednesday afternoon, Mr Gubula, who had contacted Anton from Upington, telephoned to advise that the accused and their families had asked him to formally instruct me as their attorney. As he ended the call, he said, 'This is a big relief for us, I can tell you. They are all looking forward to seeing you and Anton in Upington as soon as you can get here.' I began to mumble something vaguely comforting and confident in response. I tried to sound light and in control, unaffected by a bout of low-grade hysteria that had beset me. Instead, I'm sure I came across as a new recruit, nervously reporting for duty: 'We are preparing for our visit. We look forward to meeting you on Monday.' I telephoned Andre at his hotel and asked him to catch the first available flight to Cape Town.

4

•

A case of common purpose

Andre Landman walked into my office carrying bags and suitcases frayed from weight and travel. He dumped them on my office floor and held out his hand. He was a big man, tall and solid, and he looked younger than the sound of his voice. He was probably in his early thirties. Andre took off his suit jacket and loosened his tie. There was a swift exchange of histories and light chatter. 'So, you're at the Jo'burg Bar. Is your brother the Landman from the Industrial Court?' Colin looked at Andre, head to toe. 'You look okay for a guy who's got twenty-five murder convictions under his belt.' Andre laughed politely and I offered tea. He unlocked a suitcase and we knelt down to sift through the contents. There were maps, photographs and videos, statements, judgments and transcripts. Reams of paper, tied with pink counsel ribbon, manilla folders with big writing, pens and dictaphone tapes, bulldog clips and pads of sticky yellow post-it notes. Andre moved slowly and methodically. Nothing about him suggested fuss and no matter how I protested about the madness of the trial and the judge, Andre failed to join my wave of wholesale criticism unless he thought it helpful. As he talked about the trial, my praise for his endurance seemed inappropriate and I was relieved at the indifference he offered in response.

It was late Thursday morning. Anton had called to say he would be with us soon after lunch. From the moment they met, Anton and Andre reverberated with difference. As Anton was bold and large and sweeping in his views, so Andre was reticent, cautious and reserved. Unlike Anton, who dismissed the prospect of Judge Basson refusing us a postponement, hissing and puffing with the confidence of inevitability, Andre was unconvinced that the judge would be swayed by our presence and conviction. 'Basson's sick of this case. He's been at it long enough and he's due for long leave. He's a man, I think, who will want to clear his desk before he takes time out.' Andre's insights were obviously reliable. But whatever the judge's holiday plans, we all knew that getting a postponement was a critical step towards saving some of the twenty-five from the death penalty.

We started with the bare facts almost immediately. Andre spoke of the peculiar application of the common purpose doctrine by the court and the factors that hindered his sole representation of the accused. His delivery was low-key, almost mechanical, and as he led us through the events leading to the murder, it was clear he had to stay in the case. He had dedicated almost two years of his short career at the Bar to the Upington 25 and their families, at risk of distancing himself from his own family in Johannesburg. He was quietly obsessed with the trial and his removal from it at this stage would have hurt. His knowledge of the record, volume by volume, was meticulous. He had learnt to read the mind and the moods of the judge. His links with the Upington and Pabal-lelo communities were well-established. And most importantly, he held the trust of the accused and their families.

•

With only three short days to prepare for our appearance in the Upington Supreme Court, to secure funding and senior counsel, I was losing my ability to be attentive to Andre's story. My comprehension of the trial and its layers of factual evidence for each of the accused became muddled and I worried that any details of the case I presented to potential senior counsel would repel rather than coax their interest. There would be no short cut to the completion of this case and whoever agreed to work on it was in line for a long sojourn with adversity. We agreed that Andre should camp in a conference room for a few hours with his documents and a dictaphone and compile a summary of essential facts from the eighteen-month trial. The summary would be my prompt for discussions with advocates and the media and form the basis for applications for fast-tracked funding of the case from overseas funding agencies.

I telephoned fourteen senior counsel around the country, sounding more alarmed and horrified with each retelling of the tale. We started with a select group of advocates. Some I knew, some had appeared in other common purpose trials and all were respected political trial advocates. Most of them had never heard of the case. After I recounted the highlights, a small number were tempted. The time frame for preparation was always the stumbling block and none of them were available at such short notice to appear on the Monday. Few convinced me that they would have wanted to be available for what might follow beyond that day. What was the bottom line for preparation? A careful dissection of thousands of pages of court record, interviews with twenty-five clients and possibly their families and an array of expert witnesses, compilation of evidence and drafting argument on extenuation and mitigation. And then preparation of the record for an appeal. Months of intense work, possibly years. It was not an easy one to sell.

Andre emerged some hours later with our starting point. Combining the summary of essential facts compiled by the prosecution with the evidence from the trial, the Upington case was presented for us in manageable form. Despite being a summary, the detail was exacting. Every witness, each ordinary incident was included. With minor amendments, it is reproduced below, unavoidably fixed in legal convention.

ANDRE'S SUMMARY

In the early morning of 13 November 1985, between 6.00am and 8.15am, a murder took place in the black township of Paballelo, situated on the outskirts of the town of Upington, in the Northern Cape province. The deceased was a 24-year-old black man named Lucas Tshenolo Sethwala, who was employed as a municipal policeman by the Town Council of Paballelo. Sethwala, known as 'Jetta', lived with his mother and his siblings at house number 405, Pilane Street, Paballelo.

The town of Upington practised job reservation. Jobs were traditionally granted first to white workers, then to coloured people and, only as a last resort, to black work-seekers. Paballelo, an impoverished township of approximately 20 000 black inhabitants, was consequently beset by social problems flowing from its high rate of unemployment, such as overcrowding, evictions resulting from prohibitive rents and alcohol abuse. During the early part of 1985, classes at the Paballelo High School were boycotted by students who had complained, to no avail, about poorly qualified teachers. In the latter half of 1985, discontented youths of the township established the Upington Youth Organisation (UYO).

The UYO was keen to hold a meeting between the youth and the older members of the community to discuss issues affecting the lives of Paballelo residents and possible avenues for their resolution. The UYO youth had little confidence in the Paballelo Town Council and its elected councillors to satisfactorily address and remedy their grievances. The holding of a public meeting to air grievances relating to rent, inadequate roads and lighting, incidents of alcoholism and crime in the township, was its preferred option.

EVENTS LEADING UP TO THE MURDER

During the afternoon of Sunday 10 November 1985, a meeting was held in the local community hall, the J Shimane Hall. The hall, with seating capacity for about 700 people, was filled to overflowing with residents, young and old. The meeting was addressed by various residents who talked of poor township conditions. The issues of house rents and the use of alcohol by schoolchildren were highlighted and debated at some length. The meeting also raised the role of the Paballelo municipal police and, in particular, their malicious intimidation of informal traders trying to eke out a small living. The residents complained that some of the municipal policemen had confiscated meat from hawkers and emptied paraffin from tins on sale. The conduct of Lucas Sethwala and fellow policeman Desmond Mduli were singled out for censure.

After the meeting, a group of youths in attendance made their way down the streets of Paballelo to the township soccer field where a soccer match between the local sides, the Eleven Experience and the Paballelo Chiefs, was in progress. They danced and sang and chanted on the pitch, disrupting the game. A South African police casspir arrived on the scene and a confrontation ensued. Stones were thrown and tear-gas was fired by the police to disperse the group. Apart from school boycotts, there had been no disturbance or unrest in Paballelo prior to Sunday 10 November 1985. The confrontation on the soccer field was the first such incident in Paballelo to draw police intervention. Late that night, police reported several separate incidents of unrest, which included arson and malicious damage to property. The house of the school headmaster, Mr Xaba, was damaged as was the car of Mr Nkomozana, the Town Manager.

The tension between residents and police continued on the Monday and Tuesday. Captain Botha, in charge of the local South African police unrest unit, believed that the situation in the township warranted external assistance and he sought the help of Captain van Dyk and his riot squad unit from Kimberley. Captain van Dyk and his unit arrived in Paballelo on Monday night, 11 November 1985 and began patrolling the township streets. Captain van Dyk drove around the streets of Paballelo and addressed residents through a loudspeaker attached to his vehicle. He assured the Paballelo community that he and his men had come not to fight with the residents but to talk to them about their problems. However he stressed that the police would deal with any incidents of violence or unrest with the means at their disposal. Late that night, police shot and killed a pregnant woman, a Paballelo resident, whom they alleged had committed an act of public violence. The actions of the police and their presence in the township appeared to have the effect of reducing incidents of unrest throughout the following day, Tuesday, 12 November 1985.

Captain van Dyk and his squad came on duty at 6.00pm on the Tuesday evening and, using his vehicle loudspeaker, he again informed residents of his intentions. Using one of the residents, Zonga Mokhatle, as interpreter, he ordered groups of residents who had gathered on the streets to disperse. There was some suggestion, and rumours circulated to this effect, that van Dyk, with the help of his interpreter, had also announced that a meeting would occur the following morning on the Eleven Experience soccer field where the problems experienced by residents could be discussed with the police. Whatever the source or truth of the announcement, from about 6.00am on Wednesday, 13 November 1985, residents of Paballelo began gathering on the soccer field, an estimated crowd of 3000 people having assembled by 6.40am. Many of the residents were en route to work or pensioners who had come to the Shimane Hall nearby to collect their pensions due on the day.

At approximately 6.45am, a casspir under the command of Captain Botha arrived and parked at the edge of the soccer field. A few minutes later, Captain Botha issued a loudspeaker warning, in both English and Afrikaans, that the gathering was illegal in terms of the Internal Security Act. He ordered the meeting to disperse, giving the crowd ten minutes to clear the field. By this stage, a loudspeaker had been attached to a netball pole located at one end of the field and one by one people stood on high and began to address the gathering. After a few minutes, the national anthem, '*Nkosi Sikelel' i-Afrika*', was sung, accompanied by some people raising clenched fists in the air. After the anthem, a preacher known as

Pastor Bidi led a prayer. As Pastor Bidi began to pray, Captain Botha announced that the ten minutes had almost expired and warned that force would be used against the people if they failed to disperse. The crowd failed to disperse. At the conclusion of the prayer, as Pastor Bidi said 'Amen', police fired tear-gas canisters into the crowd. The crowd ran in various directions—some towards the male hostel, some towards the Shimane Hall and others into the township. A group of people ran to the township beer hall, a wall was pushed over and an attempt made to set the beer hall alight. As they ran from the sound of shots and tear-gas fumes, some of the crowd fell to the ground and many of the women lost their shoes in the scramble.

One of the routes of dispersal was along Pilane Street on which stood house number 405, the home of Lucas Sethwala. Some of the people in Pilane Street began to throw stones at various houses and at a police casspir parked in an adjacent street. Police retaliated by firing tear-gas over the houses into Pilane Street. A group of about 100 to 200 people gathered in front of the gate to house number 405 and shouted chants and threw stones, some of which shattered windows on the street side of house number 405. At the time, Lucas Sethwala and members of his family and the Xaba family were inside the house. The Xaba family home had been stoned on the Sunday and Monday and family members had sought refuge at the Sethwala house. At some point during the stone throwing, Lucas Sethwala fired two shots into Pilane Street from inside his house, seriously wounding a young boy, Dawid Visagie.

THE MURDER OF LUCAS TSHENOLO SETHWALA

Leaving the other inhabitants behind, Sethwala fled from his house and sought shelter in neighbouring house number 407. The owner of house number 407 requested Sethwala to leave and he ran out into Pilane Street in the direction of the Shimane Hall, firing shots from his rifle into the air. As he turned from Pilane Street into Imalie Street, he was chased by a group of people onto an open piece of land, near where the Shimane Hall was situated. As he reached what were known as the green post office houses, prefabricated structures belonging to the post office, he was caught and knocked to the ground. A state witness testified that Justice Bekebeke, later to be charged in the murder trial as accused number 10, pulled Sethwala to the ground, grabbed the rifle and struck Sethwala twice over the upper part of his body. Other people had arrived on the scene and Sethwala's body was assaulted.

Evidence led at the trial was that a group of about 60 people kicked, stabbed and threw stones at the body. A state witness who had taken refuge in house number 403, saw a person whom he identified as Enoch Nompondwana (later to be charged in the murder trial as accused number 7) run past house number 403 in the direction of the post office buildings, evidently carrying a plastic can filled with a liquid resembling petrol. The liquid was poured over Sethwala's body and he was set alight.

The police received a report that Lucas Sethwala had been fatally injured and made their way to the scene at approximately 8.10am. At the murder trial, the reports of the District Surgeon called by the state and the two pathologists called by the defence concurred as to the likely cause of death; likely, because the District Surgeon, Dr Ecksteen, failed to perform a vital test on Sethwala which would have determined beyond a reasonable doubt that he had already died at the time he was set alight. Had Dr Ecksteen tested the deceased's carbohaemoglobin value, he could have established whether Sethwala had died from the two blows to the head or as a result of asphyxiation and third-degree burns to his body. The evidence was that the second blow to Lucas Sethwala's head was so severe that the butt of the rifle broke and metal was sheared from the gunstock. The blows to his head had caused a skull fracture and extensive cerebral haemorrhaging. In the absence of the carbohaemoglobin test, the court found that in all probability, Lucas Sethwala had died from the two blows to his head and was dead at the time he was set alight.

THE ARREST OF SUSPECTS AND IDENTIFICATION OF THE ACCUSED

Justice Bekebeke, visiting his family in Paballelo from Windhoek, Namibia where he worked as a male nurse, returned to Windhoek on the night of the murder. He was arrested in Windhoek on 19 November 1985 and a few days later he made a confession before a magistrate in Upington which he subsequently contested as made under duress. After a trial-within-a-trial, the confession was found to be admissible as evidence. Another accused, Elisha Matshoba, was arrested on 18 November 1985 and he too made a confession before an Upington magistrate.

On 3 December 1985, three weeks after the death of Lucas Sethwala, an identification parade was held, made up of nineteen suspects and forty-one additional people. Three female suspects were not included in the parade. Identification witnesses identified twenty-three people who, with the three female suspects, were charged with the murder of Lucas Sethwala. Eighteen of the twenty-three accused were identified from the nineteen suspects; the further five identified were drawn from the forty-one additional people. These five had attended the parade at the request of the police, not as suspects or persons to be identified but as extras, to make up the numbers. They were subsequently arrested and charged with Sethwala's murder.

THE CHARGE AND THE COMMON PURPOSE

Twenty-six accused were charged with the unlawful and intentional murder of Lucas Tshenolo Sethwala on 13 November 1985 in or near the black township of Paballelo, in the district of Gordonia. In the alternative, the charge sheet alleged that the accused were charged with the crime of public violence in that they came together with the common purpose to violently disturb the public safety and peace and/or to infringe the rights of other members of the community and/or to defy or prejudice in other ways the authority of the state established for the maintenance of law and order, in that the accused had a common purpose to unlawfully, intentionally and violently:

  (i) participate in an unruly gathering having in their possession certain weapons such as petrol bombs, cans, bottles, stones and other weapons; and/or
 (ii) incite each other to attack the house of Lucas Sethwala and/or kill the said Lucas Sethwala and/or participate in violent and unruly behaviour; and/or
(iii) attack and damage the house of Lucas Sethwala; and/or
 (iv) threaten and endanger the lives and/or bodily integrity of Lucas Sethwala and/or the inhabitants of his house; and/or
  (v) attack Lucas Sethwala so that he died as a result of the injuries inflicted.

THE TRIAL ON CONVICTION

The trial of the twenty-six commenced on 13 October 1986 in the Upington Supreme Court, Northern Cape Provincial Division before His Lordship, the Honourable Mr Justice Jan Basson and two assessors, Mr R Kurland and Mr TJ Obbes. (Mr Obbes died in July 1987 prior to the conclusion of the trial.) The state was represented by Advocate Terence B van Rensburg, assisted by Advocate P J Loubsher, both from the Attorney General's office in Kimberley. Advocate Eben Boshoff of the Kimberley Bar appeared *pro deo* for Accused No 7, Enoch Nompondwana. Krish Naidoo and Associates instructing Advocate Andre Landman appeared for the balance of the accused for the first eight months of the trial, after which Landman appeared *pro deo* until the conclusion of the trial on conviction.

The State's case against the accused

On the charge of murder, the state contended that the offence commenced in the region of 405 Pilane Street, the home of Lucas Sethwala, and continued until the death of Sethwala next to the green post office buildings. The state alleged that although each of the accused did not personally commit the act of murder, they would each attract liability for the murder on the basis of the doctrine of common purpose. The common purpose, argued the state, was formed at the meeting in the Shimane Hall on Sunday, 10 November 1985 and/or continued until the commission of the murder. The state highlighted the following acts of the accused as being indicative of the common purpose:

  (a) most of the accused had attended an alleged illegal gathering at the Shimane Hall on Sunday, 10 November 1985 at which certain decisions were made;

(b) some of the accused were observed at an illegal gathering on the Eleven Experience soccer field on Wednesday, 13 November 1985. The state described the crowd as riotous, armed with a variety of weapons and provocative in their conduct towards the South African police, at whom they threw stones;

(c) after the meeting on the soccer field had been dispersed, a large group of people had gathered in Pilane Street near the house of the deceased, Lucas Sethwala. The state contended that those accused who were part of the group had:

- incited the group to attack the deceased's house;
- thrown stones and/or unknown weapons at his house;
- uttered certain remarks directed at assaulting and killing the deceased.

In addition, the state alleged that Accused No 1 was armed with a bottle which resembled a petrol bomb;

(d) the accused were part of a group who had chased and attacked the deceased. Some and/or all the accused had simultaneously hit the deceased with fists and/or hands, thrown stones at him, jumped on him, kicked him, stabbed him with knives and/or similar objects and set him alight.

The state argued that the common purpose to commit murder and/or acts of public violence had taken the form of an express agreement reached between all twenty-six accused deduced from their conduct.

On the charge of public violence, the state claimed that each of the accused had personally committed acts of public violence.

The pleas and defences of the accused to the charges against them

All of the accused pleaded not guilty to both charges, the main charge of murder and the alternative charge of public violence. All of the accused, except for Accused numbers 18 and 19, raised alibi defences to the charges against them. Most of the accused testified that they were elsewhere when the deceased and his house were attacked. Accused No 10 admitted that he had been involved in a scuffle with the deceased, but denied being at the site of his killing. Given the alibi defences, the identification of those charged and all the elements presented by the state as evidence of the charges were placed in issue.

The evidence against the accused

The state called six witnesses: Beatrice Sethwala, mother of the deceased; Magdalene Sethwala, sister of the deceased; and two sisters, Linerose and Roseline Xaba, daughters of the Paballelo High School principal, who, with their mother, had sought refuge at the Sethwala home after their house had been attacked some nights earlier. They were all inside house number 405 on the morning of Wednesday, 13 November 1985. The other two state witnesses were Douglas Khambule, a member of the Paballelo Town council, who lived in the house next door to the Sethwala family and his seventeen-year-old son, Desmond Khambule.

The court considered the capacity of the state witnesses to identify the accused and the reliability of the evidence given in support of this identification. The circumstances under which the witnesses identified the accused were far from optimum. Those inside the house testified that they had been afraid for some days prior to Sethwala's murder, that what they had witnessed on the Wednesday morning had happened at great speed and was chaotic and frightening, that the crowd outside the house was large and constantly moving, that some witnesses had been affected by the tear-gas fired by police in the direction of the house, that they had observed the crowd through broken windowpanes or a gap in curtains, that, at times, they had hidden under beds or in a wardrobe. Despite these factors, the court found that the four women inside the Sethwala house had had a clear opportunity for observation of the crowd and their evidence was considered honest and reliable. The court held that a single witness, Beatrice Sethwala, had accurately identified nineteen of the twenty-six accused as being part of the group in front of the Sethwala house. Her testimony sufficed without corroboration. The two Khambule witnesses were also found to be reliable.

The judgment on conviction

The court considered the evidence of close to 150 witnesses. Because of the extent of the case, the court kept a daily summary of the progress of the trial and primary aspects of evidence. This summary formed part of the 403-page judgment on conviction. Each alibi defence raised by the accused was rejected by the court and defence witnesses who testified in support of the alibis were discredited. Consequently, the accused were placed in Pilane Street outside house number 405 and/or at the site of Sethwala's murder, near the green post office houses.

In his judgment, Mr Justice Basson raised certain questions for the court's consideration of the murder charge:

1 Did the crowd form the intention to kill the deceased?
2 If so, when did they form this intention?
3 Did the accused, after the intention to kill the deceased was formed, make a contribution to the attainment of the purpose or intention?

The judge noted that given the alibi defences of the accused and their minor contribution to the court's examination of the charges against them, answers to the questions raised lay predominantly in the evidence led by the state. He held without any doubt that the evidence as a whole pointed to the conclusion that the crowd, and all the accused who were part of the crowd (except Accused No 7, Enoch Nompondwana) had been correctly identified as having participated in the stoning of Sethwala's house. Relying on the confession of Accused No 10, Justice Bekebeke, and the evidence of state witnesses, the judge also found that Justice Bekebeke had fatally assaulted Lucas Sethwala. Similarly, that Accused No 9, Elisha Matshoba, had participated in the final assault on Sethwala on the basis of a confession made by him; that Accused No 11, Zonga Mokhatle, had attacked Sethwala at the green post office buildings by stabbing his body; and, relying on a confession made to his girlfriend a few days after the murder, that Accused No 20, Xolile Yona, had participated in the attack on Sethwala. The court said that the findings in respect of Accused numbers 10, 11 and 20 were bolstered by the evidence of the deceased's mother, state witness Beatrice Sethwala, that she had seen them returning from the direction of the site of the murder with their hands in the air chanting, '*Hey, hey die hond is dood*'. ('Hey, hey the dog is dead.')

The court also singled out Accused No 18, 53-year-old Evelina de Bruin, as someone who had encouraged or incited those outside the house to stone Sethwala's home and drive him from it to his death. The court accepted evidence of Beatrice Sethwala that Accused No 18 had evidently condoned the murder by shouting on her return from the murder site, '*Daar lê die hond, vrek en brand*' ('There lies the dog, dead and burning'), and '*Hoekom help sy ma hom nie meer nie; hoekom help sy wit hondbroers hom nie meer nie?*' ('Why does his mother not help him any more; why do his white dog-brothers not help him any more?')

The court's determination of the common purpose

In answering the questions posed, the court relied on state witness evidence that a discussion had taken place outside 405 Pilane Street before the stoning had started. Members of the crowd had discussed stoning the house ('*gooi die huis*') and others had made remarks such as '*Maak hom dood*' ('Kill him') and '*Kom ons haal hierdie hond lewendig uit die huis en ons sit 'n halssnoer lewendig aan hom*'. (Come, let's drag this dog alive from the house and 'necklace' [burn] him.)

This discussion, concluded the court, had been indicative of the formation of a purpose common to the crowd, the purpose or intention being to stone Sethwala's home, to drive him from the house so that he may be killed. The court inferred from the remarks and conduct that all the members of the group were party to this common purpose and were unequivocally 'after the deceased's blood'. The stoning of the house, said the court, was an act of association with the purpose to kill, an active contribution to the achievement of the purpose. The stoning signified the commencement of the common purpose; Sethwala's murder at the post office houses was its realisation.

Implicit in the court's reasoning on the common purpose was the belief that the crowd in front of Sethwala's house was essentially made up of the same people who chased and assaulted him at the post office houses some distance away. The findings that there existed a common purpose to kill Sethwala and that all the accused were party to this common purpose from its inception were the basis upon which the court found twenty-five of the twenty-six accused guilty of murder. Having established that the crowd had an intention to kill Sethwala, Mr Justice Basson concluded that the accused who actively associated themselves with the conduct of the crowd (by stoning the house or shouting out slogans, for example) similarly had the intention to kill. The intention of the crowd was imputed to each individual accused.

The court's findings of guilt fell into three main categories:

- All the accused, bar Accused No 7, were found guilty of murder. From their conduct, the court inferred that they all had a direct or actual intention (*dolus directus*) to kill Sethwala;
- Accused No 7 was found guilty of attempted murder on the basis that the state had failed to establish that he had associated himself with the common purpose prior to Sethwala's death;
- Accused numbers 9, 10, 11 and 20 were convicted of murder as perpetrators. Despite the finding that all the accused were guilty on the basis of the common purpose doctrine and thus equally liable for the murder, the remainder of the accused were convicted as accomplices.

•

Andre's summary was an expansive and complex document and hard to comprehend in one reading. We moved from the facts to review some of the basic principles of criminal law. To secure a conviction of murder, a court must find that each element of the crime is proved beyond a reasonable doubt. Thus, in the Upington case, the prosecution had to present evidence to show that each accused had the intention (*mens rea*) to commit the illegal deed and had performed a physical act (*actus reus*) which resulted in the murder. If the accused were not able to refute the evidence and the court was convinced of the integrity of the evidence beyond reasonable doubt, a conviction of murder would follow.

The South African criminal law at the time, set out in the Criminal Procedure Act, provided that a conviction of murder carried a mandatory sentence of death. Where, however, there was evidence which suggested the existence of extenuating circumstances, the court could exercise its discretion to impose a punishment other than the death sentence. The onus was on the accused to prove, on a balance of probabilities, that such circumstances were present. These circumstances, proved by direct or circumstantial evidence, would generally include factors such as youthfulness and immaturity, degree of participation in the crime, provocation, absence of premeditation, motive and the external or situational forces which had an effect on the behaviour of each accused, reducing their capacity to regulate or restrain their own conduct (known in psychological circles as the process of deindividuation).

If the accused were able to show that the cumulative effect of these factors probably influenced their state of mind to such a degree that their moral blameworthiness or culpability (as opposed to their legal guilt) in committing the crime was reduced, the court was not bound to impose the death sentence. If extenuating circumstances were to be proved in this case and the court exercised a discretion not to impose the death sentence, we would then present similar or additional evidence (mitigating evidence) in an attempt to lessen the severity of an alternative sentence such as life imprisonment.

The trial on conviction concluded, our preparation for the next phase of the trial had two distinct components. First, we had to prepare the case on extenuation for all twenty-five accused found guilty of murder. This task was directed at evading the death sentence. Second, for those who were successful at the first stage and avoided death as their punishment, we had to present evidence which would mitigate the sentence imposed by the court and suggest appropriate sentencing options.

We had another round of coffee and took stock. What we had taken on was enormous in scale and impossible to achieve in the few days bequeathed to us by the Upington Supreme Court. Our immediate focus had to be on securing a postponement for the trial on extenuation.

Andre drew our attention to an added complication. The presentation of evidence and argument on extenuating circumstances is determined by the facts as found by the court. The Upington Supreme Court had placed the accused, beyond a reasonable doubt, outside Sethwala's home and/or at the scene of his murder, near the post office buildings. All but two of the accused had raised an alibi defence. Despite the court's findings that the accused were present, they had indicated to Andre that they would continue to adhere to their alibis and deny participation in or presence at the murder and the events leading up to Sethwala's killing.

In proving extenuating circumstances, we would plan to focus on factors that had influenced the accuseds' state of mind. Given the continued stance of the accused, we were likely to face the prospect of presenting evidence on extenuation confined to the court's findings, without the testimony of our clients to support our arguments. It was going to be hard enough to convince the court that we should have some extra time to prepare the case on extenuation. We would need more than luck to persuade Mr Justice Basson that he should accept our evidence in the absence of any substantiation from our clients.

At the end of the case on extenuation would come preparation for an appeal to the highest court in the land, the Appellate Division of South Africa. We were tempted to move quickly from the Upington Supreme Court to the Appeal Court, where the chances of a legally accurate and just decision were certainly increased. But the Appeal Court did not hear oral evidence from witnesses so it was crucial that we compiled a comprehensive and compelling record of evidence and argument for its consideration during the extenuation trial. Such a record could only result from a thorough and rigorous presentation of evidence which illustrated every possible factor that might have influenced the conduct of each accused, on a balance of probabilities. There were no short cuts and we needed extensive resources. And that meant finding the best counsel, the most qualified and well-respected expert witnesses and substantial funding.

I tried to limit our request for funding. At this stage, we simply required funds to cover the work to secure a postponement and, that achieved, we would then reassess with time on our side. Buying time meant the prolonging of life, and we decided we should make contact with representatives on the ground rather than funders in London. This way we could demonstrate the immediacy and magnitude of the case. I called Tim Bork, Director of USAID/South Africa at the US Embassy. Did I have anything in writing I could fax to him? he asked. Andre's summary was despatched immediately and we set up a meeting for Friday morning. Tim had been keen to fund political and labour cases which met USAID criteria; but for many of our clients there had been no straightforward response to this offer. Some viewed US money with contempt and the offer as hypocritical. The Upington accused, however, were not obvious beneficiaries and there was an initial reluctance from funders who were not convinced that the case was overtly political in nature given the savage murder and necklacing of Sethwala. The extraordinary mass convictions and the potential for mass hangings would be our access card to financial assistance.

•

By Thursday night exhaustion and high anxiety had taken over. We still lacked senior counsel and I realised that our strict criteria of proven ability and political persuasion may have to give a little. There was no plan to our preparations. It was more a matter of feeling our way round the exigencies of the case and trying to make a good first impression on Monday before the Upington Supreme Court. There were brief inconclusive conversations with potential expert witnesses who agreed to testify in support of a postponement. Social psychologist, Professor Graham Tyson from Witwatersrand University, who had given evidence in the Sharpeville Six common purpose trial some months earlier, was in. The Sharpeville Six judgment on extenuation was a critical starting point and we took our cue from its assessment of the evidence on extenuation in constructing our approach. We would tell the court that our evidence on extenuation required extensive contributions from a range of experts proficient in a variety of complementary disciplines. We would have to rely on them to explain the conduct of the accused. We anticipated calling a social psychologist, a clinical psychologist, a sociologist, a criminologist and perhaps an anthropologist. A postponement of the case to locate, appoint and brief the appropriate experts and a new legal team was, we believed, a reasonable request incapable of opposition.

The meeting with Tim Bork on Friday morning went well. We had in-principle funding for the postponement and our trip to Upington was secured. I called media colleagues and told them of our plan. The trial had received scant publicity. From its commencement in October 1986 until early 1987, proceedings had been held *in camera* as some of the accused were still minors. Upington was hardly a news focus: conservative, quiet, largely unaffected by the country's moods. So even when the *in camera* curb was lifted, the twenty-five convictions went virtually unreported. If the court refused our application for a postponement, twenty-five lives were under threat and the public should know. We needed media presence at court and commentary on the hearing.

It was fairly early in my legal career that I realised the value of the role of the media as a powerful ally in political trial work. The best legal skills and persuasive argument were no guarantee to a just result. Along with church groups and trade unions, political organisations and foreign diplomats, the media was an essential point of leverage when the conduct of a trial fell short of fairness or judicial independence struggled to free itself from the executive arm of government.

Despite the pull of the media, I learnt that it was unwise to litigate via the press. There was the risk of preempting court findings and attracting charges of contempt or interference with the judicial process. And there were some journalists who lost sight of the individuals and their families—parties to litigation that was unpredictable in outcome—and focused rather on 'the story' at the expense of exposure of fragile lives. But over the years, I had come to know and trust writers and editors, community leaders and diplomats who were sensitive to the vagaries of the legal process and acknowledged the parallel importance of political strategy. We became friends because of common interests and shared beliefs. I was also drawn to them because they were not lawyers and they welcomed me into an integrated world removed from relentless legal reference.

We drafted press material and made endless copies of the transcript, the charge sheet, pleadings, judgments, summaries. Our travel agent confirmed our bookings and advised that the Northern Cape was a malaria-infested zone. Prescriptions and boxes of antimalarial drugs followed. Colin, on scholarly form, had removed himself from planning and was in the library reviewing the Sharpeville Six case and the law on common purpose. Just after lunch, Andre's efforts to obtain counsel paid off. Ronnie Selvan, SC from the Johannesburg Bar accepted instructions to appear for the postponement, and by late evening Andre was en route to Johannesburg armed with Selvan's brief. Anton had returned to Namibia and would meet us in Upington at the court on Monday morning. I called him on Friday night as Colin and I sat down with our colleagues for a drink in our office boardroom. Anton was relieved. 'Well, it looks like it's Upington for life. It's a helluva place. We're in for a helluva time.' I looked forward to seeing him.

We sat down at the boardroom table and opened some beers to celebrate small beginnings. It was then that I realised that few of my partners and colleagues had any real idea of what the firm had just taken on. I began the tale in brief and the room, initially filled with the din of competing court sagas and victories of the week, fell quiet. 'Jesus Christ, how the hell did this happen?' One of my partners poured another whisky. I didn't wait to hear if his words were aimed at the firm or the twenty-five. Both were in for tough times.

5

·

Upington

For some reason, I associated Upington with dried fruit. On the outskirts of the Kalahari Desert, 850 kilometres north-west of Cape Town, Upington had streets of date palms and soil nourished by the Orange River. We boarded the Sunday afternoon 4.10 flight, South African Airways. I opened the pack of salted peanuts which arrived with my tomato cocktail and tried to make them last the full hour of the flight. One sip to two peanuts. The green earth of the Western Cape soon turned to the orange and brown of the north, the blue ocean replaced by the muddy Orange River. An oasis of green amidst parched earth signalled our descent to the Pierre van Ryneveld Airport. The climb down was uncomfortably long and turbulent to allow the plane to filter through dense pockets of hot desert air and touch base with the longest runway in southern Africa. Upington (population 80 000), reserved for whites, was perched at high altitude which combined with the heat to compound the burden we were to cart for months on end and for some of us, for years.

I felt agitated, perhaps terrified at what lay ahead. But there was an edge of excitement, of adventure, as I anticipated the beginning of a grim fight for life. For years, those feelings which set in as we began the endless descent into Upington would stay with me and turn my stomach. As we stepped out onto the tarmac, the solid heat of a late-April afternoon blocked our path. I glared at the small airport building through moving air, the neat cement ovals of flat flowers, the police in safari blue and muzzled Alsatian dogs sniffing new arrivals. The blonde Avis women in red suits, Joanna and Amy, welcomed us with sweet exuberance. They gave us keys to a 'nice little VW Golf—we thought it would suit you' and directed us to the Oranje Hotel. As we became regulars and the story of our presence in Upington unfolded, Jo and Amy disclosed which side they were on and our hire cars became smarter and bigger.

We drove into town along a straight tarred road decorated with signs warning of approaching army convoys. A turning to the right led to the Namibian border; to the left was the Infantry Battalion, bursting with men in uniform, our boys from the border. The army camp was preparing for troop withdrawal from Angola and from South West Africa, which was soon to become independent Namibia. Upington was poised to become host to troops returning from protracted and arrogant wars and refuge to white 'South-Westers' (and their capital) who feared the abandonment of their country to independence. Just before the army camp, the watchtowers of the Upington Prison rose from acres of green cabbage patches, the labour of inmates. We were to travel that road hundreds of times to visit our clients, always with dread well camouflaged.

Upington was still with the sounds of children on bicycles and lawnmowers and ticking water sprinklers. '*Stilte. Kerk*' ('Silence. Church') signs suggested a devout community, now indoors in preparation for the evening service. The heat wrapped the town like mosquito nets, clinging and containing. We drove past familiar landmarks of most small South African towns—First National Bank, O.K. Bazaars, Volkskas, Kentucky Fried Chicken, United Building Society, Checkers, Central News Agency (CNA)—and those unique to Upington: the wide avenues, a relic from years when roads were built for turning circles of spans of oxen drawing wagons, laden with *mielies* and dates and sultanas; and the two animal monuments, one to the donkey and the other, guarding the police station, in honour of the camel, which had a central role in fighting crime in the early 1900s. The Lady Di Boutique, Le Must Restaurant and the Matador Steakhouse. A blackboard outside the Matador listed respected patrons, among them, boxer Charlie Weir, who had swallowed a 1.5 kilogram steak. The name of a woman ranked with the best. She had chewed through a 2 kilogram slab. We were clearly in the land of the four-wheel drive, Springbok steaks and Windhoek lager, cracked earth and unquestioning *baaskap* (white domination).

The Oranje Hotel was like a big old ship that had run aground. The floorboards sloped under a patterned maroon carpet and cockroaches dashed under cupboards discarded in the corridors. The bar was for men only, 'ladies' were permitted a drink in the bar-lounge. The dining room was a big vault-like room, dark with red brushed-velvet wallpaper. At breakfast, trestle tables held stainless-steel vats of scrambled eggs and grilled sausages and tomatoes. It was not an 'international hotel', the receptionist confirmed, when we asked where we could consult with our clients, some of the families of the accused. No non-Europeans, non-whites, she explained, were allowed. The foyer was full of bus-tripping German tourists, Europeans in khaki shorts and felt hats with leopard-skin bands, en route to the Cape or Namibia, previously a German colony. But we were the foreigners and Upington was a whole new world.

We drove a few kilometres out of Upington keen to discover at which point the stillness might give way to a fierce chaos suggested by the murder of Lucas Sethwala. The municipal abattoir was just before the turn-off to the black township of Paballelo. Past the sign '*Welkom in Paballelo*' ('Welcome to Paballelo') was the soccer field, barren and sprawling with faded markings and tilting posts. A few metres along from the soccer field, near billboards of giant beer bottles and toothpaste was a high barbed-wire fence circling the township police station. Police vans and white unmarked cars were parked outside and men in plain clothes and dark sunglasses leaned against them making notes. Paballelo—

'Place of Playing'—was far from the river, a dust bowl with pockets of sunflowers, proud against all odds. On the kerbside, township hawkers shouted out their wares. Meat and chickens, warm cooldrinks and fruit. Lean dogs scratched at the earth and barked softly at strangers, too hungry to care. The orange dirt streets were lined with box-like two-roomed houses, each with an outside tap, few with signs of electricity. Some had patches of green and flowerbeds, and paths, lined with pebbles from a low iron gate to the front door. To the side of the front door, on the front brick wall of the house, large house numbers were painted in white. There was a feeling of arrangement in Paballelo, a sense of struggle for an order which brought some comfort. I think it came from a desperate holding on to a life that was so fragile, so easily broken down, the life condoned by those destined to rule and humiliate their fellow human beings.

The township of Paballelo was the product of government 'removal policies', which dislodged and moved black and coloured communities en masse to areas far removed from affluent white settlements. Paballelo was established in 1960 when people classified as black, living amicably with coloured residents in the township of Blikkiesdorp, were moved to a new township. Divided by a railway line, the two townships of 'Blikkies' and Paballelo, shared residents and histories and a common language, Afrikaans. But they shared little else. Only nine of the 10 000 Paballelo residents had a college education; about 7 per cent had high school diplomas. Unemployment was figured at about 30 per cent—twice the official rate for black people in other townships. Upington employers preferred to hire coloured people from 'Blikkies'. The success of apartheid was not only the separation of white from black, but also black from coloured or black from black. It was on the basis of separation that degrees of privilege were constructed, that status was accorded by legislation and that the opportunity for alliances across colour bars was diminished. The residents of Paballelo had been flung to the bottom of a three-tier racial hierarchy, kept down and deprived until eventually frustration pierced their restraint.

•

It was time to meet Andre's plane from Johannesburg and so we made our way back to the airport. I was pleased he was coming that night. He was my only link to the people, to the place and its rules and rhythms. He was one of the townsfolk and he was welcomed, possibly with pity, by many of the locals. You could almost hear the whisper as we went past, 'Shame, someone has to do the job?', the weaving of a comfortable explanation, the benevolent wisdom of the town. With Andre was our advocate, Ronnie Selvan SC, who would present our plea for a postponement in the morning. Ronnie was short, unassuming, older and relaxed.

We decided on dinner at Le Must in Schröderstraat. The owner, Neil Stemmet, asked us to sign the guestbook and recommended the calamari and the pepper steak. Le Must offered dishes with exotic French titles and Afrikaans translations which bore little resemblance to one another. The restaurant was filled with ideas from magazines and coffee-table books on interior design. The books of good taste lay casually on the entrance table alongside a bowl of coloured mints. The restaurant was a series of rooms in an old house with bold drapes and stained walls, a miniature fountain, an upright piano, carved chairs and heavy oak sideboards and a deliberate mix of glasses and cutlery. The walls were lined with the works of local artists and the music was distinctive and full of memories. There was something warm and comforting, almost kitchen-like, about Le Must. It was to become our den which stood apart from the rest of the town and dared to confront Upington's wretched insularity. Neil had created his own fantasy within the confines of a community that held its breath and shut out change. He was the perfect host to the players in a trial that would rock the coarse fabric of the town. Some months into the case on extenuation, we dined at Le Must with some visiting foreign diplomats who had sat as trial observers. I believed that the name 'Le Must' had some exotic origin and that only someone French could translate it precisely and capture the nuances of the name. Luc Almerais from the French Consulate tried to be kind. 'It means nothing,' he said. 'It has no meaning. Maybe in Upington, but not in France.'

Ronnie Selvan ordered a good bottle of red and, much to my annoyance and incredulity, dismissed my request to consult in preparation for the morning, suggesting with a disquieting air of nonchalance that we should 'play the postponement by ear'. I was to learn during the course of the trial that exhaustive preparation, a thorough knowledge of the law and persuasive argument on its correct application were not always rewarded; rather, our challenge would be the dismantling of prejudice and the introduction of doubt into the sealed minds of our adjudicators. The following morning we left the hotel early to meet with our clients at court. They were transported from the prison to court soon after eight each morning and I thought they should know what their new legal team looked like before court commenced at 9.30am.

6

•

Pleasing the court

The Supreme Court of the Northern Cape, Provincial Division, was housed in the *landdroshof* (magistrates court) on Upington's main street, Schröderstraat. On most days, from mid-October 1986, the local Magistrates Court was transformed from a court of misdemeanours and civil claims of debt and motor vehicle damage to a court of high crime, the forum for a murder trial of twenty-six residents. In just under two years, over 150 witnesses were examined and cross-examined; confessions allegedly extracted under duress from some of the accused* were contested to no avail; Mr Obbes, one of the two assessors assisting the judge on matters of fact, suddenly died; a baby was born to accused Xoliswa Dube; and the state successfully secured the conviction of twenty-five out of twenty-six accused for the murder of one man.

The courthouse was similar to most old South African town courts—Cape Dutch in style with thick white walls and a wide, polished red stone *stoep* across the front. White pillars traced the edges of the *stoep* and supported a red-tiled roof. A large Dutch

---

*   Despite being convicted murderers at the time I began representing the twenty-five, I refer to them throughout the book as 'the accused'. Aside from being an easier collective description, they always remained 'accused' in my view, still to have the highest court in the land confirm or reject the charges of murder.

gable, with a carved inscription '1939' at the top, framed the entrance and steps to the court. Sash windows were covered by wooden shutters which kept the heat and light from penetrating the front-facing *kantore* (offices). A low brick wall surrounded the building, separating it and the simple garden from the street. A single old palm tree at the beginning of the pathway to the court belied any access to justice.

The court had a sleepy feel, a lethargy that had set in amongst officials and permeated their locale. Court staff shuffled about and said '*môre*' ('good morning') and '*middag*' ('good afternoon') and not much else. People sat on benches clutching bits of paper and a child crawled on the cool stone floor. Some stood and brushed away flies, others stared at typed lists of names on noticeboards. Phones rang with the sound of a country exchange at work— stretched, dull, discordant rings which were answered with the promise of further delay. '*Hullo, hof. Hou net aan, asseblief.*' ('Hello, court. Please hold on.') We walked along a corridor past the main offices and magistrates' chambers towards the back of the courthouse. A door opened on to a courtyard and to the left was our courtroom, day residence to the twenty-six Upington trialists. Off the courtyard to the right were smaller rooms and, in particular, the room where the defence would robe for court and gather for meetings and tea breaks.

The courtroom was small by Supreme Court standards, more so for a trial of this size and import. On either side were walls of windows and the back half was filled with no more than ten rows of wooden benches with upright backs, pew-like and functional. In the centre of the court was the dock, raised and obtrusive, and on either side, a haphazard line of chairs and benches to accommodate all twenty-six accused. In front of the dock, chairs and tables with water jugs and glasses, blotting paper in flat leather folders and small lecterns had been arranged in a half-moon for the defence and prosecution teams. In the middle of the half-moon and towards the front of the court sat the judge's assistant and the stenographer with her table and equipment. Facing the front of the court, on the right-hand side, near the defence, was a small witness box. Along the walls on both sides were a few more chairs, generally occupied by the court interpreter, on the right, and members of the police, particularly the loyal warrant officer de Waal, Upington Police, who sat behind the prosecution, to the left.

At the front of the room, and a few metres above floor level, raised on a stage, were a long wooden table and three regal chairs for the judge and two assessors, one of whom, Mr Obbes, had died during the trial. Bolted to the wall and hanging outward, directly above the judge's chair, was a large South African flag. The flag was bold, assertive and hung salute-like, bringing to mind a line from the South African national anthem: '*Ons vir jou, Suid Afrika*' ('Forever you, South Africa'). There was no airconditioning in the *landdroshof* and even the flies were slowed by the hot summer air. The ceiling fans were noisy and ineffectual when the court was full. Even at the start of the morning, the court was drenched in warm stale air.

Across the table, the prosecution was setting up for the day. We walked across to their side of the court and introduced ourselves. It was '*aangename kennis?*' ('how do you do?') all round and bits of English and Afrikaans tottered between us. The leader of the prosecution team, Advocate Terence van Rensburg, was to be assisted by Advocate Jaap Schreuder, who had the stand-offish air of a newcomer to the team. Van Rensburg was pleasant and polite, slightly diffident. Both advocates wore spectacles with tinted glass and Jaap Schreuder had a neat moustache. Van Rensburg, or '*Vis*' ('fish'), so labelled by the accused for the shape and manoeuvres of his mouth, even when silent, apparently had little to say. He was keen to get on with the case and get on with his life. He had his twenty-five convictions and now he faced the challenge of shaping the punishment. I had the feeling that even van Rensburg was not in favour of twenty-five executions. It came as no surprise, however, when he said he would oppose our application for a postponement.

There was movement at the back of the court. It was starting to fill up with relatives and friends who came in and went straight to their seats as if reserved. I turned to them and mouthed a 'Good morning', and an old man in a suit and tie slowly made his way towards us, moving with difficulty on a brass-handled walking-stick. 'Miss Durbach, I spoke to you on the phone. I'm Gubula.' We shook hands. Alfred Gubula was a warm, elegant man with a greying beard. He had an air befitting his position as community leader and elder statesman. He spoke English with a slight stutter, a hesitation, and his words and tone resonated with a gentle passion for his people and their sorrow. His face was strained and his body had a slight tremor as he spoke. Mr Gubula's adopted son, Zonga Mokhatle and his nephew, Tros Gubula, had both been convicted of Sethwala's murder the previous week. We were joined by Reverend Aubrey Beukes, pastor of the *Nederduits Gereformeerde Sendingkerk* (Dutch Reformed Mission Church), the branch of the country's Afrikaner Dutch Reformed Church reserved primarily for coloured people. Reverend Beukes, a Blikkiesdorp resident and executive member of the Northern Cape Council of Churches, had been an outspoken critic of the trial and supporter of the accused and their families. He assured me that he would be in court most days and gave me his telephone number on the back of a matchbox. 'Please call if there is anything I can do to help.' Silently, I asked that he pray extremely hard for a postponement.

There was excited whispering from the gallery as Anton came into the court. He had flown in from Windhoek and Colin had met him at the Upington airport. The whole atmosphere in the room seemed to lighten as some of the families and Reverend Beukes recognised '*Meneer* Lubowski' (Mr Lubowski). He was full of energy and he towered above the prosecution as he shook their hands and told them that the case was far from over. Andre introduced Anton to Ronnie Selvan SC. Anton turned his back on the prosecution and, half-sitting on a table, asked Selvan about his plan for the postponement. He seemed mildly impressed by Selvan's reply and then walked across to say hello to the accused. It was an arrival like that of a pop star and even some of the police, who had now entered the courtroom, nodded uncomfortably as Anton greeted them in the *taal* (Afrikaans).

Advocate Boshoff, *pro deo* counsel for Enoch Nompondwana, Accused No 7, convicted of attempted murder, came over to greet Anton. He was Afrikaans, from Kimberley, a man with a kind, open face and a stocky frame whose first love was not the law. He said he'd rather be at home working with his pigs on a cure for cancer. As he spoke, I was suddenly aware of a strong police presence in the courtroom. *Sjamboks* in hand and guns on hips, some stood at the entrance with dogs and others lined the sides of the court. Five or six sat in the front row of the public gallery with their legs spread, a barrier between the dock and the free world. It seemed like overkill and there were angry words from some of the families who wanted to enter the court and were told there was no more room. Anton, in Upington Supreme Court for barely more than fifteen minutes, stepped into the fray and asked the police to show a bit of *ordentlikheid* (decency). A few police grudgingly moved and made space for relatives, and their sneering expressions suggested that Anton had been marked from then on.

Under my feet a slight rumbling moved towards the back of the court and then to the front again. Within seconds it grew louder and more distinctive. It was the sound of voices singing in unison. Our clients had arrived from the prison and were in transit in cells below the court. My heart beat against my chest and I poured a glass of water and slowly sipped at the rim. Anton and Andre left the court to robe in our small consultation room off the courtyard. Ronnie Selvan SC, already robed, was reading through his brief and Colin was talking to the court interpreter, a large black man with a round belly, a man with an obvious wealth of information. Andre came in and asked Ronnie to join him and Anton. The judge had arrived and was in his chambers and would meet them briefly before court.

I stood at our table waiting and turned to face the accused, a chorus of beautiful, full, plaintive voices, ascending the stairs in numerical order. Accused numbers 1, 2, 3, 4. The people in the gallery stood and watched in silence, some with heads bowed. A small girl ran forward and grabbed the leg of Accused No 1. He smiled and patted her head and the sergeant on guard moved between them, pointing her back to her seat. As more and more of the accused climbed the stairs, the singing filled the court. '*Senzeni Na? Senzeni Na?*' ('What have we done? What is our sin? What have we done?') For that moment, twenty-five convicted murderers held the room.

I watched the accused file into the dock and take up their positions directly behind us, spilling out onto wooden benches on either side. Unlike their lawyers, the accused seemed at ease, familiar with their surroundings. We exchanged glances and some of them smiled and nudged one another, looking at Anton with a hint of proud recognition. They knew, presumably from Mr Gubula and Andre, that their attorney was a woman. I turned to move towards them and caught a few staring at me quite intently, quizzically. Andre introduced me from left to right. Kenneth Khumalo, Tros Gubula, Abel Kutu, David Lekhanyane, Myner Bovu. They were warm and laughed and their welcome was confident and comforting. We had got just over halfway when there was a loud banging and a young policeman with orange hair came through a door on the left which led onto the raised platform where the judge would sit. '*Stilte asseblief. Almal staan*', he bellowed. ('Silence please. All stand.) His eyes darted about the court as his right hand moved to his holster. He held the door as Mr Justice Jan Basson and his assessor, Mr Richard Kurland, stepped in. A low whisper and a mumbling greeted their entrance. We nodded and bowed our heads in respect for the bench. There was a general shuffle as everyone except the accused sat down. It was Monday morning, 2 May 1988.

Basson looked down to his left, giving the signal to Ronnie Selvan to explain our presence. The courtroom was stuffy and hot and the families waved handkerchiefs and paper fans to move the air. We had been told that the ceiling fans made too much noise to stay on for any length of time. Anton leant across the table and suggested we ask the judge if the accused might be seated. Selvan started. 'May it please the court, my lord, I appear together with Advocate Lubowski and Advocate Landman on behalf of all the accused bar accused number seven.' Selvan sat down. Sitting closest to the judge, Eben Boshoff rose and announced his appearance on behalf of Accused No 7. 'Yes. Thank you. Mr Selvan?' Basson's face, framed by gold-rimmed glasses, looked tanned against his white shirt and black gown, his thick silver hair brushed off his forehead. He was almost handsome, with a sense of style. Selvan asked if the accused may be seated. Basson nodded and invited them to sit. 'My lord is aware that the accused have requested a new legal team which is presently being constituted. The new legal representatives, with no prior involvement in the case, are to prepare the case on extenuation. With respect, my lord, a formidable and time-consuming task.'

Basson was not moved to agree. Selvan kept going. 'The accused's attorneys have established the broad framework for the case on extenuation. They have spoken to some of the experts they will call, one of whom is currently in America. It is likely that the collation of evidence from these experts and the analysis of transcripts to date and my lord's judgment, will take some time before a considered case on extenuation may be put before this court.' Basson interrupted, the tone of his voice yawn-like. 'How much time do you envisage, Mr Selvan?' Ronnie looked sideways. The night before we had set our lowest bid at three months. 'Two, possibly three months,' was the brave reply.

'*Meneer* van Rensburg?' Basson faced the prosecution and changed language and pitch as if *en famille*. Van Rensburg stood and folded one arm across his chest, holding his chin with his other hand. He spoke in Afrikaans and argued that three months was '*onredelik, totaal onaanneemlik*' ('unreasonable, totally unacceptable'). He came across as if acting in the best interests of our clients, a line Basson appreciated. The accused had already endured a long trial. Now the defence wanted another long delay and then a further period for the trial on extenuation. Were the accused not entitled to the expeditious resolution of the case? Anton and I were sending notes back and forth and on to Selvan. Selvan offered an assurance. If a postponement meant preparation of a strong case on extenuation and Basson was released from the obligation to impose the death penalty, our clients would not protest the delay as justice denied. Basson looked down and began flicking through a small calendar.

By late morning, we had our postponement. One month. The case on extenuation was set down for Wednesday, 1 June 1988, the day after Republic Day. Court was adjourned without discussion and we packed our bags with great industry, eager to hold our contempt and avoid eye contact with the prosecution. Selvan had bought us some time and that was his brief. Our flights out of Upington were late afternoon and we told the accused we'd stop by at the prison on our way to the airport. In the courtyard, the families gathered round and asked questions and looked worried. Some talked to the accused and handed over clean clothing and gifts and bags of food. As we came out of the court building on to Schröderstraat, the traffic had slowed and people stood still and waited. Police motorbikes and cars with flashing blue lights and sirens, drove down Schröderstraat, a cavalcade out of town towards the prison. They were followed by yellow vans crammed with our clients, some of whom stood close to the thick black wire which sealed the upper sides of the trucks. A group of women, one or two with babies tied to their backs with checked blankets, ran out into the street and banged on the vans, yelling names and words of support. The accused sang freedom songs and as they passed us, they thrust their fists through the wire and shouted: 'Viva Upington 25, Viva Lubowski.'

One month to get a real postponement was how we saw it. One month to prepare a detailed application to court for more time. And if Basson refused, we'd tell the world and withdraw from the case, leaving him to work it out. We had met with our clients at the prison and these were their instructions. We sat with them until late in the afternoon and discussed our thoughts on extenuation. We talked about how to meet the concerns raised by the Sharpeville Six case by reference to the personal testimony of our clients and expansion of the range of expert testimony. We listed some bare minimum tasks and plotted our timetable around them. We had to read and analyse transcripts and judgments and reports. Then, with a foundation knowledge of the case, we would consult with twenty-five clients and their families and with expert witnesses, located in Cape Town, Johannesburg, Windhoek and, possibly, America. We could not do it in one month and that was what we planned to tell the court in June.

By the first week in May Anton had persuaded Cape Town senior counsel, Peter Hodes SC, to argue our postponement application. I had worked with and against Peter. With him on matters matrimonial and against him when he had been briefed by the Minister of Law and Order to defend allegations of harm made by our clients. He was perfect for the job. He was smart and a fighter and he spoke the language of the state. There was no doubt that Peter was angered by injustice and often embraced principles in conflict with those held by his state clientele. But I couldn't miss an opportunity to take the high moral ground. I called him to say how delighted I was that he had accepted the brief. 'A lucky break, a conscience brief before it is too late.' He laughed and came back in reply. 'I need hundreds of briefs like this to do the penance required. Consider me beyond redemption, Ms Durbach.'

By the end of the first week, we had confirmed three crucial expert witnesses and devised the framework for their evidence. Graham Tyson, social psychologist from the University of Witwatersrand in Johannesburg, would give primary evidence on the theory of crowd behaviour known in psychological circles as the deindividuation thesis and attest to its manifestation in the case of the Upington accused. Very simply, the deindividuation thesis argues that people in crowd situations often exhibit behaviour unfamiliar to them as individuals acting alone. Various environmental or external factors can combine in a crowd situation to influence behaviour such that someone in a deindividuated state loses the ability to regulate their conduct, becoming irrational, impulsive and atypical. Deindividuation, Tyson would demonstrate, leads to diminished responsibility in much the same way as does the consumption of too much alcohol or great emotional stress.

In the Sharpeville Six case, where the deindividuation theory was first urged as an extenuating circumstance in South African courts, the Appellate Court accepted the theory but held that the evidence presented was of a 'wholly generalised nature', not specifically related to the individual accused and accordingly, imposed the death sentence. Thus, we needed to link the theory of deindividuation to the conduct, as determined by the court, of each of our clients. To this end, Dr Herman Raath, who hailed from Windhoek, and came with high recommendation from Anton, agreed to conduct clinical assessments and draft detailed personality profiles of each individual accused. Professor Martin West, a social anthropologist from the University of Cape Town, would conduct primary research together with colleague Dr Mamphela Ramphele, soon to return from a sabbatical in America. The research would explore the impact of socioeconomic conditions in the Paballelo area—high unemployment, low incomes, overcrowding, deficient educational facilities—on the lives of the accused (and their families), and the extent to which this context of disadvantage might explain the events of November 1985 and support the application of the deindividuation thesis.

Over the next few days we briefed the experts with relevant trial material, including summaries, copies of extracts from the court record, Basson's judgment on conviction and a police video of the crowd and its dispersal from the soccer field on the day of Sethwala's death. They in turn sent us their curricula vitae, outlines of the work they proposed to undertake and the time required for its completion. I was to incorporate these in my affidavit which formed the basis of our next application for postponement. The Saturday before our appearance in Upington, the experts and lawyers met in the Queen Victoria Street chambers of Peter Hodes to prepare the application. We sat around a large table with papers spread, Peter at the head with dictaphone in hand. He drafted the affidavit by committee, with Graham, Herman and Martin adding unique points to our narrative. I would conclude that the immense scale of work was clear and necessary. And if that wouldn't persuade Basson to grant the postponement, we added that his failure to do so (and we all contributed to this line) would tarnish 'the image of this country' and 'the administration of justice as a whole'.

We arrived in Upington on Republic Day night, 31 May 1988. Upington was a town which rocked with white Republican pride, and as we drove from the airport there were flags flying and churches emptying of worshippers who had given thanks to God and the Nationalist Party. With luck, we had managed to book rooms at the Protea Hotel, a sleek modern 'international' inn where race was not a criteria for residence. Hotel manager, Willy Burger, and his wife, Kathy, a young *verlig* (enlightened, progressive) couple, extended their hospitality despite our purpose which would not have sat comfortably with their usual patrons. Over subsequent months, they administered to a growing cast of Upington 25 associates with extraordinary grace as lawyers, diplomats, journalists, clergy, trial observers and television crews demanded rooms, telephones, faxes, photocopied documents and continual room service. The legal team was housed in the northern wing of the hotel. Room number 8, river-facing, became my *platteland* (country) residence.

We worked hard to ensure coverage of the hearing. The court was full of journalists and observers from unions, the Black Sash, churches and foreign governments. Peter's performance was understated and persistent, irresistible by our reckoning. The court was inclined to give us three months to prepare. There was, however, a complication in that a postponement for three months meant resuming the trial midway through Mr Justice Basson's prearranged long leave. We were utterly accommodating and might have gone so far as endorsing our judge taking a well-earned break were there no risk of being perceived as self-serving. The *Weekly Mail* ran the story of our apparent triumph: 'Lawyers fighting for the lives of twenty-five Upington residents convicted of killing a policeman will spend the next nine months preparing argument on extenuating circumstances and in mitigation of sentence. They won the breathing space this week when an application for a postponement until 6 February next year was granted by Justice J Basson.' A nine-month postponement. No sooner asked for than given. It looked effortless in print.

7

A culture of denial

It was a simple doctrine in its pure original form, an important and respectable concept in criminal law. In its application, the doctrine of common purpose, a concept rooted in English law, was viewed as a legal expedient. If used for its intended object, it drew little controversy. At law school, in criminal law and procedure, we were introduced to the doctrine of common purpose by reference to the traditional hold-up scene. Three people plan to hold up a bank at gunpoint. One of the three will wait outside in a getaway car. The other two hold up the bank, one pointing a gun while the third person executes the robbery. Customers and bank staff panic, the gunman pulls the trigger and a bank official is killed.

The law reasons that the murder was a foreseeable consequence of the initial unlawful purpose, being to rob the bank. Although there was no causal link between the actions of the driver of the getaway car and the third person without the gun, they share liability for the murder with the gunman on the basis that the act of murder fell within the scope of the joint unlawful enterprise to which they were party. While all three will attract a conviction of murder despite the absence of physical participation in the death, their lesser degrees of involvement in the killing may give rise to differing punishments.

What became controversial and unique about the application of the doctrine in various court cases in South Africa, as in the Sharpeville Six and the Upington 25 trials, was the extension of the doctrine to ill-fitting factual circumstances. When the doctrine was extended to ensnare individuals in a crowd and spread the net of criminal liability to those with no shared plan, or commitment to collective action, it began to lose its respectability. At first glance, the judgment of Basson offended ordinary principles of criminal law. It ignored the intention and acts of twenty-six separate individuals and simply held them collectively responsible for the murder of Sethwala. To make sense of the common purpose doctrine as applied in the Upington case was hard enough for lawyers. To convey to our clients its original rationale and the evolution of its perversion and its misapplication to their situation was a doubly tough endeavour.

By the time we arrived in Upington, the doctrine of common purpose had become part of the local parlance, subsumed into the Paballelo vernacular. It was spoken about as if it was something concrete, with human qualities, capable of unleashing untold harm. Although the true meaning and implication of the doctrine as used in the Upington case may not have been fully realised by the accused, what was apparent was that a community had watched the state use the doctrine to allot random culpability in satisfaction of a political end. In consequence, the residents of Paballelo had little belief in the law and its capacity to remedy their predicament. Confronting that lack of confidence and deep mistrust was how we started our work with the Upington 25.

We had moved onto our third senior counsel in the case. But this time, Ian Farlam SC, was committed to seeing the trial through to the bitter end. Ian was a friend of the firm. We had briefed him in numerous political cases, he had asked us to represent his daughter after she was arrested at student demonstrations and he unequivocally supported our work. He was a curious mix. His fascination with Latin and Greek scholars and religion as both history and devotion made him seem older than his actual years. No visit to his home or chambers was complete without him climbing through shelves of books and journals to point to some obscure reference, followed by a reading out loud to illustrate and sometimes swamp the argument he wished to make. In his eccentric long-winded fashion, Ian would steep his argument in history and add an international law dimension. When preparing evidence or argument in a case, we would begin to feel nervous that all this knowledge was cluttering up his head and that we stood to lose our way and never retrieve our starting point, Ian would produce comprehensive and discerning written submissions and inevitably deliver a most attractive court address. Unlike Anton who was demonstrative in manner, Ian had a reserved sense of humanity, a conventionality and in Upington, he always dressed for dinner.

We returned to the deindividuation thesis and judicial criticism of its employment in the Sharpeville Six case. The testimony of our clients to support and substantiate the thesis was crucial. The court would want to know how they felt when they gathered on the soccer field and how they were influenced and governed by the psychological and physical forces which captured the crowd on the day of Lucas Sethwala's murder. The judge would want their evidence to explain common action, he would say he was entitled to hear evidence of the emotions engendered by the burdens of their daily lives and their responses to the arrival of police, the firing of tear-gas, the angry panic and flight of the crowd. Otherwise, as the prosecution argued in the Sharpeville case, if the accused did not take the court into their confidence and give evidence, the judge would have to speculate as to how they felt, and not necessarily in their favour.

We had no record of such evidence. All of the accused, bar No 18, Evelina de Bruin and her husband, No 19, Gideon Madlongolwane, denied a presence at or involvement in any stage of the murder. To try and save our clients from the death penalty, we not only needed their testimony, we needed testimony that corresponded with the court's conclusion that the accused, despite their evidence to the contrary, were present at the stoning of Sethwala's house and/or at the scene of his killing. We needed them to forgo their alibis and to testify in keeping with these findings, and to say: yes, we were there and we acted in the manner that we did (or in the manner determined by the court) because we were subject to circumstances which in all probability influenced our emotions and behaviour. If our clients testified, they would suit our purpose—to keep them off death row. But to testify in accordance with the court's findings would conflict with their original testimony. It was an unpleasant dilemma. Ultimately, it came down to an individual truth and a choice each of the accused had to make, distinct from the group.

As I explored the Upington trial and moved closer to the trialists and their community during the nine months of preparation on extenuation, I began to see the trial as a hideous manifestation of the triumph of apartheid—the cultivation of fear, kindled by violence, and a resultant stepping back from the truth. Rather than admit to attending a peaceful protest on a township soccer field early one morning or to being caught up in a crowd of stone-throwers, angered by provocative police action, the accused denied a presence, pleaded an alibi and so tracked their route to death row. As a black person, particularly in a conservative white heartland, to be in an area, to linger with a group of people, to stand on the sidelines, attracted suspicion. To admit presence, however innocent, often carried persecution. Always a suspect, up to no good. Thus, to plead an alibi was perhaps an explicable but ill-considered defence, one moulded by decades of exclusion, removal and denial. Ill-considered because once placed on the scene by witnesses of the state whose evidence appealed to the court, the accuseds' alibis were rejected and their future credibility was questionable at best.

If we were to hold out against the imposition of the death sentence and rely on the deindividuation thesis as central to our case on extenuation, we had to do what made me feel uneasy and disloyal. It was tantamount, I argued, to suggesting that our clients 'come clean'. Our show of no faith. But on reflection, it was the correct approach. We had to give our clients an opportunity to talk, if it meant the possible avoidance of the death penalty. To talk with no pressure and no hint, on our part, of any lack of belief in their word. Anton and Andre would travel to Upington Prison and spend a few days with the accused. As a group, as individuals, whatever was requested. They would talk about the deindividuation thesis and the benefit of personal testimony. They would assure the accused that lack of testimony would not be fatal to the case. But if any of them wished to speak or thought they might be of some assistance, Anton and Andre would be available to talk in confidence. It was a delicate but necessary invitation.

Anton called after day two. The exercise had proved strenuous and exacting. It was hard to keep the balance, he said. To secure the accuseds' trust, to offer hope and then seemingly cast doubt on their account of the day, 13 November 1985. Many of the accused had been antagonistic and viewed our suggestion with scepticism. There had hardly been time for us to establish a trust with our clients and within a few brief weeks of meeting we were asking them to divulge, to confide, apparently so we could save their lives. Would they feel easier if they could talk to someone else, someone who offered a greater degree of reliability, who might give them the strength to come forward without reprisal? Two names were put forward. Archbishop Desmond Tutu in person; prisoner Nelson Mandela in writing. We were being put to the test. Andre said we'd make the relevant enquiries. He got as far as calling the Archbishop's office. They were amenable to the suggestion, he reported.

A few of the accused had asked to speak to Anton and Andre in private the following day. They wanted to think about what had been said. Anton thought there might be a slight shift of explanation, a breaking through. He was excited. He would call the next afternoon with a progress report. Overnight, they had lost the will and withdrew their request to talk. One or two expressed a fear of betraying the group. The pull of the group was extremely powerful. It was a bond that would be stretched to its limits throughout the journey of the trial. Despite some initial movement, a wavering on the part of a few, the group returned to the morning consultation intact, with their final position. They were all in agreement. They did not wish to speak individually to anyone. They would not testify. They came prepared, as if to bolster their view and reinforce the group cohesion, offering considered reasons for the refusal.

To testify did not necessarily mean being believed. They had not been believed at their trial on conviction, the court rejecting their alibi evidence. Discredited at the outset, there was no guarantee, they reminded us, that the same court would now believe them at the second stage of the trial. In addition, they worried that by giving evidence which was inconsistent with their earlier version of events at the trial on extenuation, they might prejudice their prospects of success on appeal. Contradictory versions of one event given by the same accused at different phases of the trial would present the Court of Appeal with obvious difficulties when deciding credibility. With the stakes as high as they were, and the appeal being a last resort, to testify presented as a significant risk.

A further reason to support their refusal to testify was advanced by our expert social psychologist, Graham Tyson. The evidence which we anticipated the court would request related to the state of mind of the accused some three-and-a-half years earlier. They would give evidence in 1989 in relation to how they felt in 1985. If they remembered anything of how they felt, it was essential they be interviewed days, rather than years, after the event. Given their time together in prison and during the trial, such evidence, Graham argued, must be viewed as contaminated, susceptible to reconstruction and, accordingly, unreliable. 'At most,' Ian would tell the judge during the trial on extenuation, 'Such evidence would add colour to the picture but would not alter its shape and outline.'

They were compelling reasons and we wasted no further time with our fishing expedition. Rather, our expert witnesses would assemble the evidence of the accused from direct interviews with every one of them and their immediate families and through extensive analysis of the evidence already on record. From this investigation, the experts would build intellectual and emotional profiles of each accused and deduce from each of them how they might have reacted on the day Sethwala was killed. To secure a conviction of murder, the court would have had to be convinced, beyond a reasonable doubt, that each of the twenty-five accused had an intention to kill. Thus, despite the alibi defences of the accused, the court inferred an intention to kill without any direct evidence from the accused as to their state of mind. We would argue that a similar approach should be adopted at the extenuation phase, the court assessing evidence at this stage on a balance of probabilities, not beyond a reasonable doubt. Given the court's ability to determine legal guilt without direct evidence to sustain such a finding, the court should have no difficulty in again inferring a state of mind from indirect evidence provided by our expert witnesses in consultation with our clients. It was on this basis, we planned to argue, that the court should evaluate the moral culpability of each accused which would have a bearing on the punishment or sentences imposed. It seemed a logical proposal and consistent with the court's reasoning to date.

The compilation of evidence on extenuation was an immense undertaking. Some weeks into the presentation of the evidence, the *Weekly Mail* headline referred to 'Legal history's biggest extenuation case' and added sweet exaggeration, lest its readers not comprehend the full scale of the venture: 'The most massive [argument on extenuation] in legal history'.

Herman Raath, a clinical psychologist in Windhoek, Namibia, whose PhD thesis examined the acculturation of black people in South Africa in adjusting to Western society, would begin the process. He was a safe bet for the Upington Court. Conservative and traditional in approach, Herman would interview the twenty-five accused in Upington Prison, initially investigating the environment and circumstances which shaped the 'macro-system' from which they came. He would then employ various psychological evaluation techniques and diagnoses to compile an intellectual and psychological history, a personality profile he would call them, of each accused, from which aspects of personality and patterns of behaviour could be deduced. Over time, we became familiar with the TAT and the DAP tests and the TATZ test with its coloured picture cards which demonstrated responses to family relationships, handling of authority and group identity depending on the card selected.

Herman Raath's profiles of the accused would be set within the psychosocial climate which prevailed in Paballelo during the period of the Sethwala murder. An examination of the socioeconomic context, a 'context of disadvantage, discrimination and absence of rights which set the scene for the events of November 1985', would be provided by social anthropologist Martin West, Professor of Social Anthropology at the University of Cape Town and Acting Head of the University's School of Social Work. Martin's research, recognised as eminent in South Africa and internationally, focused on the social effects of apartheid on coloured and black communities living in or bordering South African towns. His work for the Upington case involved meeting all twenty-five accused, interviewing their families and other Paballelo residents, and perusing court judgments and extracts from the court record pertaining to socioeconomic matters in Paballelo along with a report of a social worker commissioned by the Deputy Attorney-General, the prosecutor in the case. He would also refer to the profiles of the accused compiled by Herman Raath.

The psychological and socioeconomic evidence would converge with the testimony of social psychologist Graham Tyson. He would seek to persuade the court, on a balance of probabilities, that the accused lacked the psychological and social resources required to commit murder. The only reasonable explanation for their common action, he would argue, was that they, and the crowd of which they were a part, were influenced by certain psychological forces operating during the attack on Sethwala's home and Sethwala himself. These forces would have an impact on crowd behaviour to varying degrees depending on the psychological make-up and social background of the individuals in the crowd or, in our case, the accused. From Tyson's work, we learnt that both situational and internal psychological forces operate in crowds—frustration (comparative deprivation), arousal (singing, dancing, tear-gas), modelling (imitating aggressive behaviour), direct provocation (police action, tear-gas) rumours and conformity pressures (conforming to group conduct). These forces could lead to an internal process called deindividuation, which produces behaviour analogous to that of someone acting under the influence of hypnosis or alcohol. We learnt of the work of scholars of crowd behaviour and mob violence like Zimbardo, Smelser, Diener, Perry and Pugh, and Gustav Le Bon, whose choice words we hoped might appeal to the Upington Court: '...by the mere fact that he forms part of an organised crowd, a man descends several rungs in the ladder of civilisation. Isolated, he may be a cultivated individual, in a crowd, he is a barbarian—that is, a creature of instinct.'

The contingent of experts was expanding, but we were not content with three. Two more experts would be asked to join this 'most massive' extenuation team. Peter Folb, Professor of Pharmacology at the University of Cape Town and Chairman of the South African Medicines Control Council, agreed to give evidence on the effects of tear-gas exposure on the central nervous system, illustrating some of the factors (arousal; direct provocation) which may trigger the deindividuated state. Professor Folb's particular research interest had been the adverse effects of drugs and chemicals on the functioning of the human body. He would show that exposure to tear-gas generally produced discomfort in the eyes, mouth and upper respiratory tract, the common sensation of suffocation and increased heart rate and pulse. The feeling of panic following these physical sensations would generally elicit a 'flight or fight' response, particularly when a situation aroused fear. 'Excitement and disinhibition,' he would say in his preliminary report to us, were 'conceivable under such circumstances'.

In selecting our last expert witness, we had moved from the extenuation phase to the mitigation of sentences. Some years earlier I had sat at the dinner table with a friend from law school and his father, a Supreme Court judge, talking about a case involving young black activists charged with public violence. I was upset by the harsh sentences imposed by the magistrate hearing our case.

The punishment seemed so at variance with the nature of the offence and the characteristics and lives of my clients, the accused. The judge was comforting, convinced we would do better on appeal but he tried to make me see how such disparity was perhaps inevitable in a divided society. It is common that the interests of society are a primary consideration when imposing sentence. I asked how courts gauged prevailing interests and societal attitudes in South African society, characterised by deep division and separate communities. Hard questions, we agreed, for any sentencing officer trying to ensure a sentence is just. The judge offered a personal insight. 'When I must pass sentence in criminal cases, I try to imagine the accused as someone I might know, who has a family and a life now disrupted. I hope then that the sentence I impose is shaped not only to fit the crime, but also to fit the individual and the life experiences which led him or her to the offence. It's much harder to do this where communities are kept apart; where your life is framed by the customs of white middle-class suburbia and the accused before you has struggled through life in a black township.'

It may have seemed presumptuous and certainly would have been difficult for the Upington Supreme Court to have reference to Paballelo community views when determining appropriate sentences for our clients. With this in mind, we commissioned criminologist Professor Dirk van Zyl Smit and his team of researchers from the University of Cape Town's Institute of Criminology to conduct an attitudinal survey of Paballelo residents. Formulated and undertaken with scientific rigour, the survey was intended to provide a helpful and valid indication of community opinion to the sentencing of the twenty-five accused. The survey and its authors never managed to get a fair hearing and Dirk van Zyl Smit was given short shrift for his trouble.

8

•

Nine months

With confirmation from Bill Frankel in London that funds were available to underwrite preparation for the trial on extenuation and anticipated appeal proceedings, we began our work. And with time on our side, I could begin to discover who the twenty-five were beyond 'the accused' with an apparent common purpose. In the beginning, the brief meetings with our clients had left little room for real contact, our focus being wedded to the narrow object of securing a postponement. Once that was achieved, we almost had to work in reverse, stripping down what we know about the case and the accused, dismantling our own hasty assumptions about group behaviour, rebuilding from scratch.

To travel the long journey of the trial, the accused had little choice but to contrive a structure which might help keep a balance when heavy weights were stacked against them. They had devised their own group language, a way of talking without giving much away. The banter and the rhythm of the group kept them strong, sometimes impenetrable. But that was the product of years of astute packaging and as we carefully peeled back their sealant and began the process of separation, we found unique individuals with aspirations and fears, loyalties and silent dreams—men and women, in fact, with very little in common.

In conjunction with the work of our experts, we traced the histories of each accused apart from the group and discovered twenty-five diverse and generally quite incompatible people, ranging in age, at the time of the offence, from 19 to 61. In his report to the court, our expert sociologist, Martin West, underscored their differences. He wrote:

> They include: the functionally illiterate and people with matriculation and beyond; the married and unmarried, with and without children; scholars and workers; employed and unemployed; sports people and artists; a few with previous convictions and most with clean records; devout churchgoers of various denominations and those without religious affiliation; people from stable homes and those from broken homes; they portray a range of economic circumstances ranging from destitute to reasonably comfortable; and they include those with no hopes and ambitions and those keen to better themselves.

With the painstaking discovery of each individual accused and their adherence to a refusal to testify, came the imperative to build a detailed profile on which we could rely in evidence on extenuation. This meant talking to their families, their employers, their friends, their priests and then returning to the accused for confirmation. For some, the exercise required delving into their psychological make-up with the assistance of expert medical opinion. Accused No 20, Xolile Yona, stood apart from the others as the most emotionally fragile. Emotionally labile, was expert psychologist Herman Raath's description. His mood changes were dramatic. Depressed and sobbing inconsolably, then confused, laughing, angry, impulsive, aggressive. He was an accomplished boxer in Paballelo and his brother Lesley had promised to take him to the Transvaal to further his boxing career after the trial. In recognition of Mike Tyson, Xolile had shaved his hair in the style of the champion. Xolile's other distinguishing feature was a wooden *afropik* which he would stick in his hair at an angle, like an elaborate hatpin. Every now and then, when he thought his hair needed touching up, Xolile would pick at it with his afro-comb, like a bird's beak at pollen.

Throughout the trial on conviction, Xolile had complained of intermittent stabbing headaches. Sometimes they were so bad, said Mrs Lydia Yona, Xolile's mother, that he would box everything in the house. When interviewing Xolile Yona, Herman Raath had queried whether his emotional lability could be explained scientifically by the presence of organic brain disease. Clearly, evidence of any neurological abnormalities would constitute an extenuating or mitigating factor. We were keen to explore this avenue. The court permitted Xolile to travel to Groote Schuur Hospital in Cape Town for neurological testing by consultant neurologist, Simon Kesler. All aspects of the journey and his tests were to take place under police guard.

On 30 January 1989, the Upington police drove Xolile the almost 900 kilometres to Cape Town. He was held overnight in a police station on the outskirts of the city. The following day, he was transported to Groote Schuur Hospital for an electroencephalograph (EEG) and a CT brain scan. Xolile told hospital staff that he had not been fed. After the examination, he was returned to the police cells and taken by Cape Town police to another police station some distance away, where a black plain-clothes policeman questioned him. Other policemen came into the room. Xolile, sobbing and rubbing his arm, later told me that they had punched him in the stomach several times, that they had attached electrodes to his head and administered electric shocks. When Xolile complained that he was hungry, a policeman wearing plastic gloves had entered the room carrying a plate of faeces and instructed him to eat it. Xolile refused. He was handcuffed and the policeman smeared the excrement over his face. The policeman beat Xolile with a *sjambok*, trying to force him to open his mouth.

When I saw Xolile on his return to Upington I was horrified at how this tough young man had turned in fear. He had a slight tremor as he spoke and he told me that his arm was sore and his body ached from beatings. I arranged for a doctor from the town to examine him at Upington Prison. He found Xolile's urine to be very concentrated with ketones present, probably, he wrote in his notes, the result of starvation or assault. Before we had even started the fight, before we had got to the Upington Supreme Court with an expectation of battle, Xolile's experience had flung me into the cycle of brutality that had led Sethwala to his death. Our attempt to assist Xolile Yona had gone horribly wrong.

I was trembling when I telephoned Major Mans at the Upington Prison. Yes, Mans said, Yona had complained to him about certain matters. They were matters, he regretted, beyond his jurisdiction. Mr Yona was a prisoner in his prison, I reminded him, under his care and supervision. I told him we intended to bring the alleged assault to the attention of the Upington Supreme Court. Major Mans offered to take up the matter with the police. I knew it would come to little. We needed the names of the Cape Town policemen and police investigations of police conduct were generally fictitious. Two weeks into the trial on extenuation, we read out an affidavit from Xolile Yona to the court. Mr Justice Basson gave us an assurance that the allegations of police assault would be investigated. We cared little about the investigation but Xolile made the news and we had made the prosecution feel some discomfort.

•

Anton had begun to spend more and more of his time working in Cape Town. Throughout the months of preparation, he and I travelled to Upington and met with our clients on a fairly regular basis to reassure them and keep them informed of our progress. Over dinners at Le Must, we talked about how odd it was to land in Upington with twenty-five convicted murderers as clients; of how we had only just begun to understand their history at a time when the task of undoing an imminent threat to their future seemed impossible; of what an enormous responsibility the trial was and how we, as virtual strangers to one another, had little choice but to take it on and adapt our lives accordingly. We began to share our own histories. I soon discovered that Anton had a bold compassion for others, an empathy with people from all sides of life. The torture of Xolile was one of many horrors experienced by the accused and their families that I would have to confront during the trial. Later, when I was shamed by the extent and display of my own feelings of hurt for the accused, because this was not the conduct expected of lawyers, I drew comfort from Anton's demonstrative way, more so that he was a man. He made me feel at ease and he welcomed the times when we talked about life, away from the law.

As we moved closer to the start of the trial on extenuation, we worked longer hours, to endless deadlines. One day, when tiredness dragged me away from hope and made me focus on the futility of our cause, Anton announced that we should drive, 'drive into the desert, through all those funny towns like Kakamas and Koekemoer and feel the earth around us. Get back to our souls'. And so we did. We tasted the dust of dry red earth as we drove past isolated *kokerbooms* (quiver trees) with their gnarled branches pointing to the sun. We bought a box of yellow cling peaches from a roadside fruit stall and drove west, towards Pofadder and Aggenys, to the Augrabies Falls, known to the Khoikhoi people as 'the place of great noise', where the Orange River thunders into a canyon below. And in the late afternoon sun, we lay on top of cool smooth flanks of rock and watched the river water fall between granite boulders, 3000 million years old. Above the roar and spray of hurtling waters, we took turns to shout out all the things that came to mind, but were never spoken, with no fear of holding back and probably, no fear of being heard.

•

Six weeks before the trial on extenuation began, just after the Christmas break, pre-trial fever struck us all in varying degrees. It became clear that the Upington case would consume me for many months and take me away from Cape Town and the rest of my practice. I did not want to give up my other clients and I fought against the reality of representing twenty-five accused in a foreign town. I wanted to have a lifeline to the world I knew, some guarantee against my isolation and a creeping obsession with the case of the Upington 25. But it was not to be. My partners at Bernadt Vukic and Potash knew better and gently distributed my files within the firm. Ian Farlam SC was gearing up at a measured pace and I realised that my impatient compulsion to get things done, to reach perfection with immediate action, would never work with him. I would need a time of total immersion in the case and have the flexibility to attend to the accused and their families, work with the experts, travel at short notice between Cape Town and Upington and Johannesburg, brief funders and the media and attack practical arrangements essential to maintaining a consolidated front.

Each day leading up to the trial was full and racked with unfinished business. We fought with the state to extract a copy of a police video which, on viewing, contrasted with critical aspects of state evidence. The video showed dust around Sethwala's home, enough to obscure the sure vision of state witnesses who had identified the accused without effort at the trial on conviction. The video was a useful device to support the work of Graham Tyson—the sound of tear-gas canisters being fired was alarmingly similar to that of gunshot; the visual evidence of panic was strong. There was an obvious wave of crowd reaction, spurred by external forces and inner fears. Enough, we would argue, to support irrational changes in the behaviour of the accused. We spent hours reviewing and reworking the reports of all the experts and then settling them with Ian's final mark. Lest we leave any stone unturned and believing optimism should have its place, Ian suggested we investigate the possibility of some accused, whom we hoped might escape the death sentence, rendering community service as punishment. It seemed a far-fetched notion given the inclination of the court. However, I set about finding another expert to investigate this prospect. I spoke to Isabel Hancock at the National Institute for Crime Rehabilitation and Prevention (NICRO) and she agreed to travel to Upington to meet some of our clients for a feasibility study.

We drew and cut, glued and indexed and copied exhibits, compiling our visual aids for the court: copies of journal articles and texts referred to by our experts; a schedule of ages of the accused, as agreed with the state; a sample of the TATZ test prompts and responses; a map of Paballelo with coloured icons and matching key, showing the trail of the day's events on 13 November 1985; and a black-and-white chart of mug shots, faces of the accused holding numbered placards. We received special permission from Upington Prison authorities to photograph our clients. They were new to us, especially to Ian and our experts, and under pressure and cross-examination a set of photographs to which we could refer would be of great assistance. The tiny photographs, strictly for our personal use as required by the prison, became hot property amongst the press and the Paballelo community, commanding black-market promises and exchange.

The preparation for the trial was never confined just to the law. We continued to plan other approaches to ensure public interest in the case and open its doors to world scrutiny. We returned to Cape Town a week before the trial to brief representatives from foreign governments and the media. All the major newspapers and television stations had a presence as did important foreign interests—American, French, German, Spanish, English, Australian, Canadian. And aligning themselves with the outside world were three representatives from the South African parliament, Helen Suzman, Jan van Eck and Tiaan van der Merwe, who stood up and reminded us that there were some on the inside who gave a damn.

On a Sunday, a few days later, the South African Council of Churches launched a campaign to save the Upington 25. 'We want to show this government that our people are being supported. That we will stand in solidarity with the Upington 25.' Reverend Aubrey Beukes stood before 1000 people, packed into the Paballelo Anglican Church. '*Ja*.' 'Amen.' Low whispers of accord greeted the *Dominee*'s (Reverend's) words, spurring him on in God's name.

He walked forward and lit twenty-six candles and invited family members to speak. Mrs Lydia Yona, mother of Xolile, rose from her chair behind the pulpit. '*Ek bid vir die wat probeer onse seuns van hierdie lot red, want ons wil hê dat hulle terugkom na ons.*' ('I am praying for those who are trying to save our sons from this fate, because we want them back with us.') Reverend Lionel Louw, former chairman of the Western Province Council of Churches read out messages of support from community, church and trade union organisations. A statement from the National Council of Trade Unions (NACTU), who were to launch a separate campaign the following day, drew applause: 'The principle of common purpose ignores the problems of the community and the naked brutality of forty years of National Party rule.'

Only some of those who attended the launch would have been aware of the hatred certain sections of the community felt for *Dominee* Aubrey Beukes. On the day before the service, a warning had been scrawled in black paint on the concrete path leading up to the door of his Dutch Reformed Mission Church: 'Beukes, you neglect us—get right or get out.' For many of the *Dominee*'s parishioners, who lived in the coloured township of Blikkiesdorp, the trial was an issue for black people, of no concern to them. Some might have resented the Reverend's stand and his commitment to highlighting the plight of people who were not members of his congregation. It was not the first warning. Pamphlets had been mysteriously distributed in Blikkiesdorp alleging that Beukes had misused church funds to finance support of the trialists. A second pamphlet portraying him with horns and a tail, blood running from his mouth, a hammer and sickle alongside his name. Beukes was labelled a 'vehicle of Satan', bent on a revolution of hate and violence—why else would he try to save murderers? The words were bent on sowing a fear of association with the *Dominee*: his revolution would turn churches into 'political gathering places' where Bibles were 'burned in great piles'. The pamphlet called on believers to stand together and 'squeeze this boil'. The same day, brake fluid was poured over his car while he was celebrating his wife's birthday at a local hotel. And then came the telephone call from the *Wit Wolf* (White Wolf), threatening death and giving Beukes a last chance to stop his campaign.

Aubrey Beukes was convinced that the reign of threats came from sources outside his congregation. Independent Member of Parliament Jan van Eck sent a dossier on the victimisation of *Dominee* Aubrey Beukes to the Minister of Law and Order, Mr Adriaan Vlok. Vlok's reply, said van Eck, was a 'horrible implicit condonation of these kinds of events'. The Minister was clearly an old hand at deflecting blame. He wrote: 'It would seem that *Dominee* Beukes through his actions has himself brought upon the wrath of the community and this has probably led to acts of revenge. Yours faithfully.'

•

The nine months that Justice Basson had granted to us for preparation seemed to come to an end with disturbing speed. Despite my equivocal resistance, I had begun to make a new life in another town, far removed from the energy and sentiments of my own. Very quickly, we learnt who was on our side and how to manage the deep antagonism to our meddling in Upington's black *skande* (shame). It was a time of concentrated exploration of a place and its people, of forging friendships and winning trust. I became accustomed to the *taal* (Afrikaans language) of Paballelo and the quiet sameness of the streets and we joked at how at home I seemed with a country practice of the law. We had migrated to a desert town and built our own community from within. In nine months we had changed our lives. It was the continuation of twenty-five others, who had initiated our journey, that we hoped the Upington Supreme Court would allow.

9

•

Extenuation

We were emptying close to thirty boxes, freighted up a day or so earlier. Documents, law books, psychology texts, studies on group behaviour and mob violence, files of evidence and office stationery. Our makeshift office and library away from home was set up along the far wall of room number eight, Protea Hotel, with chairs and a small desk in the corner. Colin and Ian and I had flown to Upington on the late afternoon flight from Cape Town. Andre and Graham Tyson, to be called as our first expert witness on extenuation, were flying in from Johannesburg in the evening. There was an urgent call from a police station. It was Anton. He and Herman Raath, bringing more documents and files, had left earlier in the day. They were driving down from Windhoek in a hired car and planned to join us for dinner.

The call was from a town close to the southern Namibian border, near Keetmanshoop. It might have been a tyre, a blow-out. Suddenly, with no warning, their car had catapulted forward, turning through the air, once, maybe twice, and rolled off the road into the desert scrub. There were hundreds of sheets of paper and bent lever-arch files strewn across the sand, flung from doors and the boot ripped open on impact. A family travelling the same desolate route had found them. They were badly shaken but miraculously unharmed. I felt afraid as Anton talked. Afraid of how we took everything for granted. Of how we had plans and never questioned their presumed outcome. For a split second, I thought of sabotage. Anton was playful, glad to be alive. He assured us they were in good care. He knew some of the police at the station, past interrogators from times of detention in solitary confinement. 'I'm here with some old friends,' he laughed. He had arranged to pick up another hire car from a nearby town. They would see us early in the morning.

It was not an auspicious start but I was determined to have a good night. To sleep undisturbed and be fresh, clear-minded for the next day. Like the night before the first day back at school, I wanted everything to be in order, polished, ready for the unfamiliar. It was hot and still, and buried in the highest corner of my river-facing room was a cricket, shrieking in the dark. I pulled myself from half-sleep and filled a glass with water and threw it, and then another, upwards against the wall, hoping to drown its voice. Not long after, perhaps the length of a half-dream, a mosquito had broken through the net curtains and buzzed above my head. I dabbed expensive dots of perfume across my bed and lay waiting for the silence brought by a successful repellent. With no pity, the dawn birds began calling daybreak from willow trees on the banks of the Orange River. It was February in Upington, summer in a semi-desert town and I was going to have to adapt to airconditioned nights and restless sleep.

We gathered for an early morning breakfast at a big round table in the corner of the hotel dining room. It would become our table, reserved for the *prokureurs* (lawyers) by the dining staff. Some of the kitchen staff, while clearing plates or pouring our tea, whispered that they knew the accused. They were from Paballelo and they worried about what might happen. It was Monday, 6 February 1989 and we were off to court for day one of the Upington 25 trial on extenuation. We drove down Schröderstraat the short distance to the Upington Court to unload all our materials. The police had cordoned off a section in front of the court with yellow tape and waved us on. Vans with pacing, growling dogs inside were parked on either side of the prohibited area. Police with batons and dogs pushed in amongst a crowd of people waiting on the pavement. I started to walk towards a queue which stretched towards the front door of the court. Some in line had been there since 7.00am to make sure they got a place in the courtroom. Mr Gubula, near the front, was leaning on his stick. We had arrived, he said, minutes too late. A small group of youths had staged a protest outside the building. They had stood with placards and shouted 'Viva Upington 25' a couple of times. The police tore down their posters and hit them with *sjamboks* until they crouched to the ground.

The front door of the court was heavily guarded. Maximum security was on show. Police checked our every bag and case and then allowed us entry to the building. Once in the courtroom, Johanna, who served us tea from a stainless-steel pot and thick porcelain cups, called me and asked if I would go to the front. '*Daar is 'n probleem. Hulle sê daar is nie plekke vir al die mense buite. Xoliswa se ma en Innocentia is verbode. Kom, Mevrou, asseblief, kom.*' ('There is a problem. They [the police] say there is not enough room for all the people outside. Xoliswa's mother and Innocentia are being denied entry. Come, Miss, please, come.') Johanna had worked in the kitchen of the court for over a decade, sweeping, cleaning, making tea. She was aunt to Accused No 16, Xoliswa Dube. At the door, the police were arguing with Mrs Dube. I insisted there was enough room in the court and asked that Mrs Dube and Innocentia, Xoliswa's baby daughter, be allowed in. Baby Innocentia, not even a year old, was in a pink party dress with a tiny petticoat underneath. The police told Mrs Dube to sit Innocentia on a table at the door. They took Mrs Dube's bag and emptied out the contents. To complete their malicious search, they prodded Innocentia and checked the folds of her petticoat. There was a shuffle at the door. Those who had been turned away squeezed together and raised their arms, passing plastic shopping bags over heads towards me. They were food parcels and clean clothes for some of the accused, their names scribbled in big, uneven letters on the outside.

I returned to a full courtroom and the accused positioned in the dock. There was great chatter and reunion between them and families and friends. It was their first court appearance for almost a year and there was a sense of excitement and expectation, like an old stage show returning to town. We were guaranteed a long run with packed houses every day. There were new faces in the gallery, a welcome bank of support. From Cape Town and Pretoria came diplomats: Charles Crawford and Mick Frost representing Britain, Andrew Goledzinowski from the Australian Embassy, Gillian Milovanovic and Ron Trigg of the American Embassy and Morgan Kulla from the US Consulate, John Schram and Ross Stubbert of the Canadian Embassy, Luc Almerais from the French, Remert Cohen and Peter Mollema from the Dutch, and for the Spanish, Alfonzo Sanz. Pilot and diplomat, Gerhard Dedic, had flown down to Upington in a six-seater plane to represent Austria. He was tall and blond and very striking, clearly a man who enjoyed the good life. Like a magnanimous host, he invited his colleagues from other nations to fly, courtesy of Austria, back to Pretoria. There were nervous declinations except from Anton, who asked if a detour to Windhoek was possible. Brian Currin from Pretoria, Director of Lawyers for Human Rights, Pierre van der Heever from the South African Council of Churches, Mary Burton, President of the Black Sash and Sash executive member, Muriel Crewe and representatives from the media, international and national, arrived throughout the day.

The court was ready to proceed. Ian Farlam SC took the plunge and outlined our case on extenuation. The court had determined the guilt of the accused and their participation in the common purpose. Working within the confines of these findings we would seek to show, on a balance of probabilities, that the accused were not wholly cognisant of their actions found to have caused Sethwala's death. Our experts would demonstrate that a combination of factors, historically and socially based, explained the conduct of the accused sufficiently to waive the imposition of the death penalty.

Graham Tyson, slight and bearded, papers under his arm, walked to the witness stand and took the oath. All eyes were on the professor and social psychologist, head of the University of Witwatersrand's Division of Experimental Psychology. He stood in the box, tilting forward, nudged his glasses onto his nose and waited for his cue from Ian. For two full days Graham, author of a contemporary study on mob killings in South Africa, sought to explain how twenty-five people with different home backgrounds, intelligence and personalities could have come together to perpetrate a murder in broad daylight, with no attempt at stealth or disguise. 'None of the mob tried to mask their identity...though it is obvious they could be identified easily. Even after the deceased fired his shotgun from inside his house, the crowd continued to throw stones, regardless of their personal danger. The attack itself was irrational: the first two blows with the butt of the shotgun killed Sethwala, yet the mob continued to assault him for between four and ten minutes. What rational purpose could that serve, especially when it logically increased the chances of being caught or identified? The only reasonable explanation for this behaviour seems to be that the accused were deindividuated.'

Given the great variations between the accused, the events of 13 November 1985, argued Tyson, could not be explained in terms of a group of people brought together by prior disposition or criminal intention. His reading of reports by clinical psychologist Dr Herman Raath and social worker Mrs Nelmie Barnard suggested that the behaviour of the accused was totally out of character. The murder of Sethwala originated from a spontaneous outburst, lacking in any rational plan or common purpose. Tyson, referring to the extensive court record, listed, with painstaking detail, factors and incidents which illustrated the irrational conduct of the accused, the complete lack of awareness of the consequences of their actions. Earlier in the hearing, Mrs Beatrice Sethwala, mother of the murdered policeman, had testified that Accused No 15, Boy Jafta, and her son, Lucas, were 'like brothers', Boy was 'almost like a son' to her. Former policeman, Accused No 21, Albert Tywilli, had been the dead man's best friend. Their actions in the context of their relationship to Sethwala and his family, said

Professor Tyson, suggested they were deindividualised, indifferent to how others saw their behaviour.

Tyson moved on to highlight psychological forces operating in the crowd which could have led to, or enhanced, the process of deindividuation. Arousal, rumours, frustration, modelling, direct provocation, conformity pressures. Rumours that Paballelo's mayor was a sizeable sum in rent arrears, yet avoided eviction, unlike other residents, were likely to have heightened feelings of frustration and tension amongst an impoverished community. Rumours that the meeting to discuss rent and other grievances was organised by police. The breaking-up of the meeting by the police, in the face of such rumours, would have increased frustration and anger. The stone-throwing, the angry shouts from people in the crowd, the sound of gunshots as tear-gas was fired by police, uncertainty whether live ammunition was being used, the effects of the tear-gas and panicked attempts to get away would all have served to arouse the crowd. 'This, coupled with people's frustration, would have led to intense anger and greatly increased the possibility of violence. People would also be more susceptible to suggestion and more likely to act without thinking of the consequences. Arousal feeds on itself and tends to grow rapidly. Things happened quickly and there was no chance for the arousal to dissipate.' Where there was deindividuation in a mob situation, modelling—a copy-cat reaction by members of the crowd—was likely to occur or increase. Some of the accused, given their aggressive natures, could unwittingly have led the mob by starting to throw stones, with others modelling their behaviour on that of others. An internal pressure to conform may also start to emerge. 'It's very similar to what happens at concerts when a performer is given a standing ovation.'

At the afternoon tea-break, we brought in a large cake from a *banketbakker* (confectioner) in Schröderstraat. It was the thirtieth birthday of Accused No 2, Tros Gubula, and we sang 'Happy Birthday' and shouted 'Hip Hip Hooray'. Later in the evening, we reviewed the day and the quality performance by Graham Tyson. We sat in the garden of the Protea Hotel, with drinks around the pool, and looked out at the Orange River and the orange sunset. Graham was concerned that his presentation had escaped the judge's comprehension, that his thesis would be viewed as fanciful. 'Ag, Graham,' Anton leant forward into the circle, 'you were a complete star.' At that stage of the trial, we were still naive enough to be encouraging. Dinner at Le Must was filled with conversation about independent Namibia and deindividuation and whether, as Gaye Davis asked in her *Weekly Mail* article at the end of the week, a mob could have a mind. We left Anton and John Carlin, Southern African correspondent for the English *Independent*, close to midnight, still arguing about the best economic blueprint for Namibia.

On the second day, Tyson continued to examine the conduct of the individual accused against the backdrop of his social and psychological analysis. When he came to Accused No 10, Justice Bekebeke, 27-year-old nurse, guilty of dealing the two blows which killed Sethwala, the courtroom became still, holding its breath. 'Justice Bekebeke is a person of above-average intelligence, with realistic ambitions, unfulfilled largely due to factors beyond his control. This, in itself, must have led to feelings of relative deprivation and of frustration. He is someone who cares about the welfare of others as evidenced by his becoming a nurse and wanting to become a doctor. His caring nature together with an awareness of the problems in Paballelo may well have caused him to become involved in trying to solve them. He is not an aggressive hoodlum, but an intelligent, mature and decent person, with a lot to offer his community. Yet he acted in a barbaric manner. This court has found Justice Bekebeke had an intention to kill the deceased. One would have expected someone with his intellectual ability to have planned the murder more carefully, executed it more discreetly. The degree to which he was aroused and deindividuated can be gauged by the frenzied manner in which he caught and killed the deceased.'

Tyson concluded that it was highly probable that all of the accused were deindividuated to varying degrees. Like Justice Bekebeke, most of the accused, he said, had acted out of character:

Kenneth Khumalo, 32, former councillor and colleague of the deceased, 'Sensitive to social situations and unsure of himself', likely to conform; Tros Gubula, 30, another conformist, 'not the sort of person who would want to stand out as different'; David Lekhanyane, 24, 'a responsible young man, with high moral standards'; Myner Gudlani Bovu, 28, a trainee teacher with 'high aspirations and a reservoir of frustration, aware of the inequalities around him'; Zuko Xabendlini, 32, 'poor self-image and unassertive, timid nature'; Elisha Matshoba, 23, 'an outstanding young man, quiet, studious and talented, an active churchgoer, of exemplary behaviour'; Barry Bekebeke, 22, brother of Justice, 'sensitive and artistic, intelligent and ambitious'; Ronnie Masiza, 22, 'a responsible and exemplary young man, despite the unfavourable circumstances in which he grew up'; Boy Jafta, 23, a friend of the deceased and treated as a son of the house, whose 'life seemed to revolve around soccer'; Elizabeth Bostaander, 22, 'quiet and reserved, high moral values, exemplary student'; Evelina de Bruin, 57, 'very traditional, low frustration tolerance, under stress appears to act impulsively', and her husband, Gideon Madlongolwane, 61, 'traditional and loyal'; Albert Tywilli, 26, the deceased's best friend; Neville Witbooi, 20, 'a phlegmatic character'.

Low intellectual ability, lack of sophistication and a poorly developed system of values were suggested as factors leading some accused to being swept up by the events of 13 November 1985: Jeffrey Sekiya, 24; Sarel Jacobs, 22; Roy Swartbooi, 22; Ivan Kazi, 21, 'the emotional and intellectual sophistication of a 12-year-old'; Xoliswa Dube, 20, 'naive, a childlike nature', and Wellington Masiza, 26, brother of Ronnie. A few exhibited a tendency towards aggressive behaviour and were thus easily provoked: Abel Kutu, 22; Andrew Lekhanyane, 28, brother of David, 'an explosive personality, hostility to authority'; Zonga Mokhatle, 30, 'lack of a strong value system and a tendency to respond impulsively with aggression' and Xolile Yona, 24, 'strong resentment to authority figures'.

Graham completed his evidence and took a solitary evening walk to settle his mind before his cross-examination by the state began the following day. Anton, Colin and I committed ourselves to an exercise program for fear of going soft in the limbs from sitting long days in court. We joined the Suid-Afrikaanse Spoorweg Ontspanningsklub (the South African Railways Recreation Club) for three months. The secretary of the club, Paula Pieters, signed us up as short-term members for the sum of R4-75 each and dropped off a key to the tennis courts. Andrew Goledzinowski agreed to be our fourth and arrived on the courts in bright floral board shorts down to his knees. They were evidently high fashion in Australia. It was a strange, languid game. The high altitude and warm dense air meant that the balls bounced higher than normal and flopped back to earth at low speed. We started out with energy and a keen competitive streak. But one by one we slowed down as heat and fatigue combined, and we shuffled about on the court, barely scooping the ball over the net. Colin declared he was suffering from deindividuation and needed a beer. He invited us to 'model' his behaviour and join him for a drink at the pool before dinner. We followed suit, like the copy-cats of Tyson's evidence. I think we were all beginning to enjoy our new evening ritual.

•

'Poor self-image and unassertive'; 'the emotional and intellectual sophistication of a 12-year-old'; 'low intellectual ability and a poorly developed system of values.' There was something I found disturbing in the way we presented the accused, something unsympathetic, clinical, demeaning. In a written report, these descriptions were tolerable, the results of a psychological investigation, contained and private. But now, as we broadcast their details in the presence of each accused, as they heard them, perhaps compared them, in the presence of one another, I felt their inner beings being pierced open.

The accused, however, as they often did, brought me to a reality. They knew that the individual profiles compiled by the experts were necessarily uncomplicated, expedients framed in technical language, compliant with traditional viewpoints to suit a narrow purpose. Inevitably, evidence on the scale required had to be accessible and capable of simple categorisation by the adjudicators. The presentation of evidence—the reading of lengthy reports and extracts from weighty texts, expositions of complex theories, 'scientific' and 'lay' accounts of crowd behaviour—seemed often endless and dull. Most of the testimony of our expert witnesses was given in English. Afrikaans was the preferred language of the judge and the prosecution. It was also the language of our clients. Clearly, technical evidence in English did not have wide appeal. A few of the accused persisted and made notes and offered suggestions. But throughout much of the presentation of our case on extenuation, many of them sat and whispered, exchanged gossip and fantasies, drew, wrote notes and, on hot afternoons, closed their eyes and rested their heads, inured to harsh descriptions of the self.

10

•

The accused

Life at Upington *Gevangenis* (Prison) for months on end was desperate and colourless. Meals were often inedible and too hurried
to break up the day. Worse, they were out of sync with usual time:
breakfast at 7am, lunch at 11am and dinner at 3pm. At least on
court days, lunch accorded with standard time and dinner was
closer to 5pm. Boredom and hunger, particularly during the long
afternoons and barren nights, were common complaints. We
invented a small distraction: preparation of lists for the Friday
afternoon shop and door-to-door delivery. We drafted a house rule.
Shopping lists had to be handed to us each Thursday before court
adjourned. If a list was not handed in, the accused would miss
out. There were no exceptions and no latecomers allowed.

The lists were very detailed and gender and hobby specific.
Xoliswa Dube and her friend, Elizabeth Bostaander, Accused
No 17, liked Je Taime body spray and Dolly Varden hair gel. The
men went for Brut and Brylcream. Friday afternoons, before our
flight to Cape Town, we would load shopping trolleys at Checkers, the O.K. Bazaars and Upington's art supplies shop. Packets
and boxes would fill the boot and back seat of our hire car and
we would speed off to the prison, squeezing in just before 4pm
closing time, with our orders for delivery and distribution. Boxing

magazines for Xolile Yona, photo-comics on young doctors and nurses in love for Elizabeth and Xoliswa. Nine bottles of glycerine oil, eleven of Dawn cocoa butter, seven tubes of Colgate toothpaste, Lux soap and Lip-ice. Cartons of Chesterfield and Gunston cigarettes, Peter Stuyvesant for Accused No 1, Kenneth Khumalo, dried sausage and salami, pockets of oranges, boxes of Ouma's rusks, 7 Up cooldrink, fruit chews and Make-a-Litre powdered milk. Elisha Matshoba, Accused No 9, artist in residence, produced lists of exhaustive particularity: 'Drawing lead pencils: B, 2B, 4B, 6B; drawing brushes: 000, 2, 8, 14; fixatives, drawing inks (vermillion), A4 Creative Sketch Book. NB. The pencils must be Staedtler or Royal Sovereign.' And he would add, '170 packets of matches, 10 x 500ml Bostick glue (for wood), sandpaper, twine, clothes pegs and varnish,' for ship-building.

There were two distinct schools amongst the accused: the artists and the athletes. From the artists and crafted from thousands of burnt matchsticks, came 'arks of faith', model matchstick boats, carefully structured during hours of confinement. Steamboats, pleasure cruisers, elaborate ocean liners; expressions of dreams, reminders of journeys away from captivity, away from death, Christmas gifts from prison. Elisha Matshoba, Justice and Barry Bekebeke, Zonga Mokhatle and Wellington Masiza were master shipbuilders. Kenneth Khumalo used broken wooden clothes pegs to build a church, a birthday present for his wife. Xolile Yona, the 'ox-wagon king', made miniature wagons, reminiscent of those used by the Voortrekkers during the Great Trek migration northwards in the 1800s. He had also led the construction of a matchstick model court, a gift for Andre, complete with public gallery, models of the judge and assessors, tiny books piled up before them, the dock and benches for the accused. Teams of helpers would burn the ends of matches and then position them on a ship's hull to signal stripes and design. Green plastic 7 Up cooldrink bottles were cut into portholes and windows, and faces from magazines became passengers, looking out to sea.

The athletes had approached the future head-on, and in anticipation of spending long periods in jail added soccer gear to their shopping lists. '*Andy, u weet mos laat ons vir 'n lang tydperk gaan in die gevangenis bly. Aangesien ons 'n paar manne is wat sokker speel, gaan ons u vra om asb vir ons sokker boots en sokkies met skeen gards koop want ons will sokker gaan speel.*' ('Andy, as you know, we are going to spend a long time in prison. Seeing that a few of us play soccer, please will you buy us soccer boots, socks and shin-guards so we can play soccer.') Underneath the request, they placed their orders:

'Sarel—Adidas; size no. 9½ shin-guards with socks

Roy—Adidas; size no. 7 shin-guards with socks

Neville—Adidas; size no. 7 knee-cap with socks. And ankle-guard.' Ronnie, Jeffrey and Elisha were also team hopefuls. I wrote to the South African Council of Churches about this request. Saki Macozama from the Council was able to help. Some weeks later, a short time before sentence, Saki arrived in Upington with a large cardboard box filled with Adidas products—boots, socks, shin-guards of all types and bright blue T-shirts. The Upington 25 soccer team was fit for play.

•

Elisha 'Sgibo' Matshoba, Accused No 9, was an integrated kind of man. Both creative and sporty: he had a soft, robust appeal and his face sparkled with a mischievous charm. Elisha sang for the Upington gospel group, Voices Unlimited, and as leader of the Pathfinder church youth group, he had become an accomplished actor, his dramatisation of biblical themes attracting far greater interest from churchgoers than Sunday sermons. He played a smooth game of soccer and was rated as a tennis player of some prowess, earning the nickname 'Boris Becker' from Paballelo residents and fans. But it was his art that gave him most pleasure. He was born in the Karoo desert town of De Aar in 1966 and his work as an artist was a feature of De Aar's Nozwakazi township. He decorated township houses with intricate house numbers and painted 'Nozwakazi Town Hall' on the local civic building. Art was his favourite school subject and he spent each day in court keenly observing, soaking in every scene and each participant for portrayal in pencil sketches and drawings of coloured ink, the judge, defence team and witnesses his models.

Elisha's father, Mr Abednego Matshoba, was his greatest fan and during a visit to Upington he hovered near journalists, bursting to report on the excellence of Elisha as son and artist. His own story drew more coverage however. As a black pensioner Abednego Matshoba had little chance of raising the train fare to Upington to see his son. During the Christmas season before the trial on extenuation began, he played Santa Claus in the sweltering heat of midsummer at Ellerines, a department store in the small desert town of De Aar, asking customers to make a wish. On some days, standing for hours in his heavy costume and long white beard, the heat was extreme. He fainted, he said, on two occasions. He raised the fare to Upington and arrived some months later to discover that Elisha had become a contender for death row and would not be returning to De Aar for some time.

There were three women on trial. Xoliswa Dube, Accused No 16. Elizabeth Bostaander, Accused No 17, and Evelina de Bruin, Accused No 18, close to sixty years of age, mother of ten and wife of Gideon Madlongolwane, Accused No 19. Xoliswa and Elizabeth, both high school pupils at the time of their arrests, would sit close together in court, whispering behind interlocking fingers, often dressed for a day, even a night, out on the town: Xoliswa in high-necked white frilly blouse and Elizabeth in black, a lace dress with low-cut back. During the trial on conviction, Xoliswa gave birth to her daughter, Innocentia, Xoliswa's show of innocence to the world. Xoliswa's pain was compounded when she agreed that Innocentia should be taken away from her mother—and the lice in prison. Instead, she would come to court each day and be breastfed during adjournments. Innocentia went to live with Xoliswa's mother in Paballelo. Each day Mrs Dube would bring her to the courthouse by taxi as she was too heavy to carry the six-kilometre journey which many families would walk. Innocentia had inherited her mother's sense of dress, arriving at court most days in a tiny party frock with billowing petticoat. She would sit in the gallery, propped up on her grandmother's lap, and peer at the dock. When Xoliswa came into court and turned to face her girl, Innocentia would break into a shiver of joy, hands held out in a jig of delight.

There was no doubt that Xoliswa had a good eye for quality. Her courtroom trysts with Elisha, however, posed a dilemma and she sought counsel of a non-legal kind. Her letter was a refreshing invitation to focus on lives which went on in spite of the trial. A folded note was handed to me with 'Andy' written in the top left-hand corner. Underneath, a discreet bracketed '(No 16)' suggested its sender.

Ek weet regtig nie hoe om dit te stel nie maar ek het dan nou op (Sgibo) No 9 verlief geword. Ek het hom regtig lief. Ek weet dat hy ook vir my lief is maar daar is die probleem van sy meisie wat in ons pad staan. Hy het my wel gevertel dat hulle twee nie meer lief vermekaar is nie. Tog voel ek sleg want Sgibo se meisie is lief vir hom. Ek wil nie probeer om mense seer te maak nie; want ek sal ook nie daarvan hou dat ander my moet seer maak nie.

(I really do not know how to put this but I have gone and fallen in love with [Sgibo] No 9. I really love him. I know that he also loves me but there is the problem of his girlfriend who is standing in our way. He did however tell me that they no longer love one another. But I feel bad because Sgibo's girlfriend loves him. I do not want to hurt people because I would not like it if others hurt me.)

Xoliswa's dilemma threw me a little. I had been so consumed with the trial that my own needs and fears and hopes beyond this life in Upington had surfaced only to be pushed aside and discarded. For a brief spell, Xoliswa, a young woman and mother, wanting and daring to love, turned my mind towards my own complexes in life and love. I resisted the pull and got on with the task of writing a reply. I reasoned that if Sgibo, Elisha as I knew him, had told her that he and his girlfriend no longer loved one another, Xoliswa could love him, particularly in circumstances where the chances of his old girlfriend finding out about his new love seemed remote. Xoliswa read my reply once and then again and blushed. A further note came down the line.

Baie dankie Andy. Ek is baie bly om 'n suster soos u te kan hê wat ek op kan vertrou en 'n mens baie kan verstaan. Ek is baie jammer vir die No 16. Ek vra om verskoning vir dit van u suster Xoliswa.
(Thank you very much Andy. I am very happy to have a sister like you in whom I can trust and who can understand a person well. I am very sorry about this No 16. I ask for forgiveness from your sister Xoliswa.)

We had spoken to one another and shared something special, breaking the barrier of lawyer and client. This was to be our secret, as sisters.

Some of the twenty-five were content to sit on the rim of the group or be in their own worlds, shy and afraid, never trusting the words they were tempted to speak. The outsiders had reason to be so. They were the five 'extras' (Jeffrey Sekiya, Sarel Jacobs, Roy Swartbooi, Neville Witbooi, Ivan Kazi), brought to the identity parade by the police not as suspects, but as fill-ins. The less outspoken accused were also silenced by the madness of their predicament, bewildered passengers dragged along on some mysterious trip. Zonga Mokhatle, Accused No 11, survived by entry to his *skemerwêreld* (twilight zone), scoring *dagga* through the prison network of deals and trade-offs. There were those who stood out, who felt comfortable to lead and were looked to for their leadership. They were the spokesmen, the managers and the brave when those around them began to flounder and lost their will. To my eye, Myner Bovu, Justice Bekebeke and the brothers Andrew and David Lekhanyane shared a sensibility about the trial. They came to it each day as if to a job, aware of the boundaries within which we had to juggle ideals and limitations. They seemed devoid of expectation, but clear about their needs and they approached disappointment with a wise composure, as if inevitable and intrinsic to their task.

Myner Bovu, Accused No 5, was a student teacher at the Cape Teachers College at Fort Beaufort at the time of his arrest, home

for the holidays. In his late twenties, Myner was completing the
second year of his three-year course. He lived with his father, a
frail man in his late eighties, in a small house in Paballelo. Mr
Bovu was a municipal worker. Myner was concerned for his father.
He wanted him to retire but the trial had severely delayed his
chances of becoming a teacher and supporting his father. Myner
played soccer for the Paballelo Chiefs and he sang in the choir of
the Ethiopian Church of South Africa. He liked to amuse, to laugh
and he liked it even more when we laughed with him. His envi-
able quality of being able to lighten hard times belied a depth of
intelligence and a curiosity for knowledge and understanding.

When our case on extenuation began with its difficult theories
and complex deductions from psychology and sociology, Myner
would borrow court transcripts and texts from our experts. He
would read and wrestle with detail and concepts and reduce them
for lessons in the prison, held each evening after court. Myner,
Justice Bekebeke, Kenneth and David would tirelessly guide their
fellow accused through the maze of evidence and cross-examination
by the state and ensure that despite their failure to testify and the
ennui that had taken hold, they were not mere observers. I knew
when their teachings had hit a chord of recognition. Sometimes,
after the prosecution had presented a fact or a conclusion for the
court's consideration and van Rensburg would pause to let his
wisdom sink in, the accused would utter a collective 'yoh!' or 'tssss'
of incredulity or rejection, shaking their heads from side to side.
When Farlam, or 'the old man' as the accused would call him,
dismissed a claim of the state with swift disregard, a short whisper of 'ja' would mean we had won strong approval from the dock.

In the judgment on conviction Mr Justice Basson had found
that Justice Bekebeke, Accused No 10, had inflicted two blows to
the head of Lucas Sethwala with a rifle. These two blows were
fatal, said the court, and 'could cumulatively and individually
have caused the death'. When I met Justice 'Basie' Bekebeke, the
call to treat him as the primary perpetrator of a murder was
immediately hopeless. Justice was twenty-six, tall and elegant
and immediately engaging and empathetic. His face was beautiful

and striking, a bone sculpture of dark and polished brown. He had grown up in Paballelo and his family was well known and respected. I visited Susan Bekebeke, mother of Justice and Barry, at their home before our trial began. She and her husband had wanted the very best for their children, to learn and to work as hard as they could. Basie, she said, with a sad pride, loved to read and he drew well, mostly portraits. For Christmas, he had used his time in prison to build her a matchstick ship. She turned and pointed to his masterpiece. The model ship sat high up on a mantelpiece, almost life-size in the tiny front room of the Bekebeke home.

In 1985, Justice had planned to attempt matriculation. He had spent the previous four years training as a nurse at the Windhoek Provincial Hospital, before returning to Paballelo to write the matric exam. He wanted to care for people, to become a doctor. At the time of the murder, he was visiting his family on a break from work in Windhoek. On 13 November 1985, one image plagued his mind. The rest, we never spoke about. He saw Lucas Sethwala shoot a young boy in the spine. The harm to the child filled Justice with a horror and a rage, a rage he found difficult to comprehend, perhaps difficult to constrain. In the telling of this tale, some may see the lure of false sentiment, even delusion. But however harshly I would judge the acts attributed to Justice, I could not swear that Justice Bekebeke had acted with an intention to kill.

The Lekhanyane brothers were one of three sets of brothers convicted of murder: Justice and Barry Bekebeke, Ronnie and Wellington Masiza, Andrew and David Lekhanyane. Their father, Reverend Lekhanyane, was Minister of the African Episcopal Church. The Lekhanyane family set up home wherever the church could offer the Reverend a post and contributions—they moved from Beaufort West to Pampierstad, from Upington to Graaff Reinet. The family had always been impoverished. David wanted to become a mechanic and studied at the Moremogolo Technical College in Kimberley, earning a Certificate of Merit for 'Earnest Endeavour in Study'. When Andrew left school, he worked at

Sam's Meat Market in Upington and then for an electrical contracting firm where he learnt to make switchboard boxes. His wages went to his parents one week and to his girlfriend Elsie Vice and their three young children the other. Andrew and David had a dread of poverty. Their father's financial struggle had clearly shaped their desire to become self-sufficient, licensed men of trades.

Of all the sets of brothers, the Masizas were hardest hit. When Ronnie and Wellington were convicted of murder, their father, Eliot, a labourer and security guard, suddenly fell ill. On a visit to Mrs Virginia Masiza, she sat in a chair, a heaviness in her body and in her voice: 'There is a terrible pain in my heart.' She heaved her chest and stared at the floor. 'Life is very hard for me now, because my children were helpful to me. With their own hands they helped to build this house. When they were convicted, my husband grew sick and when the judge refused them bail, he was so shocked and grieved about their terrible plight that he grew weaker and weaker. He never recovered. He died of a broken heart soon after.' Mrs Masiza was struggling with life.

Kenneth 'Pinkie' Khumalo, Accused No 1, was well known. He was title-holder, the named accused in the official case citation. I think he felt a certain responsibility, that in some way he carried the other accused, that their lives depended on his. Kenneth behaved accordingly. On most days of the trial he wore a suit and tie. With his clean-cut looks and square-framed glasses, he presented a sharp intelligence. He read widely, he was eloquent and liked to lead discussion. He was listened to and commanded respect from those around him, but if pushed, he would enter the fray. To give the full picture, Kenneth's overtures could sometimes border on being self-serving.

He was born in Upington in 1956 and completed his schooling in the Eastern Cape. His ambition to become a lawyer was thwarted when he was unable to secure admission to Fort Hare University. He was married with three young children and he provided the sole income for the family. Kenneth had various jobs in Upington and the family moved to Windhoek where he found steady work at a general dealer. The family were forced to return to Upington at some stage and Kenneth became unemployed once again. In Paballelo, he was drawn to local politics and his popularity secured his election unopposed as the first mayor of the township. He resigned as mayor in order to draw a decent income and at the time of his arrest he was employed as Treasurer of the Paballelo Town Council.

He moved like a polished fighter from the streets and he watched before he spoke his mind. His style was to draw me apart from the others, to whisper into my ear, to take me into his confidence. Kenneth was serious and concerned and he retained the stature of a man in authority, usually some distance from the rest of the accused. He was persuaded by the deindividuation thesis and approved its application to the group. But in private, he would insist that he was a man who would always keep his head no matter the extent of madness in his midst. Kenneth was a man in control, at least for the time being.

11

•

Days on trial

The state cross-examined Graham Tyson for four full days. It seemed an unnecessarily long time to make a simple point: that Tyson had failed to follow the 'correct [scientific] procedures' in establishing whether the twenty-five had been deindividuated. Tyson stood his ground, content that the procedures he had adopted reflected the requirements of the law on extenuating circumstances: that evidence of an accused's subjective state of mind and emotions could be established either through their own testimony or through extensive investigation and interviews undertaken by expert witnesses. Despite his cool approach in court, Graham became despondent and unnerved as each day fell into the next and there seemed no end to his inquisition. Graham and his young family had to make a Qantas flight. They were leaving South Africa to live in Australia where Graham was to take up a university teaching post shortly after his arrival. We were worried that the prosecution would learn of Graham's plans and prolong his cross-examination and so rattle his fortitude. But to them, Graham played a man of endless patience, with time to answer questions, no matter how pointless and repetitive. The state concluded its cross-examination two days before his departure. We drove at a dangerous speed to the Upington airport and Graham just made the last plane to Johannesburg. 'What a way to leave the country,' he turned to say a last goodbye. 'I'm sure they'll be alright. Do they have the death penalty in Australia?'

Martin West's cross-examination by the state was comparatively brief. The reason may have been that one of his primary tools of evidence was a socioeconomic survey commissioned by the town council of Paballelo. Martin had discovered the existence of the report, *Paballelo: socioekonomiese analise, Desember 1987*, (Paballelo: socioeconomic analysis, December 1987) conducted by Rademeyer and Van Wyk, urban and regional planners and development economists during his research for the case. We requested permission to review this public document and Martin told us of an amiable but unsuccessful visit to the Town Clerk's office to effect its release.

Mr Tienie Nortje came to Paballelo as Town Clerk shortly after Lucas Sethwala's murder. He prided himself on being tough but fair and, reported Martin, he claimed to understand the black mind, an insight he had acquired despite his allegiances apparent from his office decor. A South African flag stood firm on his desk and a large painting of President PW Botha hung above his public service green leather chair. Mr Nortje showed Martin the report, the cover and the index, but he was sorry he could not oblige him with access to the findings. The document was private and confidential, Nortje said, and even if he could have given Martin a copy, it would have been too costly to reproduce. We had no alternative but to subpoena Mr Tienie Nortje to court with the document and so discovered the basis for his reluctance: the survey presented Paballelo as having the highest levels of unemployment (30.9 per cent compared with the national average overall unemployment rate of 18.2 per cent), domestic overcrowding (965 additional families on 1421 occupied residential sites) and the lowest levels of income as compared with averages in black townships across the country (92.4 per cent of Paballelo breadwinners earned less than the Minimum Living Level in August 1987 of R557-00 per month, with 57.5 per cent earning less than R250-00 per month). The survey was a bolster to our argument on extenuation from an unexpected, but in the eyes of the court, wholly reliable source.

The residents of Paballelo, said Martin West, were 'the most disadvantaged [in Upington] in terms of facilities, employment, schooling and opportunities for advancement. They were without the direct political representation which could engage those who controlled their lives. They had little confidence in their Town Council. They were third-class citizens in Upington, which is a conservative area in terms of white politics, subject to all the controls and restrictions placed upon black people generally.' Paballelo itself was a 'relatively quiet, conservative area. Crime was reportedly fairly low by township standards, and there was less "unrest" than in some other areas [during the riots which spread across the country] in 1976 and 1985. But this in no way detracted from the underlying frustrations and sense of deprivation. I would expect, in fact, the more conservative areas to keep things bottled up, and to explode periodically. Precipitating action on 13 November 1985—the breaking up of the meeting (given perceptions of some that it been called by the police), the firing of teargas by the police—combined with this history of deprivation, harassment from officialdom and the conservative nature of the area, could have led to a crossing of this threshold of frustration, contributing to an explanation of the behaviour of many of the accused, whose actions on the day seemed to run counter to what we know of them as individuals.'

Martin's evidence laid the ground for a debate we were to have with state witness, Dr CP de Kock, a sociologist attached to the South African Human Sciences Research Council (HSRC) and a regular lecturer at the Defence and Police Colleges on crowd dynamics and control.

Dr de Kock would argue that the murder of Sethwala was not a 'spontaneous isolated outburst' but an orchestrated incident which had to be seen in the context of unrest around the country, as part of a countrywide mobilisation of blacks, the aim of which was to make the country ungovernable. The existence of this emerging pattern or strategy of hostility from black people towards figures of authority in particular was, he assured us, supported by his research in areas of unrest in black townships. Under examination, he disclosed his methodology: when conducting this research, he had generally been accompanied by policemen.

De Kock chose to support his 'orchestrated plan versus spontaneous incident' argument by extensive reference to a chapter on revolutionary violence he had written for a book published in 1988, *South Africa: The Challenge of Reform* from his work. For some reason, Dr de Kock had forgotten an extract which supported the argument of Martin West. In our cross-examination of de Kock, Ian Farlam quoted from the chapter, reminding the doctor of his published words: 'Almost without exception, non-violent action involves masses of people in highly emotional causes...The people involved are already highly frustrated, they have a high level of aggression and regard the system as non-legitimate (and they also regard the agents of control as non-legitimate). As a result, non-violent direct action can very quickly be transformed into violent direct action. All that is required is a triggering incident (a spark) which is usually provided the moment the agents of control arrive on the scene.' Luckily, de Kock still agreed with his previous position but he did tell the court that this did not mean that police should not take action. 'One of the greatest problems in this country is whether the police should use minimum force.' De Kock left us with his quandary: 'The question is, has minimum force in fact worked in the South African context?' Mr Justice Basson thanked Dr de Kock for his testimony and for throwing 'much light on the matter'.

The night before Martin returned to Cape Town, we had a whole new batch of guests for dinner at Le Must. Among them was Joyce Mokhesi, sister of Francis Mokhesi, one of the Sharpeville Six sentenced to death in December 1985 in the Safatsa common purpose trial. In November 1988, Francis and his co-accused had their death sentences commuted, his to twenty-five years imprisonment. Joyce had been a critical force for the Six. She had travelled around the world campaigning for their freedom and she and her husband, Peter, had arrived in Upington to bring good wishes and advice to the trialists and their families. We were also joined by MP Jan van Eck, John Battersby from the *New York Times*, photographer Anne Day, Mercia Andrews from the education trust, the South African Council for Higher Education (SACHED), which supplied the accused with all their educational needs for studying by correspondence in prison, foreign correspondent David Beresford, who wrote for the *Guardian*, Arlene Getz of the *Sydney Morning Herald*, Marius Bosch of the *Cape Times* and Herman Raath, who was next in line for cross-examination. We had a toast to Martin and to 'spontaneous outbursts' and then to Anton, who arrived late for dinner to announce that he had been elected to the SWAPO Central Committee.

David Beresford declared that he had no choice but to take me to task. 'That was some lead, Andy. Your Mr Nortje. Thanks for the tip-off.' He was dabbling with sarcasm. David had been keen to interview someone who might give him an insight into how those who ruled the town had reacted to the trial, an official perspective on its impact on the community. I had suggested he contact Town Clerk, Mr Nortje. I told him about Martin's conversation, how he 'understood the black mind' and of his damning report on the township which was now accessible as part of the public record of the trial.

Delighted with his find, David called the Upington Town Council and asked to be put through to Mr Nortje. 'Hullo, stores,' came the reply. 'Is that Mr Nortje?' asked David with the requisite respect for a man in authority. 'Ja, speaking,' was the curt reply. David introduced himself and asked if he might meet Nortje the following day for a few minutes. He was interested in his views on the Upington trial and its impact on the town for an article for an international newspaper. 'Ja, okay.' There was a faint nervous giggle from Nortje. 'What time would suit you?' 'Ag, anytime, just come to stores and ask for me, I'm in supplies.' David replaced the receiver and felt uncomfortable. Something worried him. The busy Town Clerk available to speak to a foreign journalist at the drop of a hat; a senior public servant located in 'stores', no less 'supplies'. It didn't hang together, something was amiss. David had little time and wasn't going to risk it with the wrong man. He called back the next morning to cancel. 'O, hell man,' Nortje was clearly put out. 'I told my wife and the family I was going to be in the news, on TV. Anyway,' he mumbled 'suit yourself.'

It transpired that David Beresford had been caught out by the intricate needs of racial division. Apartheid infrastructure dictated that Upington town and Paballelo township each have their own (different) town clerks. David had called the Upington Town Council and had been put through to Nortje, an employee of the white administration; the Mr Nortje he had desired was the (white) Town Clerk of Paballelo township. In a pure apartheid town, no assumptions could be made that the town council would administer to white and black inhabitants alike. The divisions were stark and reinforced by separate councils with attendant bureaucracies. It was a simple case of one clerk for each colour. Amidst riotous laughter at apartheid's expense, Mercia Andrews, an old hand at activist politics, nudged my arm and said that the two men dining opposite our table had been taking an eager interest in our conversation. She had a hunch that they were plain-clothes police. 'Trendy dressers they may be from their ankles up,' she said, 'but look at their shoes. Always a dead give-away.' I bent down and lifted the tablecloth for a clear view. Sure enough, sticking out from their cool blue jeans were two pairs of familiar brown lace-up regulation boots, police issue. Martin and I changed the flow of table-talk. We thought we should give our visitors a complete night out. Martin was a mean pianist and we took to the upright and belted out a couple of old standards in the true 'spontaneous outburst' tradition.

•

The state's counter witness to Herman Raath was a forensic psychiatrist in private practice in Bloemfontein in the Orange Free State. Dr Johan Fourie was a stout man with a close-fitting jacket and a ginger beard which stood out like a grass skirt from underneath his chin. His area of speciality was depression amongst black people. He was impressed with Dr Raath's profiles drawn up for each accused and believed they were well formulated. He argued, however, that if the profiles were to be of any real value, the accused should have been asked to recall their emotions on the day of Sethwala's murder. During our cross-examination of Fourie, we reasserted our view, supported by the research of renowned experts in the field, that a recollection of emotions experienced by the accused on a particular day some four years earlier would be inaccurate and unreliable. Dr Fourie acknowledged he had not read the works of the expert we specified, one of the foremost researchers in the field of memory retention, nor had he heard of a second expert mentioned. But his own resources would suffice. He dismissed our view by reference to his ability to recollect exactly what he was doing and how he felt the day that Prime Minister Hendrik Verwoerd, architect of apartheid, was assassinated. He was able to recall his memory of emotions with such precision because, he said, pushing out his chest with heartfelt pride, he 'admired HF Verwoerd's ideology and policies'.

Dr Fourie demonstrated a similar insistence in relation to the extensively documented theory of deindividuation. He had doubts about the 'unproven' theory of deindividuation, doubts, he declared with confidence, which had been confirmed by two of his former colleagues at the Department of Psychiatry at the University of the Orange Free State medical school, not a school known for its research or writings on the subject. Having dismissed the validity of the theory, he then negated its applicability to the accused: Kenneth Khumalo, Dr Fourie told the court, had acted 'with calculation rather than in a deindividuated state during the events leading to the killing of Constable Sethwala'. Under cross-examination by Farlam, Dr Fourie conceded that he had come to these conclusions without reading the judgment of the case on conviction or a summary of the evidence led at the trial. Dr Fourie had an obvious trust in his own intuition. Perhaps he thought the usual tools for shaping evidence—textbooks, research articles and findings, transcripts from the court record—would cloud his ability to speak from the gut.

Mr Justice Basson, comfortable with this approach, asked Dr Fourie for his views on the conduct of Xolile Yona. Fourie offered an unexpected suggestion. He recommended that, given Herman Raath's testimony pointing to Xolile's impulsive behaviour and faltering memory, Xolile should be sent for thirty days' psychiatric observation. And so the state requested, and Basson agreed, that Xolile Yona be sent to Bloemfontein's Oranje Hospital for psychiatric assessment to determine whether or not he was criminally insane. If so, he faced life as an inmate at a state asylum.

It was a procedure that might yield an alternative to death by hanging but one which filled Xolile with terror. His trip to Bloemfontein, like his journey to Cape Town's Groote Schuur Hospital for neurological testing, would be under police custody and Xolile feared similar police treatment, at the time the subject of an investigation ordered by Basson. To allay his fears, Herman Raath accompanied Xolile in the back of a police van to Bloemfontein, a distance of almost 600 kilometres. In an article in the *Independent* after their return, John Carlin wrote: 'Herman Raath reported that Xolile could not have looked more meek, frightened and childlike during the drive. Stepping from the van in Bloemfontein, out of Herman's care and into that of the police, his top lip quivered. If Mr Yona is found not to have been in full possession of all his faculties during his alleged part in the municipal policeman's murder, he will become what is legally called "a state president's patient", which means that in his new life as inmate of a state institution, he would come under the guardianship of President PW Botha, a volatile and short-tempered individual who, in the view of many inside his own party, has only a tenuous grip on reality.'

The treatment of Xolile Yona was not the only instance leading us to request the court to investigate police handling of our clients. Two weeks into the trial on extenuation, Xoliswa Dube was diagnosed with suspected appendicitis by a prison doctor. She was admitted to the Upington General Hospital for an emergency

Photos were taken at the beginning of the extenuation trial so that the legal team, who had not previously met their clients, could recognise each of the accused. Justice Bekebeke, Accused No 10, is on the left and Evelina de Bruin, Accused No 18, is on the right.

Advocate Anton Lubowski and Mr Alfred Gubula during morning tea in the courtyard of the Upinton Magistrate's Court at the start of the trial on extenuation. (Photo Anne Day)

The Magistrate's Court in Schröderstraat, Upington, which housed the Supreme Court for the duration of the trial. (Photo Jillian Edelstein)

Waitresses outside Upington's Le Must restaurant. Owner Neil Stemmet played host to the Upington 25 defence team, witnesses, supporters and media most nights during the trial. (Photo Jillian Edelstein)

Sarel Jacobs, Accused No 23, and Elizabeth Bostaander, Accused No 17, on the Eleven Experience soccer field in Paballelo. (Photo Jillian Edelstein)

From left to right: Abel Kutu, Accused No 3, Elizabeth Bostaander, Accused No 17, Neville Witbooi, Accused No 25, and Sarel Jacobs, Accused No 23. (Photo Jillian Edelstein)

From left to right: Mrs Susan Bekebeke, mother of Justice (Accused No 10) and Barry (Accused No 14), Shadrack Madlongolwane, son of Gideon (Accused No 19), a friend of the group, and Mr Jack Bovu, father of Myner (Accused No 5). (Photo Jillian Edelstein)

Mrs Virginia Masiza, mother of Ronnie and Wellington (Accused Nos 12 and 13) during a candlelight meeting in Paballelo of the families of the Upington 25. (Photo Jillian Edelstein)

Innocentia, daughter of Accused No 16, Xoliswa Dube. (Photo Jillian Edelstein)

Adelaide (Tutu) and Mbulelo, youngest daughter and son of Evelina de Bruin, Accused No 18, and Gideon Madlongolwane, Accused No 19. (Photo Jillian Edelstein)

Accused No 22, Jeffrey Sekiya, is granted bail pending the Appellate Division hearing of the appeal against his conviction of murder and sentence of six years' imprisonment. (Photo Jillian Edelstein)

Mr Phillip Tuys and Mrs Maria Kutu, mother of Abel (Accused No 3). Mr Tuys drove the families to Pretoria Central once a month to visit the accused on Death Row. (Photo Jillian Edelstein)

A matchstick model ship made by the Upington 25 during their time in Upington Prison. (Photo Ronnie Levitan)

Advocate Andre Landman with Accused No 16, Zuko Xabendlini, and Accused No 21, Albert Tywilli, outside Pretoria Central after their release from Death Row. (Photo Andrea Durbach)

(Left) Gideon Madlongolwane, Accused No 19, shortly after his release from Death Row. (Right) Kenneth Khumalo, Accused No 1, walks to greet well-wishers shortly after his release from two years on Death Row. (Photos Andrea Durbach)

Outside Pretoria Central after their release from Death Row: (back row from left to right) Gideon Madlongolwane, Wellington Masiza, David Lekhanyane, Tros Gubula, Kenneth Khumalo, Zuko Xabendlini; (front row from left to right) Andrew Lekhanyane, Albert Tywilli, Myner Bovu, and Boy Jafta. (Photo Andrea Durbach)

appendectomy on a weekend. She was kept under police guard throughout the weekend, her guard being a young Afrikaans policewoman. On the Sunday evening, Xoliswa went to the bathroom to wash herself down. She felt tired and sore and took her time. When she returned to her ward, she noticed the curtains around her bed were half-drawn. Through the curtains, she saw the policewoman, her guard, and a man embracing on her bed. '*Hulle was besig om te vry*' ('They were busy necking') she explained. The police guard instructed Xoliswa to wait outside in the corridor where she stood for almost half an hour, feeling cold and sick, faint from severe pain. In the morning, she was discharged from hospital and driven to the court in the back of a police van.

She was told to wait outside the courtroom until her co-accused had arrived from prison. I found her in terrible pain, holding her waist, leaning against the door to Court. She told me that after she had had her operation, she had been discharged from hospital. She had been brought to court by the police who drove at high speed, causing her to slide around and bang into the sides of the van, compounding her pain. She hobbled into court, hardly able to walk or sit in the dock and we sought permission for her readmission to hospital for a period of supervised recovery. Ian, expressing concern about the police transport, told the court that I would take Xoliswa to hospital in our car, accompanied by a police guard. Basson declined our offer. Such an arrangement, said the judge, posed a security risk.

I visited Xoliswa at the hospital after court that day. There was no sign of her guard. She had taken the trouble, however, to ensure her charge could not escape in her absence. Xoliswa lay on her bed at an awkward angle. She was manacled to the bedframe, one arm raised behind her and handcuffed to the bedpost. Somehow she had managed to fall asleep. We took a statement from Xoliswa a few days later and she told us that each time her guard left the ward, she would handcuff Xoliswa to the bedframe. Sometimes the pain was so great, she would pass out and wake up to find the guard unlocking the handcuff on her return. Xoliswa sighed and shut her eyes. She was tired and needed to rest. As we got up to go, she opened her eyes and said: '*Hoekom kan 'n vrou hierdie dinge doen? Sy gee liefde vir haar man op een dag en op die ander, sluit sy my op net soos 'n hond.*' ('How can a woman do these things? She gives love to her man on one day and on the other, she locks me up like a dog.')

•

Sometimes, I forgot that I was the only woman on the team. We were so enmeshed in the day-to-day focus on the Upington 25 that our individual traits and needs became secondary, often articulated in relation to the trial. Although I worked with men who would never openly define my responses to issues or events as related to my gender, I was given and assumed certain roles which I played with an unabashed ease.

We worked long and hard, and often stress took its toll. There were long nights when the air was hot and still and we worked in our rooms with extended families of mosquitoes, when perhaps we drank too much with dinner and ate anything with lots of sugar. And there were mornings when simple fairness and compassion from the court had been too big an ask, and over lunch in my room, Anton and I would order in a whisky and a packet of Camel filters and wait for the dread to subside. My way of believing we could keep sane and healthy was to make sure that at least one meal a day was balanced and full of essential nutrients. So each morning I played housewife with Le Must's Neil Stemmet. Before we left for court, Neil would call and we'd plan the dinner menu together, mulling over options—fish, green vegetables, perhaps rice, a big salad for the table and fruit for dessert. One morning, as I was confirming our dinner and opting for fresh fruit rather than a sticky Cape brandy pudding, Anton arrived at my door, anxious to get me to court. I explained that I was talking to our chef and suggested that he go ahead without me. Anton insisted on staying to listen with mock seriousness to my conversation and then turned to join the others waiting nearby. 'It's so good that you're in charge of catering. I'll let the judge know you're doing the menu.' When Colin got flu or Ian lost his voice and I forbade them to leave their rooms at night, making them gargle and suggesting garlic and ginger, Ian christened me 'Florrie', as in Nightingale, with the greatest respect.

I looked forward to the visits of the women in the media who'd come to do a feature story or follow-up reports. We became good friends and I enjoyed being able to flop into a pyjama party familiarity with them. We talked late into nights filled with laughter and dreams of life after Upington, and with them I felt safe to say that I longed to escape the overwhelming responsibility of the trial and return to ordinary life. Esther Waugh of the *Pretoria News* always had the *skinner* (gossip). She was tall and blonde and straight down the line. We would be sworn to secrecy and with grand gestures and a deep voice, Esther would divulge the inside stories long before the official version appeared in her paper. Her tales of political intrigue were high drama for a girl anchored down in Upington.

Gaye Davis had been a senior journalist for the *Cape Argus* and an active vigilante of press freedom. We had known one another for some years. She had covered many trials in which I had acted and she was an unobtrusive and effective ally. When the progressive *Rand Daily Mail* was forced to close and give way to the dictates of economic survival over critical perspectives and rigorous commentary, a few brave and committed journalists got together to establish the *Weekly Mail*. Gaye became the Cape Town correspondent for the *Mail* and she was one of the first journalists who took to the case of the Upington 25 and broke it open to the world. She was dedicated to the accused and the Paballelo community and was a solid and consistent presence throughout the trial. Gaye's incisive reporting and support, which often went beyond mere newspaper duty, sustained us all through some rough times.

Soon after the trial on extenuation began, Lynda Schuster arrived in Upington to do a cover story for the *Christian Science Monitor*. She combined a serious intensity and an attractive quirkiness which I was sure, enabled her to maintain her rare post. A Jewish American and the *Monitor's* Southern African correspondent, Lynda had an extraordinary history. Before her posting to Africa, she had spent time as a correspondent in Nicaragua where she had met a Scandinavian photographer. They fell in love and a few weeks after their marriage they travelled to a trouble spot on assignment. Lynda's husband was fatally injured in a skirmish and for five days Lynda was presumed dead by her family and the *Monitor*.

Lynda had a strong appetite for the stories behind the news and she liked to talk to people and to listen. One Friday afternoon, with time before our evening flight home, I suggested an expedition that I thought might suit her quest. The Upington Museum was housed in a small cottage and a barn-like structure on the banks of the Orange River. Its curator, *Meneer* (Mister) Stuurman, was thin and bent, and clearly one of Upington's oldest residents. The skin covering his throat was stretched and wrinkled and fell in neat folds onto his chest. His thick-lensed glasses protruded from his tight compact face. He was proud of his town and its history and thrilled to display its relics to two visitors. His tour was conducted primarily in Afrikaans, although he was polite enough to answer Lynda's queries in broken English. At the start, he insisted we sign his visitors' book, lest we get away without boosting the numbers.

The cottage was a reconstruction of an original Upington *inwoner's* (resident's) home, with old furnishings and a fine array of kitchen utensils. We moved to the barn which was previously a church hall. The centrepiece was an old *kerkorrel* (church organ) and the walls were lined with aged photographs of families and members of the congregation. Upstairs was an attic, packed with a collection of curious objects. There were jars of sand, old coins, dried snakes and rusted biscuit tins. Mr Stuurman settled in to show us each item. Lynda was far more interested in his views on the trial. 'O, ja, I know about that case,' he avoided eye contact with his interviewer. 'And what do you think about it?' Lynda exuded a charm that would have made him want to give a shame-fully honest reply.

By this stage we were walking back towards the cottage and we stopped at the entrance to the museum grounds. Mr Stuur-man was shaking. His answer snapped out of his taut frightened mouth. 'I'll tell you how I think about that business. When I see a black coming up the road, I cross over to the other side.' 'Oh, really,' Lynda's slow drawl had a quizzical tone. 'And why's that, sir?' 'Why! Why because they cut off your head and then they set it alight.' It was a shocking image and one obviously shaped by small-town myths of fear, by decades of mistrust and minds locked in by hate. We thanked Mr Stuurman for his time and promised to send more visitors his way. We mumbled that we hoped that they got as far as the museum with their heads still on and Mr Stuurman nodded with appropriate gravity. A year later, I received an invitation from Lynda to attend her wedding to an American diplomat in Liberia. White South Africans were not on the guest list of the Liberian authorities. At the bottom of the invitation she wrote: 'Let me know if you'll come. We'll smuggle you in as a wedding gift.' From Upington to Liberia. It was more or less how I expected Lynda might travel through life.

•

The presence of the media at the trial was fundamental to the maintenance of public interest in the case. The support of jour-nalists and newspaper editors both in South Africa and, more so, internationally had triggered political leverage by foreign govern-ments and pressure groups when judgments went awry. As lawyers, we were determined to hold onto a confidence in the legal system to deliver justice in the end, but the heavy knocks and punches dealt to the accused throughout the trial made it hard for us to engender an equivalent trust in our clients. They did find some solace, however, in the consistent coverage of the trial and their lives in the press and on radio and television. This exposure lessened their feelings of isolation and gave them hope that the forecast for their lives did not necessarily rest with one man.

I often wondered whether Mr Justice Basson had any idea of the extent to which he and his court had catapulted the Upington 25 and their community onto the public stage and contributed to their broad education and politicisation. No matter what he chose for them, be it freedom, imprisonment or death by hanging, they had travelled too far to believe in simple destiny shaped by circumstance. During a trial of almost five years, with overt displays of cynicism and racism, frequent reminders of police harassment and brutality and the misuse of legal doctrine for political ends, the twenty-five had debated legal theory, questioned interpretations of fact, swapped academic texts with expert witnesses and read the mainstream and alternative press cover to cover. Their discussions with embassy officials from around the world, foreign correspondents, documentary filmmakers, trade unionists and church men and women invited to monitor the trial filled the breaks in proceedings during the day, and at night and over weekends their prison cells hummed with new ideas and questions and debate. This disparate group of unskilled labourers and young scholars, an illiterate domestic worker, an ex-policeman, a town treasurer, a professional boxer and a railway worker with no initial purpose, no common thread, had been thrown together to pursue a cruel and intense education, but one which ignited their imagination and left a taste for cultivating opportunity.

•

My weekends in Cape Town were short and unsettling. In some peculiar way, I had become accustomed to Upington. It was the site of my primary and immediate life and those central to it and more and more it was Cape Town that felt strange and distant. There was little time to spend with people and it was hard to draw them in, to make friends and family feel part of a life so removed from their own. There were trips to the office to prepare for the week ahead and collect mail and boxes of gifts and clothing from all over the world for the accused and their families. Then there were the standing orders for newspapers unavailable in Upington. The *Weekly Mail, Die Zuid Afrikaan, Vrye Weekblad, South, City Press*. Ten of each. Essential reading for the week. Monday mornings in the dock, the accused would huddle round and skim through the papers to see if there was any coverage of the trial, then look for articles by journalists they had come to know: Jacques Pauw, Max du Preez, Henry Ludski, Connie Mlusi, Marius Bosch. The serious subscribers would then divide up the papers and arrange times for exchange.

Through the funders, letters of support and small allowances would pour in from pen-friends in England, Sweden, Holland and Denmark. Some afternoons after court, we would gather at the Nompondwana home for letter-writing, helping with replies to overseas mail that we would take to Cape Town for posting. Zonga Mokhatle's mother recited her letter for me to write down. It was to Nina Norgaard in Denmark: 'I'm now 81 years old, being a pensioner. By receiving your letter, for me was a relief, perhaps, although I really don't know how I could get the pain off me, living in a country of tears rolling everyday. I'm so happy to have a contact from so far away. Please don't stop writing, Nina, let's be friends forever. Best wishes, Martha Mokhatle.'

The mothers and wives of the accused who had recently established the Dependents Committee had cause for grand celebration when one day cargo arrived from Australia. My South African friend Penny Andrews, working as a legal academic in Melbourne, had followed the case with care. She had organised a vast clothing drive for the families of the accused, particularly for those with babies and young children. Clearly, Melbourne had fine taste in children's apparel. It was an extraordinary load. To ensure equal and appropriate distribution of the clothes and to talk in general about the ongoing needs of families of the accused, I invited the Dependents Committee to meet on the lawn of the Protea Hotel. Tea would be served.

At five o'clock, the committee arrived dressed for tea, some with hats and scarves covering their heads from the afternoon sun.

My guests included Elsie Vice, girlfriend of Andrew Lekhanyane, Caroline Tywilli, sister of Albert, Mrs Sarah Johnson, mother of Boy Jafta, Lydia Nompondwana, wife of Enoch, Mrs Susan Bekebeke, mother of Barry and Justice, Mrs Dube, mother of Xoliswa, with baby Innocentia, Francis Gubula, sister to Tros and niece of Alfred, and Mrs Yona, mother of Xolile. In accord with the afternoon ceremony of my upbringing, some residue from a Cape colonial heritage, I suggested an order of tea and assorted cakes. There was little enthusiasm from the committee. So I proposed Coke or Fanta, ginger beer and 7 Up and there were some takers. To shift the formality of the occasion, I joked that maybe we should throw caution to the wind and order a round of beers. There was a chorus of approval and I placed a final order of one pot of tea, one ginger beer and seven beers, and a platter of chocolate eclairs, apple strudel, slices of *melktert* and swiss rolls. We moved through the business of the meeting fairly quickly and onto other matters. There was talk of childhood and families, love and sorrow, women and work. Francis Gubula told us that her Xhosa name meant lawyer and there was raucous laughter and cheers of support when I returned with Anton's black gown, draped it around Francis and begged her to take on the case in my stead.

12

•

Absent testimony

On a Thursday morning in mid-March, towards the end of the presentation of evidence on extenuation, I decided to stay at the hotel and swan around my room, pretending to be at leisure. I felt a need to do things domestic: hand washing, read, condition my hair, order room service, make lists. Close to noon, Anton called me from court. The judge wanted to make an announcement and had asked that I be present. Anton had no clues and I feared the worst as I tore down Schröderstraat. I was queasy from waves of anticipation and furious with myself, angry that the judge had caught me playing.

I entered the court and proceedings began. I nodded at Basson, with apologies, and he unwound a smile and welcomed me, a benevolent gesture. 'Mr Farlam,' he began, 'as the case on extenuation currently stands, I have to say that it will be difficult to find extenuating circumstances without the testimony of the accused. What I have in mind is to postpone the case until June to consider the evidence and allow the accused one final opportunity to give evidence in extenuation before we proceed to hear concluding argument.' He then turned to the court interpreter, a short round black man who slouched in his chair, waiting for the occasional prompt to speak. Looking directly at the accused, the judge emphasised each word and waited for the echo in Xhosa: 'The seriousness of this case can not be underestimated. If I find no extenuation, I am bound by law to impose the death sentence. I will have difficulty finding extenuation without your testimony. The evidence led by the defence and the state has concerned the state of mind of the accused on the day of the murder. From the evidence led so far, certain detrimental inferences can be drawn. At this stage, I cannot say whether those inferences will be just.'

I shifted in my chair. It seemed a manipulative strategy and Basson's words made me feel restless and uncomfortable. He forged on with apparent largesse: 'The accused have a lot at stake and it is of the utmost importance that the court record be complete. I will grant one last opportunity for you to reconsider your decision not to testify in extenuation. I will adjourn until 9am tomorrow when I will hear what you have decided.' It might have been easier, certainly more straightforward, if the judge had dismissed the case of the defence, sentenced the accused and ended it there. He clearly disliked our approach, he was unimpressed by the complexity of the argument and our challenge to his preferred comprehension of the case. No guarantees, but it seemed unlikely that the testimony of the accused would dramatically shift his stance. It was a cruel manoeuvre and if nothing else, it undid the accused at a critical time. It was a swift escort to destabilisation.

The refusal to testify was not a foolish, stubborn stance, a case of stroppy clients taking the high moral ground. They had sound reasons for their absence of direct testimony, clearly and repeatedly articulated but there was no point in further attempting to convert the judge to our view. The absence of trust between accused and judge was complete and beyond retrieval. As far as the accused were concerned, the judge did not see them, did not listen to them. They were a faceless group conforming with an image and role firmly fixed in his judicial mind. They had no confidence in his objectivity, no desire to let him into their worlds. It should have come as no surprise that Basson's invitation to bare their souls was met with derision. It was the pain which accompanied their contempt that made me wonder why we played by the rules.

'We will not talk. You can't drag this out. It's cruel, we've had enough. Just sentence us and be done with...' It was an unusual outburst from Kenneth Khumalo, perhaps out of character. His voice shook and he started to choke and sat down. He'd given others permission to speak. There were sounds of anxiety, shuffles, whispers and intermittent calls of 'no' to the judge. Xolile Yona began to wail and beat his palm on the table, over and over. 'I don't care. I don't care. Give me the death sentence. I want to die. Let me die.' People in the gallery started to cry and it felt as if a swell of grief and anger was rising in the court beyond our control. Kenneth, quickly recomposed and concerned to stay a spiral of disquiet, leaned across to Xolile, begging him to sit down. Others closest to Xolile tried to talk to him, to calm him down. With all his might, Xolile, the boxer, lashed out, punching those around him with extraordinary force. One of the accused went down, hitting the floor with a chilling thud. Anton's big frame stepped forward and locked Xolile in a bear hug. They struggled with each other and finally, six policemen came to quell Xolile's rage and drag him down into the cells below.

Amidst the noise, Basson took hold of his wooden gavel, beat the table and declared court adjourned, turning his back on the brawl. We stood in shock, no words came out and slowly Gideon Madlongolwane spoke in quiet defence of Xolile: 'We all feel like Xolile. His anger is our anger, our disappointment. I have no more hope. It keeps being broken. I am tired.' Xoliswa Dube nodded in agreement and, pleading with me, took my hand: 'I just want it to be finished. I can't sleep for thinking about my baby, my Innocentia.' We all needed time to slow down, to think, to separate. How to placate the accused, how to engage the judge? The police began to clear the courtroom and usher the accused from the dock. I told them we would be back after lunch with some ideas for discussion.

Tense and exasperated, we had little desire to talk over lunch and we returned to court without a masterplan in mind. Standing around the table in the centre of our consulting room, I poured cups of cold tea and we agreed that things could not be left as they were. There had to be an immediate resolution and a postponement until June was unthinkable. We thought we should talk to the judge and fathom his appetite for compromise. But first, we had to gauge the sentiment of our clients. The accused and their families sat in small groups, bent over, some with heads down, others staring ahead, silent and waiting. The strain of a protracted high-security trial had already taken its toll; the possibility of its further extension would push many close to the edge. We arranged with the police that we would talk to the accused and their families in our small consultation room, away from the prosecution and the court. The police could, if they liked, stand guard outside.

The room was crowded and stuffy. We huddled around the table, chairs turned against the door and we talked in hushed tones. The accused were stern and resolute. They would not testify, not in June, not in December, not in their lifetime. Zonga Mokhatle pushed forward from the back of the room, his eyes wild, his mouth quivering: 'If Basson postpones this trial, if we delay it more, I will take my life, tonight at the prison. I do not need to wait for tomorrow, I know what he will say. I cannot live like this anymore.' This was no empty threat. Zonga spoke with a desperate intonation and I felt his distress. There was a murmur of support through the room. It was a disturbing cry from Zonga and foolishly, not one I had anticipated.

We promised to talk to Basson and agreed to meet again later that evening in the prison. We went out into the courtyard. The accused moved slowly, deliberately. Some of the men stopped and tapped a policeman on the arm for cigarettes. Mrs Kutu, mother of Abel, Accused No 3, a round gentle woman with few teeth and a *doek* on her head, came towards me and shyly asked if we could talk. I knew Mrs Kutu well. She came to court every day and sat listening and smiling, always patient. We returned to the consulting room and sat at the table while the advocates stood drinking tea, stirring in sugar long dissolved. Just standing and stirring, faces empty of expression. Mrs Kutu had four lumps of sugar, no milk. *'Andy, jy weet Abel is 'n goeie man.'* ('Andy, you know that Abel is a good man.') She pulled a small lace handkerchief from her sleeve and wiped the tears from her face. *'Hy kan nie hierdie saak verder verdra nie. Hierdie Basson is regtig 'n klein man. Wat het ons teen hom gedoen? Andy, asseblief, vertel hom. Abel is my seun, hy is onskuldig.'* ('He can't bear this any longer. Basson is such a small man. What have we done to him? Andy, please tell him. Abel is my son, he is harmless.') I tried to make her see Basson differently, to instil some hope. 'No, Mrs Kutu, the judge is a big man. He is clever and I think he will see that he must change his mind.' Mrs Kutu wiped away the last tear, ready to go outside and be strong. She smiled and said *dankie* (thank you) and I turned away from the door and sat on the edge of the table facing the window, wondering at the world outside. For the first time, in the presence of my team, my men, I started to sob, with no shame and no shield.

I had weakened and my ability to put up a fight had been suspended temporarily. I had a sudden sense of a very deep fear of failure. Anton moved towards me and sat close, like gentle insulation from exposure. 'It all feels so relentless, so pointless really. I'm tired of trying to hold on to hope. I'm tired of trying to make people feel better when inside I feel that they know my game, that we cannot win this one.' Anton nodded and put his arm around my shoulder. He lowered his head and made a soft sound. I looked at him but he kept his head down. My guard, my mister tough, was weeping with me.

There was a knock on the door. More parents wanted to see us. I pleaded with Anton to stop the crying, to stop my crying. We had to be brave for them. To show vulnerability would scare them. Then I drew on my own internal shock tactic. Remember: to show weakness would delight the state. Never let them see you down. Within minutes I was ready for the next delegation, doing all I could to instil a belief in the judicial process and its capacity to render justice. We were carefully balanced and we had to show Basson that we had the stamina and the faith to carry on, no matter how long it took. It was important to get the state on side, to take the prosecution into our confidence and let them have a glimpse of the crisis unfolding amongst the accused and the urgent need for management of the situation. Van Rensburg was clearly concerned. He knew about talk of suicide and that it should not be taken lightly. There was agreement that we request a meeting with the judge.

Basson invited us to sit. His chambers were dark with heavy wood panels and glass cabinets stacked with law reports and texts. A ceiling fan turned above us and prints on the walls depicted dull scenes from the olden days. A calendar and a pad of blotting paper bound by leather lay at the front of his desk. He sat back in his chair. Ian thanked Basson for his time and said that we were anxious about the mood of the accused. It was unlikely they would testify and they had not responded well to the suggestion of a postponement. To postpone the trial at this stage, we all believed, would be intolerable for the accused and generate unbearable strain. There had been talk of suicide. Basson said nothing, but I felt it was a lull before the storm. Van Rensburg took over. He agreed it might be detrimental to the trial if we postponed it now, and certainly a delay might have a bad effect on the state of mind of the accused. There was an uneasy silence as we waited for a response. We looked at one another and back at Basson. He radiated a quiet anger. 'I hear what you say,' he began. 'I will agree to continue the trial tomorrow but I must warn you,' he was looking at us, the defence, 'I will not be pressurised by the accused and I will not be manipulated by threats of suicide.' I think we looked sufficiently chastened. He moved his elbows onto the desk and clasped his palms together. 'The trial will resume, but in the circumstances I may not be able to deliver a good judgment. I cannot give any assurances. Please convey this message to the accused.' I assured the judge our clients would be told his every word.

I tore back to the hotel to call Herman and pleaded with him to come down the following day. I told him what had happened in court and that the accused were emotionally battered and may need help to pull them through the next few days. I rang the prison and arranged for Anton and me to meet with the accused at 6pm. I told the Major that we had some good news from the judge which he had asked us to pass on to our clients. We arrived at the prison to find the accused listless and visibly sagging. Their relief that the trial would continue the following morning was tepid. It was couched as a small victory, but deep down they knew, we knew, how the judge would rule in the end. Now, it was just a matter of time.

In the morning Herman Raath was at court. He had hitched a ride with an army jet, care of the South African Defence Force. Old allegiances can always be resurrected in times of need, he quipped. His dedication to the trial and his care for the accused was unmatched and they felt easier with him present. My diary note for the day was short: 'Trial continues. Ian begins argument on extenuation. Thank God.'

•

The trial back on foot, there came an interesting and fortuitous change in the law. We would soon conclude our summation of the evidence led on extenuation, and would be followed by the state and its concluding argument. The court would break for two months to write its judgment on extenuation and sentencing of the accused would follow. A few weeks earlier, the Criminal Procedure Act had been amended, expanding existing provisions for community service as an alternative to jail sentences. We invoked the new provision and Justice Basson agreed to an order allowing us to take advantage of the new amendment and the special procedure it established.

Basson asked the National Institute for Crime Prevention and Rehabilitation of Offenders (NICRO) to convene an evaluation panel to assess the suitability of the accused for community service as an alternative to imprisonment and to investigate possible facilities in Upington for the rendering of such service. Basson's order to NICRO for pre-sentence evaluation was the first under the newly amended Criminal Procedure Act. Granting such an order in respect of twenty-five murderers was a brave move on his part, but lest we rose too far into euphoria, Basson was quick to maintain some distance from his decision. He issued a warning: 'This request came from the defence and the granting of it should not create expectation.' At least we knew where we stood.

There were no planes out of Upington to Cape Town on Thursdays. We would have had to fly north to Kimberley or Johannesburg and then hope for a connecting flight south to Cape Town. It was the Thursday before the Easter weekend and we were waitlisted on the Cape Town flights. By lunchtime there were still no seats and the thought of Easter in Upington sent us into a dark panic. We had no option but to charter a flight on a six-seater. It was a tough choice. Four airless days in a town closed down or a trip over craggy mountains and deep seas in a sewing machine. There was one consolation. I had organised an exhibition of the Upington 25 collection of matchstick models at a Cape Town gallery in mid-May and small-plane travel provided a cost-effective opportunity to transport the models under our personal care. We boarded in the late afternoon, Colin at the back and Ian and I in the middle. Ian bent down, almost to his toes and squeezed into his seat, his head grazing the roof of the plane. The pilot, in long socks and safari shorts, was at ease and predicted fine weather for most of the trip.

We travelled well for the first hour and then as we moved towards the coast, we had a direct hit with turbulence. We dropped like a yoyo and then sprung back up, before plummeting again, Ian's balding head colliding with the ceiling. He felt his head for damage and there was blood on his hand. Ian had just accepted a six-week appointment as an acting judge and worried that a cracked skull might disqualify him from exercising judgment. I was more concerned about air safety at this stage, worried that the roof had splintered from the impact of Ian's head. But the pilot was relaxed and tried to distract me from my fixation with the fuselage. It was time for a break, he said. His wife had packed some sandwiches and a flask of tea. It was when he turned to offer us a tupperware box of ham and tomato on white bread, his eyes off the 'road', his back to controls, that I hyperventilated and became semi-conscious until we touched ground at Cape Town airport.

The exhibition of artworks by the accused and photographs taken by Eric Miller of their families and the people of Paballelo drew crowds to the Baxter Theatre Gallery on a Sunday evening. Patrons of art and supporters of the Upington 25 packed the gallery to hear Dr Mamphela Ramphele, renowned activist and academic, Mary Burton, President of the Black Sash, open the exhibition of work of 'intricate and intriguing creativity from a hopeless and barren place'. On exhibition were matchstick ships and Xolile Yona's Great Trek miniature ox-wagons. In the centre of the gallery was a model of the Paballelo Roman Catholic Church made by Kenneth Khumalo from broken wooden clothes pegs and matchsticks. Inside his church the detail was magnificent: pews of sucker (ice lolly) sticks, walls lined with snippets of wrapping paper, as if stained glass, and cake candles on the altar.

The ships were popular and a committee was established to co-ordinate and distribute orders from the public, with proceeds of sales going to the Upington welfare fund which supported the families of the accused. The Centre for African Studies Gallery at the University of Cape Town asked to host an extended showing of the exhibition and the university bought two models as did the South African National Gallery. The most prestigious order came from London: a model was required as a present for the seventy-sixth birthday of Father Trevor Huddleston, an Anglican priest sent to South Africa in 1943 to administer to the black township of Sophiatown. Father Huddleston had become a legendary figure within the black community, a 'dauntless warrior' for their rights. It was a great honour and thrill for the accused that their prison art was in demand from such high places.

The break had been necessary. It meant that we had a few weeks to consolidate, to pull together the threads of the trial and catch our breath in preparation for the unpredictable time that lay ahead. Although I was able to have some distance from

Upington, the temptation to speculate was always present. How the court would view our evidence on extenuation was fairly clear. But the gamble was how many accused would face a sentence of death. I did the numbers in my head, with endless variations and interpretations, and each time I figured a number that offered no comfort. To have even one client sentenced to death brought a terror to my heart. Perhaps the break from the raw intensity of the trial would allow Justice Basson some time for clemency to break through.

13

Beating back the fear

The weekend before the Upington Supreme Court was to deliver the judgment on extenuation, Colin and I travelled to Johannesburg. We had been invited to a seminar to present a paper on extenuation and the common purpose doctrine, using the Upington case as illustration. The seminar, which focused on political trials, brought together judges, attorneys, advocates, legal academics and human rights scholars from around the country to discuss the practice of law under states of emergency and legal developments in political trial work. The gathering, at a retreat of thatched *rondavels* in the Highveld, an hour or so out of Johannesburg, came at a crucial time. It was a welcome distraction from the Upington routine and allowed us to meet with valued colleagues and friends who could share experiences and offer advice and direction. I was a newcomer to the rules and the rites governing statutory killing, the judicial taking of life, and I was dreading the events of the impending week with all my heart. To spend two days with lawyers who had endured something similar, who could share their post-trial retrospection and demonstrate a revived strength despite defeat and sorrow, was an important source of comfort.

On the Sunday morning, hours before our flight to Upington, Lloyd Vogelman, a clinical psychologist at Witwatersrand University who administered to death-row prisoners, gave a chilling account of the day-to-day lives of death-row inmates and the lead-up to their execution. He spoke of the small cells with high ceilings and a window out of reach, a wooden plank bed fixed to the wall, old blankets for covering. Of overhead lights which burned in the cells for twenty-four hours each day, of difficult sleep often replaced by fantasies of suicide. He told us how prisoners marked for execution would be given seven day's notice of their hanging before being transferred to a group of cells which housed prisoners awaiting death. In the 'pot'—where prisoners 'stew before they die'—necks and bodies were measured for the rope. On the day before an execution, prisoners would receive a final family visit if the cost of travelling to Pretoria and emotions permitted. That night, the last supper of a whole deboned chicken would be served and the prisoner given a small stipend to buy a treat at the prison tuckshop.

I remembered particularly Lloyd's description of the night before an execution when prisoners held an all-night vigil. Lloyd spoke of the singing of hymns and the banging, the shouting and the wailing from behind prison walls. Inmates reached out to each other with song; a gentle, constant chorus of impending death. The singing would continue through the night and accompany the early morning visit from the *dominee*, the prison chaplain, which meant that the prisoner had thirty minutes before being led to the gallows. A policeman would fingerprint each prisoner to ensure that the right one was to be hanged. There would be a doctor in attendance to certify the prisoner's death. A white hood, with a flap over the face, would be placed over the prisoner's head. His hands tied, the rope would be pulled tightly around the neck with the knot next to an ear. The executioner pulled on a lever which opened a trapdoor and the prisoner was dropped, sometimes pulled back up and dropped again until his neck was broken. From the time of the first drop, it usually took 13 to 15 minutes for a prisoner to die. Stripped naked, the executed would be carried on a stretcher to a coffin which was nailed up and taken to a graveyard. Family members would not see the body or the grave site. They simply received a notice giving the number of the plot which housed the grave.

To cope with the fear of execution, many myths circulated on death row. One of them, said Lloyd, was that when you were hanged, you did not die but rather dropped beneath the floorboards, landing in the Government Mint where you worked to make money for the government. The mountain that existed behind the prison, so the myth went, was the earth dug out to make room for more prisoners to toil and keep government coffers full.

The prisoners sang, the prisoners were measured, the prisoners were dropped to their death. The prisoners, faceless subjects of research and myth. As I listened to Lloyd's precise description, the prisoners of his paper started to blend with the bodies and faces of twenty-five people I had come to know and for whom I cared deeply. Not all of them, thank God, would be sent to death row, but just how many might have to endure this cruel underworld depended, to a large extent, on how the dice of Justice Basson touched down. Our guesswork leaned in favour of twelve or thirteen—the state seemed set on the latter—and the suspense surrounding the final figure had become intolerable. Lloyd's clinical account of what lay ahead turned my soul and I prayed for some intervention that would prevent me from going to Upington that night.

I raised my hand to praise Lloyd's work and to plead that his paper be sent to judges in the hope they if they read it, they might waver before their office compelled them to take a life. I was mid-sentence before a room of tough and esteemed legal counsel, when, without any warning, I slid into a shock of uncontrollable sobbing. The fear for the end of the trial, for the inescapable, had sat with me for weeks and it had decided on an untimely release. I tried to stop my crying and resume a cool, resilient exterior and continue sober discussion. But seconds expanded to minutes before I could fully compose myself, made difficult by the deep silence in the room and the round-table layout which allowed for sharp focus on my display of impropriety. I had spent the previous weeks battling with changing images of the unknown ordeal, of how we would approach the judicial recitation: 'I sentence you to death.' Lloyd's paper had introduced a sense of some reality and triggered the distress I'd tried hard to check. But his research did not prepare me for what was to come. I don't believe anything really could.

•

We left the seminar after lunch, with wishes of good luck and support. Anton, Andre and Herman Raath met us at Jan Smuts Airport in Johannesburg and we flew to Upington, glad to be together again after the recess. I was grateful for Herman's return. He had only recently revived his psychology practice in Windhoek after deserting it for five weeks to present his testimony in support of extenuation and assist us with the cross-examination of state witnesses. I had asked him to leave his practice once again, this time to counsel the accused and their families in anticipation of the sentencing. Perhaps more importantly, they would need him to guide them through the painful separation at the ending of a trial which had stretched its players far beyond their worlds and then bonded their every cell for life. And I needed Herman to be there for purely selfish reasons.

Judgment on extenuation was scheduled to commence on Tuesday morning, 22 May 1989. The trial on extenuation of Xolile Yona, Accused No 20, had been scheduled for the day before, separated from the main trial to hear evidence on his criminal capacity. Xolile had spent the requisite thirty days at the Universitas Hospital in Bloemfontein under observation. A panel of psychiatrists had assessed his ability to appreciate the nature and gravity of his actions at the time of Lucas Sethwala's murder. We were content with the conclusions drawn by the panel. In their view, Xolile was fit to stand trial. He was not criminally insane although he was clearly prone to manifest a tendency towards aggression when provoked. On the basis of the evaluation, there was a strong likelihood that someone with Xolile's psychological make-up would have become deindividuated when subject to the external forces present on the day of Sethwala's death. Mr Justice Basson had not hidden the fact that he had been unimpressed with the evidence on deindividuation presented thus far. Anton, leading the team in the absence of Ian who had taken up his six-week appointment as an acting judge, was anxious about his ability to shift the judge's inclination in respect of Xolile. He ordered room service, preferring not to join us for our welcome-home dinner at Le Must.

It seemed as if we had been away for a long time and it was hard to come back knowing that an awful finality was on the cards. We were tense and a little distant from one another, perhaps in preparation for an ending and the possibility of change, a new direction which might lead us all into something different. Before too long, we were reconnected by the spirit of the twenty-five. The next morning, they entered the court, slowly climbing the stairs from below, singing the national anthem, '*Nkosi Sikelel' i-Afrika*' and carrying three matchstick ships at shoulder height. One of them, four-storeys high, had two small banners tied between its masts, with the words 'ANDREA' and 'DURBACH' written on them in thick blue ink. Another, an elaborate steamship, was a gift for Anton. The third was brought for show. Boy Jafta placed it on the dock and asked me how I had enjoyed my holiday. I looked puzzled. I hadn't been away. 'Yes you have,' he laughed, pointing to the portholes on the boat. 'You see,' insisted Boy, 'I gave you a cruise on a luxury liner.' Staring out from one of the portholes, with pop stars, sports heroes and babies on either side, was my face, a photograph cut from a women's magazine which had featured an article on the trial.

Our presentation of Xolile's case was short and uneventful and in symmetry with our evidence throughout. Xolile's inherent frustration with the world had evolved from his history of exposure to social deprivation; this factor, coupled with his temperament, his anger at the police intervention on the day of the murder and the frenzy of the crowd had unleashed a latent tendency to aggressive behaviour. All these factors, said Anton in summary, would have predisposed him to a high degree of deindividuation. The prosecution saw Xolile differently. '*Yona was een van die beskuldiges,*' argued van Rensburg, '*wat 'n politieke motief gehad het—hy wou die woonbuurt onregeerbaar maak.*' ('Yona was one of the accused who had a political motive—he wanted to make the township ungovernable.') The bench's comments on the submissions were bland and perfunctory. That some conclusions had already been drawn during the court recess may not have been an unfair explanation for this lack of enthusiasm. The court adjourned just before lunchtime and Basson confirmed that his judgment on extenuation would commence the following morning.

We were lucky to have some breathing space before the onset of despair which accompanied the next few days. After lunch, we drove to the prison to meet with our clients one more time before fate took its course. We hardly spoke; a simple exchange, a checking-in was about all we could muster. I had promised to organise a meeting of family and friends in Paballelo that evening. Mrs Yona, Xolile's mother, had offered to host the gathering. En route to Paballelo from the prison, we stopped in at the hotel to collect Herman and Gaye Davis who had returned to Upington to cover the judgment for the *Weekly Mail*. The meeting was called to explain what we thought might happen over the next few days—the handing down of the judgment on extenuation, the procedure after its conclusion, the appeal against the judgment, our continued representation of the accused and work with the families. I wanted to ensure that they felt everything would remain intact until we'd achieved nothing less than they deserved. Herman had agreed to talk about doubts and expectations, the shared agony and the need to be bold.

As we drove into the township, the warm May evening carried a strange calm, perhaps a mixture of the predictable and the inevitable. We sat outside on a tiny red stone *stoep* and patch of grass and earth, the township streetlights glaring down at us. Behind the trim garden hedge children ran with rims of steel across the gravel and peeked through twigs to watch us at work. Their silent scrutiny began to boil into high-pitched whispers and stifled giggles and Elsie Vice jumped at the hedge with a stick to scold them and sent them scuttling down the dust road, dogs barking at their heels.

It began to grow dark and some of the women lit candles and swayed, singing hymns of comfort and songs of hope and freedom. Herman coaxed deep fears from those who could bear to speak and tossed them back and forth until they had almost dissolved. Gaye spoke from behind: 'We will make sure the world hears about your story. They will know what has happened.' There was some laughter and much crying and then we were asked to gave thanks to God. The women, always the women at meetings, at court with food and a change of clothing, making decisions— the wives, sisters, mothers, aunts—stood up one by one to speak while others translated. They thanked the lawyers, praised the experts and prayed that the world would step forward and let justice be done.

As we walked back to our car, the women surrounded us with fists clenched in the air, ululating. They would never let a meeting, however sombre and painful, complex and hopeless, end without a collective show of unity and strength, a beating back of fear. 'Don't worry about us, Andy. We are strong. Let us give you our strength,' they shouted as we drove down King Street and back into town. It was a strength that I craved and honoured and one which at the time, surfaced from sheer will to protect myself from pain.

14

•

Judgment

Over three sluggish days, the Honourable Mr Justice Basson read out, word for word, his 200-page judgment on extenuation. He was a serious man with a strong sense of duty and he was going to render the judgment by the book. At the end of each day, I would be given those portions of the judgment already declared, a keepsake of the day's achievements and a reminder that we would resume the painful process the following morning.

'Taking into account the above factors cumulatively and in the absence of direct evidence by the accused, we find that in the case of Accused number...no extenuating circumstances were present.' Given Basson's indications throughout the presentation of our case on extenuation, there were no real surprises in the cumulative factors he cited in support of his findings against extenuation. He conceded that Paballelo residents had valid community grievances but concurred with the trial judge in the Sharpeville Six case who said that extenuating circumstances could not be claimed when people aired their grievances by 'sowing death and destruction'. Had the possible political motives of the accused been fully investigated and had they testified as to their feelings on the day of the murder, said the judge, 'their apparently irrational behaviour might have seemed rational'. Without the testimony of the accused, there existed a vacuum as the court had no factual basis on which to decide their state of mind at the time of the murder. Any evidence on deindividuation amounted to 'pure speculation' and in rejecting our argument that the accused had acted in a deindividuated state, Basson pronounced that 'an accused with no other defence has no right simply to call on deindividuation in a last attempt to spring free from the consequences of his crime'.

The events of 13 November 1985 amounted, in the view of the Honourable Justice Basson, to a politically motivated 'semi-organised revolt' in which symbols of authority were targeted. Although, on the evidence, he could not find a plot to kill Seth-wala, the overall plan of the accused was clear: to act against authorities and informers. In dismissing provocation as an explanation for the conduct of the accused, Basson was convinced that the crowd 'knew' that the police would use force if the meeting did not disperse. 'It is difficult to believe the people could be provoked by the tear-gas. They made its use necessary by their actions.' We had argued that Sethwala's shots into the crowd and his wounding of the young boy on its outskirts were provocative acts giving rise, in all probability, to an uncontrollable rage on the part of the crowd. These were not provocative deeds, said the judge: 'With such a heavy stoning of Sethwala's house, the crowd could surely have expected the deceased to defend himself... to talk of provocation on the part of the accused is utter nonsense. The people who attacked the home of the deceased did so because they had decided to drive him out of the house and kill him and not because there had been any provocation.'

Our contention that most of the accused had played a minor role in the murder, that they had participated to a lesser degree, was also rebuffed. It was 'not necessary' for the state to prove that all twenty-five took part in the actual killing to a lesser and greater degree, said Basson. The accused had associated themselves with the common purpose by stoning Sethwala's house with the clear intention of driving him out to kill him. The act of association with the common purpose to kill was sufficient for the court to determine twenty-five separate convictions of murder.

We would tally the scores each day. Tuesday: Accuseds 1 and 2, Kenneth Khumalo and Tros Gubula, no extenuation. Wednesday: Accuseds 3, Abel Kutu, 9, Elisha Matshoba, 12, Ronnie Masiza, 14, Barry Bekebeke, 16, Xoliswa Dube, 17, Elizabeth Bostaander—extenuation. The court found that Abel Kutu's 'low intellect' and the 'concrete infantile way' in which he approached his environment had probably influenced his mind on the day of the killing. Elisha, Ronnie, Barry, Xoliswa and Elizabeth were saved by their youth and their 'emotional immaturity and low intelligence'. They had not committed the crime, said the judge, 'as a result of some inherent evil'. No extenuation could be found for Accuseds 4, David Lekhanyane, 5, Myner Bovu, 6, Zuko Xabendlini, 8, Andrew Lekhanyane, 10, Justice Bekebeke, 11, Zonga Mokhatle, 13, Wellington Masiza and 15, Boy Jafta. By Wednesday night the tally was extenuation: six; no extenuation: ten. By midday Thursday, the gap would widen beyond our reckoning.

With Basson's narration, the last few accused had to wait three days and two nights before they knew their fate; a prolonged diagnosis. Over the period, we had little choice but to devise our own absurd distractions from this senseless and insensitive exercise. Herman sat behind me and taught me how to breathe to lessen anxiety spasms which would clamp my chest. As the pressure of anticipation grew causing unbearable strain and panic, I slipped glucose and vitamin B and C capsules to the accused and their families. Herman dispensed sedatives. Anton amused some of the accused, demonstrating the prowess of a computer diary bought in New York after attending one of his meetings with Sam Nujoma. He was entering addresses. Andrew Lekhanyane had a go: 'Lekhanyane, Andrew. Maximum Security, Pretoria Central. No phone.' Andre read law reports in preparation for an appeal he was to argue in Bloemfontein and Colin surprised us with his sketches, portraits of courtroom figures for his Upington portfolio.

As each day dragged by and the familiar prelude to a finding favouring the imposition of the death sentence was announced, I would turn my chair away from the judge to talk quietly to my clients, sometimes joking about the mad formality he displayed. For the first time, I felt it safe to show a gentle contempt for his office and his rigid adherence to the harshest of laws, and so turned my hostile back to the bench. The accused showed a dull resignation, leaning forward with chins on folded arms, some spilling out from the crowded dock. We touched and clasped hands and I reassured them that we'd be fine on appeal. Those furthest from me or keen to discuss something in private, requested pen and paper which would be sent along the line. We then entered into correspondence. Some notes stood alone, begging no reply.

> The judge found us guilty. He thought he could make us accept guilt by forcing us to talk about our feelings. He must stick to his guns and we'll stick to ours. He has chosen to carry his load. We are not prepared to carry it for him. No 1 (Kenneth)

> *Die regter smile die manier hy onreverdig is en Koerlan raak rooi. Hulle het ons skuldig bevind. Voor die saak begin het. Dis hoekom hulle uitsprak so nonsens is. Ek weet ek sal gaan hang. Wanner die regter vriendelik praat dan is hy eers skelm. Ek ken hom baie mooi soos my broer.* No 11 (The judge smiles in his unjust manner and Kurland [the assessor] turns red. They found us guilty. Before the case began. That's why their judgment is nonsense. I know I shall hang. When the judge speaks in a friendly manner then he is at once a rogue. I know him well like my own brother. Number 11)

The notes and letters signed from 'No 1' and 'Number 11', from 'number 16', about 'number 9' reminded me of my precious response during the early days of preparation when I was appalled by the accused referring to one another and to themselves by number. During the days in court, they were rarely addressed by name by the judge or the prosecution and the use of numbers rather than names was reflected in the various judgments. To my mind, this practice served to strip the accused of their individual characters and traits, of their history and of their intention; it allowed individual liability to be ignored and deemed them murderers by association with a group. Initially, my assumption was that the accuseds' use of numbers to refer to or address one another was bitter proof that the dehumanising process endemic to a trial of this nature had triumphed. But as I got to know them and discover the intricate ways in which they managed their lives together, I began to read their manner of address as a deliberate mimicry of judicial posture, an expression of affection for one another and of pity for a man who feared humanity.

The accused employed this approach as they tried to transcend the *danse macabre* played out before them each day of the judgment. Their method was an interesting, if bizarre, match for the judge's performance. With each finding of no extenuation which signalled a mandatory death sentence, they would smile and chuckle, mouth 'Congratulations', mime the clapping of hands and lean forward to pat a back or shake hands with the condemned. Then they would face one another and busily mimic the measuring of necks. To those who were granted extenuation and would be spared the death sentence, they offered commiseration and brushed make-believe tears from cheeks.

The court's treatment of the evidence led on behalf of Accused No 10, Justice Bekebeke, left little doubt in our minds or in his that he would receive the death sentence. When Justice was told that no extenuating circumstances could be found in his case, Zonga Mokhatle, who sat next to Justice in the dock, showed comic exaggerated disbelief at the news and clapped his hands wildly, this time distracting Justice Basson and throwing him off guard. This apparent lack of respect caused the judge to bark at Anton who was calling up electronic diary details of someone famous for Myner Bovu. 'Please, Mr Lubowski.' Anton looked up and stood to face the judge. 'There are some accused who are clapping their hands and laughing. It is very disruptive. Please would you warn them to stop this immediately or they will face serious consequences.' Anton assured the judge that a reprimand would follow and turned to Zonga and winked. He sat down and bowed his head, scoffing under his breath. 'They're being sentenced to death, for God's sake. What must I say—"If you don't behave, you'll be in big trouble?" '

•

On the Wednesday, the second day of judgment, David Beresford from the *Guardian* met us outside the court at lunchtime. He had spent the morning on tour, visiting Paballelo and moving through the town, getting a feel for the place and its people. He announced, to the delight of the other journalists, that a contingent of pro-South West Africans had that morning arrived in Upington on a trail of protest against Resolution 435 and Namibia's (South West Africa's) looming independence. They were en route to Pretoria, hoping to coincide their arrival with 31 May, Republic Day. They had chosen Upington as official resting place and were to address the town at a rally that night. It was rumoured that Eugene Terreblanche, old blue eyes of the *Afrikaner Weerstandsbeweging* (AWB, the Afrikaner Resistance Movement), was to play master of the meeting. There was general agreement that the citizens of Upington would be devotees of the man on horseback, with rifle cocked and Nazi-like insignia covering his thick upper arm. He would stir this town. The locals knew about the spectacle that night; few, however, had noticed that their town was host to the largest murder trial in South African legal history.

We walked back towards the hotel as a convoy of painted cars and *bakkies*, flags and banners advanced on us from behind. They stared ahead with mad intensity, sharply focused on their cause, on their words for fighting change, heads held high. As they closed in, Anton turned and stepped onto the road in their path. He thrust his fist into the air and roared: 'Viva SWAPO.' I flinched as we laughed. I feared the hatred these foot soldiers had for those who challenged their view of the world, their hold on their world. I was angry at Anton's bravado and I walked on ahead.

After lunch, I decided to delay my return to court. I was tired of the unchanging rhythm of Basson's readings and I wandered down to the government pre-fab in Smitstraat which housed the

Department of Social Work and Welfare to see Mrs Nelmie Barnard, social worker and probation officer. Mrs Barnard, assisted by the National Institute for the Prevention of Crime and Rehabilitation of Offenders (NICRO), had been asked to undertake the evaluation procedure to assess the suitability for community service of those accused who exhibited extenuating circumstances sufficient for the court not to impose the death sentence. It was becoming apparent from the judgment who the likely candidates might be for assessment and I thought it would be useful at this stage for Mrs Barnard to acquaint herself with those individuals on paper. I explained my visit and handed her the various expert reports and background information. Once Justice Basson had read out the judgment on extenuation, we would know which accused would be sentenced to death and which of the twenty-five would face sentences that precluded the death penalty. It was the latter whom Nelmie Barnard would assess in an attempt to shape their sentences away from prison terms to orders of community service.

Nelmie Barnard was young, pretty and straightforward. She asked if I'd stay and talk a little about the case, apologised for her poor English and offered me a cup of *rooibos* tea. We spoke in Afrikaans. Nelmie Barnard had graduated from the prestigious Afrikaans University, Stellenbosch and her round as social worker was predominantly based in Paballelo. She was quietly angered and concerned about the effects of the case on the community, and the emotional battering heaped upon the families whom she visited and counselled. She sensed their pain and wanted to reconstruct the lives of those who suffered. 'Mevrou Barnard' (Mrs Barnard) was a familiar name, often mentioned at family meetings as someone who would help obtain a grant or an extension when rent was dangerously overdue. 'Mevrou Barnard' talked to children who wouldn't go to school, who could no longer endure the ache of separation from their mothers and fathers on trial. She was a background figure who, against heavy odds, did much to restore the image of Afrikaners among the black and brown *inwoners* (inhabitants) of Paballelo.

I left Nelmie Barnard's office feeling remarkably buoyant and refreshed and returned to court for the remainder of the afternoon session. As I sat down at the bar table, Boy Jafta, Accused No 15, was told that no extenuating circumstances could be found in his case. Herman Raath, in his testimony, had highlighted Boy's acute emotional immaturity which, he argued, did not tally with his age in years. This conclusion had not been challenged by the state and appeared to have been accepted by the court as uncontroversial. But not even his age or immaturity of spirit was sufficient to save Boy from the death penalty. A heavy mood descended on the courtroom. It was a shocking finding, inconceivably cruel. A gentle man, with a warm round face laden with a childlike sensitivity, Boy had turned twenty in March 1985, eight months before the murder of Lucas Sethwala. Had Boy been twenty years of age or younger at the material time, that factor of itself, said Mr Justice Basson, would have constituted extenuation. The additional eight months, however, took him out of the realm of 'youth' and into the category of a convicted accused awaiting execution.

There was a ghastly wail from the gallery. Mary Malote, the woman who had mothered Boy from a young age when he had lost both his parents, stopped the cry with both hands across her mouth. Francis Gubula and Lydia Nompondwana shifted along the wooden benches to get closer to Mary, comforting her with sweets and handkerchiefs. Boy, stared at the judge, puzzled and disbelieving, not quite sure how to react. He began to whimper in the dock, trying hard to hold back tears in the presence of his tougher co-condemned. He looked at me, pleading for a change of mind and I winked back, an inane gesture of solace. I couldn't move from the cold panic that froze my body. Eight months had separated this boy from life—it was a finding so unexpected. Then the tug of responsibility triggered an urgent need to double-check. I was frightened that we may have overlooked a crucial point of argument. I raced through pages of the transcript, tracing clues to our submissions in the case of Boy Jafta. We had incorporated all the relevant and decisive factors—his age in years, his emotional immaturity, his inexperience—and read together, they presented a clear picture of youth, a strong case for extenuation. But it was too late for restatement.

Not even emphatic words of reassurance could eradicate the feelings of guilt and horror I felt for Boy and for his family, and those feelings were brutally reinforced each time I later visited him on death row at Pretoria Central. Painfully shy and sensitive, Boy would quietly beckon me to a corner of the consultation room after my discussions with his co-condemned, reticent to talk out loud. He would whisper that he was sore in his heart and missed his mother and Choice, his best friend, very much. He worried that they were destitute and struggling to pay the rent. He felt bad, he said, as he'd let them down, and then tears would fill his eyes. I would hold his hand and hope he could not feel the trembling of my limbs as grief and shame muddled through my heart.

I looked around the court and met Herman Raath's eye. He shook his head and then let it drop between his knees. The judgment on extenuation had made frequent reference to the profiles that he had painstakingly compiled after days of consultation with each accused. So as not to jeopardise his private practice, he would often conduct these interviews over weekends. He told me of hot, empty days in the prison and Saturday nights in his hotel room with a plate of sandwiches and an in-house movie. And of lonely Sunday afternoons at the Upington golf course hoping members might need a fourth. An Afrikaner and one-time corporal in the prisons service, Herman had dared to question his society and move on to write his doctorate on the psychological effects of apartheid on black South Africans. A dedicated professional with an unyielding integrity, Herman's work in respect of each accused had been candid, the bad aspects of each character thrown together with the good.

Herman had heard the state and the court accept his profiles, he knew that they considered his work sound, thorough and in line with professional standards. So much so, that the judge had relied on his clinical assessments to underwrite the findings on extenuation. There were moments, however, when Basson, rather than acknowledge the completeness of Herman's work, had used the unappealing features contained in some of the profiles to sustain an absence of extenuation, and so a sentence of death. As the likely death penalty toll rose to ten, as soft, young Boy Jafta joined the ranks of the condemned, Herman became riddled with self-doubt. Outside the court, drawing hard on successive Gauloises cigarettes, he asked for answers, repeating the same questions, unimpressed by any explanation offered. Anton, who had travelled a similar intellectual track and had endured the pain of breaking rank, tried hard to persuade Herman to rise above the disingenuity and cynicism embodied in the judgment. I began to worry about Herman's strength to counsel the accused—he was crushed and needed time out.

After court, the legal team, experts, press and observers had been invited to a concert in Paballelo. I invited Herman for a pre-concert drink. We were quiet and dull, worn down by the day. We sat on the lawn of the Protea Hotel near the pool and Philemon, our waiter in black fez and red jacket, poured Windhoek lager and asked if 'they' would hang. Looking out across the Orange River, we were audience to another perfect sunset and the evensong of crickets. Our spirits lightened, I dressed for an evening out, thrilled to be doing something that reminded me of normal after-hours city life.

The concert invitation had come from Raymond, a member of the Paballelo Blacksmiths, a vocal group originally founded by two of the accused. The special evening performance began at 6pm in the front yard of Raymond's house. The Blacksmiths wore bright, bold tunic tops and stood in a half-moon formation, intently watching one another's faces, keeping pace. Their voices were charged with vigour and rich with exquisite harmony. 'Where were you on the 13th of November 1985—Upington 26, Upington 26.' Raymond introduced the song as a dedication to the accused and they sang it to several cries of 'more'. Raymond had his sights set on stages far from Paballelo and, as I left, he asked if I could talk to the 'guys' at Gallo Records about a recording contract. He thought we had contacts for every occasion. 'We're going to be stars,' he said, 'we'll make this place famous.'

After the concert, Herman seemed a little less troubled and I decided we should try for further diversion and eat at a new restaurant called Le Raisin. This was a big departure from tradition and we agreed that Neil should never know. He had called me at the hotel at lunchtime to ask for an update on judgment and to make sure we would be dining at Le Must that night. He was to be host to a visiting netball team from a nearby town. New faces and lots of fun, he promised. It was not what I had in mind so I lied and said we needed a night at home. Even dinner at a new restaurant could not draw Herman. The judgment of Boy Jafta had come back to mind. Herman excused himself saying he was tired and felt sick to the core.

•

It is hard to focus on the Thursday, the final day of judgment on extenuation, to sift among the memories I remain so desperate to forget and meddle with emotions now deeply stowed away. We were all very tired and even reckless by then, and, we thought, pushed as far as we could go. But the events of the day drew us back to full alert. We were constantly tested and there was no room to give in or lose a hold; everything happened at great speed and with critical effect.

The court was filled to capacity, police lining the gallery and marking the windows and doors. The accused rose into the dock from the cells below, slowly, calmly climbing the stairs, singing in Xhosa 'Senzeni Na?' 'What have we done?' What is our sin…it is our black skins. They have caught us, now they are trying to kill us. What is our sin? What have we done?' It was the day that Evelina de Bruin, aged fifty-seven, and her husband, Gideon Madlongolwane, sixty, were told they would be sent to the gallows. Boy Jafta wasn't young enough to escape death; in the case of Evelina and Gideon, advanced age, unlike youth, was not considered an extenuating circumstance by Basson.

Gideon and Evelina, dock partners for almost three years, pressed their shoulders together and fumbled for each other's hand, clutching tightly, heads bowed. Of all the accused, I sat closest to Evelina and now, facing her, I took her hand and started to speak, hoping to distract her thoughts. 'You're going to be fine, Evelina, this is just the beginning. We have a long road ahead and the sooner we leave this court and get to Bloemfontein [seat of the Appeal Court], the better it will be for us all. Things will be different then, I promise you.' The court was very still. There was gentle sobbing from the gallery and flutters of pink and white, as tissues were passed up and down rows. Gideon raised his head and looked at the judge with pity and loathing. Evelina stared down at the floor, tears dropping onto the glass of her big square spectacles. Herman sent her a small white envelope with a sedative inside. Lomar, the court stenographer, had stopped tapping keys. She shook her head, her orange brush of hair swaying from side to side and I think I saw Mrs Claasens, the judge's registrar, shed a tear. Evelina didn't flinch. She didn't hear the judge, she didn't hear me, she didn't respond to my touches or utter a sound. She was detached, as if she had quietly taken her leave, numbed by the immensity of incomprehension. The judge is mad, he must be mad, Anton murmured.

Just before lunch and close to the end of the judgment on extenuation, Andre sent me a note. At the tea adjournment, he had engaged in simple chatter with some of the policemen on guard in the courtyard. They had been deployed from Kimberley, home town of the judge, the nearest major centre to Upington, a few hours drive east. Andre had asked them when they hoped to return home. Probably tomorrow, was the answer. They were to be in attendance until those found lacking in extenuation were formally sentenced to death and driven out of Upington to Pretoria Central, death row. Tomorrow? Yes, said the policemen, for reasons of security the condemned would be moved tomorrow and arrangements to that end were under way.

Ian's appointment as an acting judge meant his absence from the case until the first week of June. Our insecurity and the accused's distress about Ian's temporary absence from the trial had been lessened to some degree by a meeting we had called prior to the end of the previous court term. Judge Basson and the prosecution had agreed that sentencing of all the accused would take place once Ian had fulfilled his obligations on the bench, and the date for sentencing of all the accused had accordingly been set for Friday, 2 June. This arrangement would allow for the presentation of Xolile's psychiatric assessment to establish whether or not he was criminally insane, Basson's reading of the judgment on extenuation and preparation of our case in mitigation of sentence for those accused who had established extenuating circumstances and faced punishment other than death. Most importantly, it would give relatives of the accused who lived far from Upington time to travel to the town to see their family members before their transfer to death row or to prisons hundreds of kilometres away.

The information from the Kimberley police, however, warned of a breach of this agreement. Perhaps it was only a rumour intended to instil fear and confusion. But Andre knew the machinations of this town better than most, the quiet underhand strategies devised with little fuss and no apparent collusion between the trustees of the state. He was adamant that we should not be caught out, that we should burst their silent plan. My dilemma was whether my belief in the endurance and integrity of the words given by a man of high office should give way to Andre's gut feeling.

We returned from lunch eager for delivery of the last verdicts on extenuation. They were positive, the last five accused—Jeffrey Sekiya, Sarel Jacobs, Roy Swartbooi, Neville Witbooi, Ivan Kazi— would escape the death sentence by virtue of their youth and limited intellectual capacity. To find to the contrary would have unleashed considerable dismay. These were the accused not arrested as initial suspects, picked up from the streets of Paballelo, rounded up by police as extras, fill-ins at the identity parade. Identified by the state's key witnesses, they became suspects, were charged and convicted of murder. That these five men were permitted the benefit of extenuation was an enormous relief. That I momentarily saw the bench as reasonable and fair-minded, and smiled at Basson a smile of genuine, albeit short-lived warmth, was clearly a case of misplaced gratitude. I had temporarily forgotten that these men had a positive claim on their right to live.

I began to sense insidious movement in the court and outside. Policemen walked in and out of the courtroom exchanging typed documents with Mrs Claasens and then tiptoed across to chief investigating officer de Waal, an ever-present figure, infamous in Paballelo for his determination to crush a harmless militia of slingshots. The police would place documents on the table in front of de Waal and point to the spot where he was to sign. His signature secured, they walked back to the door, bowing their heads in deference to the judge, whispering to one another with the smugness of conspirators clinching a deal. I looked at Andre for some guidance. He was passive, there was little we could do, his body seemed to say. I felt frantic, fearing the plotting and planning that had taken place behind closed doors. I scribbled notes of alarm to Anton and Colin and then at 3pm, judgment was concluded.

We were due to adjourn until Thursday 1 June, three days later, when Ian would be back to present evidence in mitigation of sentence for those accused who had proved extenuation. The following day, all of the twenty-five would then be sentenced: the fourteen who failed to prove extenuation would be sentenced to death; the remaining eleven for whom extenuation had been found, primarily on the basis of youth and 'sub-normal intelligence' would be sentenced to jail terms or, hopefully, periods of community service.

Suddenly, the court emptied of policemen and, without warning, the judge hit us hard, a merciless finishing stroke. 'Mr Lubowski,' said Basson, 'for practical and security reasons, sentencing of the fourteen will take place tomorrow morning. Court is adjourned until 9am.'

15

•

A court case, not a burial

It was perhaps a naive, although warranted, belief that all the accused would be sentenced together. The Upington accused had sat together through months of allegations, evidence and argument. They had been convicted as a group and classified as such by the state and the bench. Perceived by their community and the world who cared as contained, linked by their torment, the very least they could expect was to be sentenced together, to move towards an ending as a whole. It was essential that the pride, support and love they had derived from the commonality of their experience was sustained and went with them into the next phase of their lives as the Upington 25.

The judge had originally determined the day of sentence for the first Friday in June, an agreement made with the prosecution and our defence team. With the date settled I had contacted family members who did not live in Upington or the surrounding districts, so that they could make arrangements to travel to the town over the days following the judgment on extenuation. This would allow them time to see the accused—their sisters, sons, mothers, fathers—before their sentence and possible removal hundreds of kilometres away to Kimberley Prison or Pretoria Central. David and Andrew's father, the Reverend Lekhanyane, had called to say he was motoring from Graaff-Reinet with Andrew's three young children. Evelina's brother, Reverend Benyani, and her eldest son, Welcome, were to travel from Namibia; we would collect Adelaide and Mbulelo, the two youngest de Bruin–Madlongolwane children, after school and bring them to court to spend an afternoon or two near their parents. Adelaide and Mbulelo were our most important assignment. If Evelina and Gideon were to be sentenced to death and moved to Pretoria Central, Adelaide and Mbulelo had to spend as much time as possible with them before sentence. Death-row prison regulations prohibited children under sixteen from visiting condemned prisoners. I worried that Adelaide and Mbulelo might never see their parents again.

There was a rumble from the dock, loud whispers from the gallery. Anton was locked on his feet. I tugged at the sleeve of his gown. He leant down and I whispered a rush of words. 'Tell him he agreed. All the accused would be sentenced *together* when Ian returns. That's still our belief. And the accused think the same. Many of the families are now travelling to Upington to be here for sentence next week. It's cruel to do this now.' Anton pushed his hair off his forehead and tugged at his collar to let the anger out. He spoke with a slow, difficult dignity and, trembling, pleaded with the judge to stand by our agreement. Cloaked by the law, Basson presented the reasonable approach: 'If you can show me a rule or regulation which requires me to allow families to be present for sentence, I will hear you.' Anton sipped at a glass of water. 'My, Lord, with the utmost respect, perhaps at this stage of the trial we should not be too concerned with the letter of the law, with rules and regulations. What we are asking for now,' he ventured, 'is compassion.'

The courtroom was silent. It seemed as if everyone had shifted forward in unison, perched to hear Basson's reply. His eyes were cold and fixed on Anton and there was a slight edge to his voice. Basson's words were sharp: 'Mr Lubowski, this is a court case, not a burial.' Anton dropped his head and with remarkable restraint asked for a short adjournment.

Basson allowed the adjournment and Colin raced off to the small court library in search of legal authority for our proposition. He returned with miraculous speed, balancing law reports on both hands and textbooks containing commentary on relevant statutes. There was no authority directly on point, he advised, but sufficient material to make out a case. Court resumed and Anton continued to battle, but reasons of security and practical arrangements already in place won out. The judge announced his decision: 'The case has been a long one dating back to 1986 and the court can find no justification for postponing sentence. Security and the administration of justice require that sentencing occur as soon as possible. As far as I'm concerned, the accused will not be prejudiced by this decision.'

I heard a shuffle behind me and Kenneth Khumalo, Accused No 1, former mayor of Paballelo, a serious man with a business-like manner, leapt to his feet, tears, like small bits of glass, across his cheekbones. Demanding his right to remain with the other accused until the trial's conclusion, he pleaded with Basson, a last desperate attempt to hold on to time: 'When you sentence our co-accused who may not get the death sentence, you may say something which could have relevance to our case on appeal.' His immediate plea was rational, and then he began to sob, his veneer of control falling away. 'Please allow us our dignity to remain with them to the end.' Kenneth's co-accused were uneasy, clearly disturbed by this unusual display. I feared his cries might trigger an outbreak from the other accused and moved towards him, begging him to be calm for the sake of the twenty-five. Kenneth was close to hysteria and difficult to comfort. Nomfaswe, his wife, rushed forward from the gallery, calling his name. Basson ordered silence in court and Nomfaswe was pushed back by a man in uniform. Xolile Yona banged his fists and stood up in the dock, pleading with the judge to change his mind, to give him another chance. Basson, angered by Xolile's direct address to the court, instructed him to sit down. 'If you must talk, you should address the bench through your legal representatives,' warned the judge. Boy Jafta began to weep and the police closed in on the accused.

With his hand on his holster, the young policeman who was guard to the judge swung open the back door of the court and smartly ushered the judge and assessor from the room. Basson, mid-sentence, still issuing words above the low din, turned to face the room: 'Court is adjourned until tomorrow,' and he was gone. Some of the accused began to sing 'We are marching to Pretoria', sung during the Anglo-Boer War by British troops as they marched on the South African Republic and occupied its capital, Pretoria. From the gallery came a surge as family and friends, sobbing and calling the names of the accused, their hands stretched out to touch them through the barrier of police blue, crushed one another in their panic. Hurried plans were made for the morning; requests for items of clothing, food, money and for special friends and family members to come to court to say goodbye. We stood back, watching, impotent. Police and prowling dogs gathered in the courtyard outside, simmering for action; inside, they tried to separate the gallery from the dock, shouting and shoving the accused down the narrow stairwell leading to the cells below.

The touch of police. The tap of a *sjambok* on a shoulder, the grab at the back of a neck, a white hand raised and eye meets eye. I had seen this prelude to battle many times. Then came the scornful exchanges and scuffles. Police jumped over tables and benches with batons drawn, chairs fell to the floor and the beatings began. The courtroom was filled with screams of terror and angry voices as police and accused locked in hate. No one was in control. It was an open brawl. Anton pulled police from accused; bigger than both, his strength and raw courage saved both parties from serious injury. Baton-wielding boys from the riot squad chased elderly friends and relatives from the gallery. Evelina de Bruin, frightened and bewildered, took refuge under the defence team's table. I crawled to her and held her soft shoulders, rocking her back and forth. She was shivering and slowly I took her hand and led her out from under the table. I wanted to move her towards the stairwell to the cells, away from the threat of harm. She tightened her grip around my fingers and limped behind me. A policeman, his baton pointed at Evelina, raced towards us and shouted: '*Kom, haastig uit die hof uit, mevrou*' ('Come, hurry out of the court, madam'). He dug at her elbow with his baton. 'Don't push her,' I said, 'she's trying to get away as fast as she can. Let her be.' 'You keep out of this,' he spat, his boyish cheeks puffy and red. I looked up and saw a video cameraman standing above us on a table, his camera rolling, pointed down. Throughout the scenes of chaos, a tall, wide, bullish plain-clothes policeman had stood atop the judge's table filming the scene for the South African Police Video Unit. 'I've got you on film, lady,' he grinned, smug, repugnant. He bellowed a raucous laugh, joined by colleagues at his feet.

We packed up our books and papers, keen to get away from this mad scene. I looked across the bar table into the gaze of senior advocate for the prosecution, Deputy State Attorney Terence van Rensburg. 'You see what you've done,' he accused, quick to get in first and deflect what was coming his way. I walked over to his table. 'Why the mean, indecent change of plan, *meneer*, the failure to advise and give us notice? We could have avoided the bitter and unhelpful events of this afternoon. We had everything organised—visits by family members, counselling by our psychologist. We could have prepared them slowly and humanely.' Van Rensburg swallowed and brushed his hand across a dry mouth. 'I've been involved in cases like this before,' he assured me with the air of an old hand, a dealer in the death penalty. 'If you don't act quickly, they go berserk. The sooner we move them out to Pretoria, the better. That way, it doesn't give people a chance to think about it. It's easier for them.' There was no real purpose in this exchange, no chance of common ground. He was obviously a man trained in the field.

I went down to the cells to check on the accused. I told them we would call their families and bring them food and clothing and some money later at the prison. There was little time left in the day and much to do and I was anxious to leave. The accused scribbled notes on small pieces of paper, reminders for their families, messages and shopping lists. We walked out to the back of the court, where the police vans were parked. Myner Bovu thrust his list into my hand as he climbed into a van bound for his last night at Upington Prison. We waved them on, feeling listless and remote. As we walked back to the courtroom, I read Myner's note. 'One litre of table wine, one girlfriend, a little soft light, five litres of Ballantine whisky, cigars and ten kilograms of *versagting* [extenuation].' At the bottom right-hand corner of the note he had written: 'Only joking.'

•

Back at the hotel, Reverend Aubrey Beukes and his wife were waiting for us in the corridor outside my room with some of the families, hoping to hear that the judge had agreed to postpone the sentencing. It was not to be and the Reverend sat on a chair with his head in his hands and asked God to forgive Justice Basson. Journalists, spread out on the carpet, sipping beers, jotted words in notebooks and put in calls to bureau chiefs. Neil Stemmet telephoned from Le Must to reassure us that there were people in Upington, white people, who were horrified at the news. He wanted us to know we had their support and said he feared for the future of our country.

I was light-headed. It was indecision, not knowing where to begin, what to do first. There were tens of telephone messages to return, continual calls to be answered, a last big shop for those accused travelling to Pretoria, and a sorting out of their debts. We had to obtain medical supplies, transfer educational facilities and books, convey last-minute messages to families and friends, meet with senior prison staff to ascertain the extent of the rights of condemned prisoners, and arrange a meeting with the fourteen at the prison. All these tasks, which we had planned to complete at a measured pace with maximum effect for all, now had to be completed within hours.

We started by ordering tea, an after-court ritual initiated by Ian which closed each day and helped centre our thoughts. Trays of tea arrived, and the room filled with pots and sugar bowls, milk jugs and glasses, tens of cups and saucers and as many people on the floor, on beds, on windowsills. We issued a 'press salute', a single call to an agency that would, within minutes, alert the media in South Africa and beyond to the issue of the day. The media responded with overwhelming speed and interest, hungry for the next implausible instalment. Mary Burton, National President of the Black Sash, had arrived in the morning from Cape Town to observe the trial. With no prompting, she settled in and quietly managed each call, as if part of the team from the start, pruning information to the barest details in between priming me for interviews with radio stations from around the world. She fielded calls from the hotel management and car-hire reps, begging us to give up rooms or a car for television crews arriving for the following morning. We replenished drinks and tea as bare comfort for the relatives who arrived to watch and wait with us. Mr and Mrs Bekebeke offered to host a family meeting and prayer service at 6.30pm. Andre drew up shopping lists: fourteen cakes of Lifebuoy soap, fourteen toothbrushes and tubes of toothpaste, Palmolive shampoo, boxes of Ouma rusks, tennis biscuits, dried fruit, sweets, asprin, magazines. Herman and Andre drove to the supermarket with forty minutes before closing time and Colin called the prison to request an after-hours meeting with prison staff and the accused. Permission was granted for 8 o'clock. As we left the hotel to drive to the Bekebeke home in Paballelo, we remembered pocket money for the fourteen condemned, for their first few weeks at Pretoria Central until regular funding could be secured from the South African Council of Churches. The banks had closed at 4 o'clock. Colin had his bank card and emptied his auto-bank account. The balance came from personal loans and an advance from our hotel.

The meeting at the Bekebeke home was crowded and close. We tried to put the parents at ease. We told them that the accused would be cared for in every way and that family visits to Pretoria would occur as often as possible, bearing in mind the distance from Upington of 850 kilometres and the cost of travel; that the accused would receive pocket money, medical and psychological care and continue to study; that colleagues from Johannesburg and

Pretoria would visit them in between our visits from Cape Town. Herman reassured the parents, saying he would be available to counsel them and the accused during the months ahead. 'Mind you,' he added, amid much laughter, 'after doing their shopping this afternoon, I'm not sure my services will be necessary. They are going to be too busy to see me, washing and cleaning, eating and reading.'

We introduced the foreign correspondents and visiting journalists who had joined us for the prayer service. Mr Gubula rose to speak. He said that before the accused were convicted, no one knew about the trial. The community had felt isolated and removed from outside help. 'But now, the world is with us in our pain. We thank you for your work.' As he spoke, the men and women nodded in agreement and whispered shy sounds of appreciation. Mary Burton stood to bring greetings from the Black Sash executive and from women around the country. She told Evelina's family that the Pretoria branch of the Black Sash would care for Evelina and watch over her. Martha Malgas, Evelina's sister, sat huddled in a chair, her head bent, occasionally wiping a tear with a handkerchief which she'd twisted and turned throughout the meeting. We were told the next day that after Evelina had been sentenced to death, Martha had collapsed outside the court and was taken to hospital. She had suffered a stroke which left her paralysed on one side for several months.

It was growing dark and there were smells of woodfires and evening meals being prepared. Mrs Bekebeke handed out candles which we lit. Final arrangements for the morning were confirmed: we would collect the older family members at 8am and drive them to court to secure a seat; we would call employers to request an hour's absence from work for those who feared they might lose their jobs. Aubrey Beukes ended the meeting with a prayer and we stood, heads bowed, under a navy sky, feeling comforted and at peace, fortified by solidarity. We moved through the meeting, leaving the families swaying to hymns, eyes tightly closed, oblivious to our departure.

•

Herman, Andre and Colin drove straight to the prison with shopping bags and boxes for distribution. Anton and I went via the hotel. I still had to call some of the families who lived far away. I needed to warn them of the imminent sentences before it was too late and they travelled long distances to no end. As we drove, I imagined each conversation, each opening line, over and over and I dreaded what had to be done. Anton waited in the car. I crossed Schröderstraat and walked towards the Protea Hotel. At the entrance to the hotel, tucked away to the right, was a man I recognised as a policeman. I'd seen him at court and we knew one another simply to nod. He was dressed in plain clothes, smoking a cigarette, waiting, possibly to meet a friend. As I got closer to him, he stared at me with cold dark eyes. I slowed my step and said: '*Naand, meneer*' ('Good evening, sir'). He held my gaze and said: '*Jy's dood*' ('You're dead').

My legs felt heavy as I walked into the foyer of the hotel, ignoring Leanne's call from reception about messages. I ran down the corridor and locked the door of my room behind me and fell onto my bed. I curled my legs up underneath my body and lay very still. I kept hearing his words. '*Jy's dood*.' Push it away, I told myself, start the calls. I dialled the number for Evelina de Bruin's brother in Namibia. Reverend Benyani's voice was shrill. 'How can this happen? We must see her. We will be there tomorrow afternoon. Make them wait for us until then, please.' I fought back tired tears and telephoned Reverend Lekhanyane. He had left for Upington some hours earlier. I ran back to the car refusing the temptation to look behind me, to see if the night policeman was still there. I started to tell Anton what had happened. It all came out like a tirade, an exhausted mix of fear and anger. Anton didn't speak. He looked at me as if to try and then he seemed to change his mind and turned on the radio. A few days earlier, he had bought me a new Joan Armatrading tape which he played continually, in the car, in his room. He rewound the tape to the beginning and we drove to the prison as Anton and Joan sang 'The devil I know'.

•

A week after my meeting with the policeman outside the hotel, when we had returned to Upington for the sentencing of the remaining eleven accused, I stopped in at my room after court one evening before dinner at Le Must. The room smelt of cigarettes recently lit. Two cigarette *stompies* (butts) had been left on the carpet near the door and there were burn marks on the weave, made, it seemed, with some degree of deliberation. On the right-hand side of my bed, up towards the pillows, near the telephone, was a large indentation, the mark of someone who had sat there not that long ago. Files and notes and transcripts of the court proceedings piled up against a wall at the far side of my room had been disturbed, left open and taken out of the order that I carefully constructed each day. I felt invaded and watched and that night I lay awake for hours convinced that someone other than Sera, who cleaned the rooms and cared for us, had a key to my room.

The next night I was too tired to eat. I ordered soup and toast and left Le Must early, determined to catch up on sleep. I entered my room and went to draw the curtains across the wall of windows that looked out over the hotel lawns and the dark Orange River. As I glanced out, I noticed two figures standing down below, in direct line with my view. Leaning against the fence which separated the hotel from the river banks, standing in the frozen night air, they were looking up at the hotel. They were the night shadows of male figures. One of them had arms folded across a broad chest. Every few seconds, the other moved a tiny orange light from his face down to his side, and then up again. As my vision sharpened, I saw a cigarette. From then on, my imagination took over, keenly directed by rising fear. I equated the figures below with the carriers of the cigarette stubs left on my carpet, with the marking on my bed. I believed they could watch my movements, trace shadows from the inside of my room.

I knelt down below windowsill level to undress and crawled along the carpet to the door. I piled three or four chairs on top of one another and pushed them against the door, a home-built alarm system to warn me of intruders. I stacked chairs for another two nights and only stopped when Anton came to visit me to tell me of his invitation to an urgent meeting with exiled Namibian President-elect, Sam Nujoma in New York the following week. It took me a few minutes to unload the chairs and open the door. Anton queried the banging on the door from the inside before I let him in. 'What's actually going on here?' He was puzzled by the gathering of chairs so close to the entrance. Two of them had fallen on their side in my hurry to dismantle the guard. I explained, hopelessly embarrassed and we laughed and talked of fear and how we store it. Anton had fears, terrible fears, and he struggled to keep them at bay. He got up, needing to move away from the topic and walked down to the hotel bar, returning with two brandy and cokes and his tape recorder which crooned his favourite Julio Iglesias. I hadn't had a brandy and coke since my Standard Eight school dance. The chairs came down and my fear evaporated, in some part due to the sheer nuisance of my own cumbersome method of self-protection.

•

Captain van der Merwe and Andre met us at Upington Prison entrance. The Captain was sorry, but no foodstuffs or toiletries or books were allowed at Pretoria Central. The shopping, the bags and boxes, lay stacked in the corner of the Captain's office; a futile and expensive expedition. For some reason we'd assumed prison rules and privileges were universal. We walked down the passage of grey linoleum tiles to the men's section of the prison. Prisoners on their hands and knees moved to one side to let us pass. Tied to their hands, under their palms, were oblong brushes of bristle and on their knees, yellow dusting cloths dipped in floor polish. As we walked, they started moving again, shuffling backwards, their hands moving in swift circles, like human polishers. The Captain told us we could collect the accuseds' bundles of belongings the following day to give to their families. He continued with the new rules. The accused would not be allowed to further their studies. 'You are, however, at liberty to lodge an application with the Commissioner of Prisons for special study permission.' He was trying to help. The prisoners would be forbidden work, television or videos; sport and visits were only by prior written permission. Thirty minutes of exercise each day was the standard. The accused were no longer awaiting sentence, he explained, and their sentence was death. They had changed categories and prison classification and life in Pretoria Central would be different. Very different. If we had any further queries, we should not hesitate to ask. The Captain left us to meet our clients.

We had grown accustomed to the amiable staff at Upington Prison, to the relaxed atmosphere, to the privileges and favours. I knew those came with time and knowledge, with a recognition of the accused as complex human beings, with a belief that the accused had the capacity for good. They would have to earn this understanding all over again. For the time being, they were a bunch of convicted murderers, new arrivals at death row, with no history and a fixed destiny. With their altered status came a switch, a different approach even from the officials who knew them well at Upington Prison. The staff had become rigid and anxious about suicide attempts. 'The night before the death sentence is a bad night for us. We have to watch them. But your guys seem in good spirits.' We were led into a big hall where we saw the thirteen men, watched over by warders who peered through a glass wall. Herman visited Evelina in the women's section. Boy Jafta pulled his maroon tracksuit top over his head, a gift to him from the South African Council of Churches. He asked me to give it to Choice, his girlfriend. 'By this, she can remember me. Tell her I wore it often. She must wear it every day.' The others talked amongst themselves, jostling one another, joking, trying to keep it light. We talked to them briefly. There was little to say and we shook hands and wished them strength for the long night ahead. A tingling filled the air, a tension, a strange excitement and shouts of 'Amandla' and 'Long Live' trailed our steps along the hallway from the prison.

•

On schedule, we arrived at Le Must just before 9pm. Our table was a feast of colour and taste. Mary Burton of the Black Sash met us at the restaurant with various members of the Upington news team—John Carlin, Gaye Davis and David Beresford. Marius Bosch from the *Cape Times* and Connie Mlusi from the *City Post* joined us after filing their stories for the morning. Neil paraded back and forth, bursting with pride, the adoring and attentive gourmet. He served a house specialty, springbok (venison) pie which was an enormous success and our host wallowed in the universal appreciation. Neil bent down and whispered in my ear. 'I've been thinking. I would like to make a special dinner for the families and the accused. Perhaps we can take it to the prison tomorrow. I could do steaks and salad. With a peri-peri sauce. Something simple.' Dinner conversation was in anticipation of the following day. How would Basson deal each blow? What would we do next? Is an appeal automatic. Amidst references to the last supper, Neil called me to the telephone. It was Mr Gubula, he said. It was urgent.

Alfred Gubula spoke softly. In the background, I could hear people shouting and crying. 'It's terrible, Andy. You have to come. It's very bad down here,' Mr Gubula explained. After the meeting at the Bekebeke home, the families prayed and then walked down the streets of Paballelo with lighted candles, singing hymns and freedom songs. They were joined by a few township teenagers, mostly girls, who swelled their numbers and their song. As they walked towards their homes, police vans and trucks drove towards them and encircled the gathering. Policemen jumped to the ground with *sjamboks* and batons. Their barking dogs followed, ready to maul. The police kicked and whipped the bodies of the old and young, men and women. Mr Gubula was breathless. He was silent for a moment and then continued. They *sjambokked* women across their faces, across their breasts. They stood on the stomach of a pregnant woman who fell as she tried to run from their rage. Dogs were set on the group, tearing at clothing, biting through flesh. A young boy tried to leap across a wire fence, chased by police and dogs. He was caught by the fence, lacerated and punctured by a rusted post. There were bodies everywhere, bleeding. Most were young, maybe thirteen or fifteen-year-olds. Some were still, kicked and clubbed unconscious. They were thought to be dead. So far, said Alfred Gubula, twenty people had been taken to hospital.

In front of me sat a table of boys in brown uniforms and solid boots, laced to the shins. They were army boys on their night off. They slapped Neil on the back and ordered monkey gland steaks and bottles of beer. I stared at them and for one brief moment I thought I might ask them for help. I had stopped listening to Mr Gubula and I told him we'd call him straight back. I didn't want to know, I didn't want to care, not any more. I walked over to our table, reluctant to stop the swing of mid-dinner talk. There was a stillness as I spoke. Anton, sensing my withdrawal, my numbing, called Mr Gubula and said some of us would be there soon. Gaye Davis grabbed her bag and keys and offered to drive to Paballelo and take statements and assess the damage. She would telephone us from Gubula's house with an update. I sat back and watched our guests take charge. Mary and John then David left the table. Slowly, the day lost focus and images of carnage filled my head. At some point, Neil tentatively offered dessert.

Ian went to bed. I sat with Anton and Andre and Colin, waiting. An hour or so later, Reverend Beukes stopped in at Le Must on his way back from the hospital and reported that things were pretty grim. 'And they wonder why we turn to violence.' Beukes lit a cigarette and ordered coffee. John Carlin made reference to the Reverend's words in his report for the *Independent* that night: 'The wonder, if anything, is that they don't turn to violence more.

Why, how the milk of human kindness has not curdled into hate. How the nobility still remains.'

I stayed awake for hours. I called home to find out news from the city, from a suburban world happily insulated from life on Schröderstraat. I tried to sleep but thoughts and pictures circled in my mind. Pictures of a pregnant woman, her stomach kicked in by policemen's boots. The boy impaled, his limbs cut by fence wire. Dogs tearing at flesh. I pictured Basson and wondered if he was sleeping. In the morning, he would sentence a group of people to death. Then he would travel home for the weekend to be with his family and tend to his farm. Far away from the wounds he would inflict on Paballelo, oblivious to the wounds of this night. At three o'clock I had a bath, hoping the warmth and water might bring sleep. I lay on my bed and listened to the still, still night. And then I heard the rain and a secret joy and comfort clothed my body and I drifted into sleep. With the night rain came a sense of safety, a reasoning that those with evil and injurious intent would be forced to stay inside. I liked to think that the rain was a shelter from harm, and now at last I could rest with a slight easing of my anxious mind.

I woke at 6.30am, disturbed by the ringing of a telephone. It was Friday, 26 May 1989. The beginning of the day of death for the Upington 25, and the press and the world were up in search of headlines. Pushed under my door was a collection of papers and faxes and notes from media already in Upington requesting a press conference after court. I dressed as I thought one should on such a day, in black, and went to the hotel dining room for tea. It was still early and the room was almost empty, just two travelling salesmen sitting one at either end, one of them tapping on a pocket calculator. I sat near a window. The rain of the night had slowed to a gentle drizzle. One of the cooks came out from the kitchen with a plate of sausages, mushrooms and fried toma-toes. 'It's a special for you this morning.' She lowered the plate onto the table and looked outside at the rain. As she turned to leave she said: 'God is crying for them.' The dining staff took turns to bring me a clean cup and saucer and fresh pots of tea.

This way they could stop to talk. They had heard rumours in the township. Was it true that fourteen would be sentenced to death? Would they all be hanged? What was to happen to the old couple? Soon after eight, Anton arrived looking drawn. By now, the dining room was buzzing with television crews, reporters, embassy officials. Anton sat down and tucked in to the sausages and mushrooms. It was good-luck food, I said, and insisted he clean the plate.

16

---•---

May the Lord bless you, my lord

We drove up to the court. Queues of friends and relatives of the accused stood on the pavement. One by one the police approached them and asked their reason for being there. They had a better chance of getting in if they were close family. We stopped to talk to those in line, to see if we could help, to answer questions. Some wore bandages around their heads and limbs, others had welts, dog-bite wounds or open gashes on their arms and faces, signs from battle the previous night. As I entered the courtroom, my eyes were drawn to a thick band of blue that spread from wall to wall. Riot police had stacked the front row of the public gallery taking space from those who legitimately should have filled it. They were on alert. Lining the sides of the court, in the court-yard, at the front, ready to guard the judge. People in the gallery jostled for space and then came the familiar rumbling from below. The voices of the condemned, led by Kenneth Khumalo, travelled up the stairs from the court cells and we rose to greet them.

The police stared ahead, unmoved as the fourteen stood in the dock and sang 'Nkosi Sikelel' i-Afrika'. As they ended the hymn, one of the police guards standing at the front called the court to order. There was silence and Judge Basson entered in robes of crimson red, the official judicial dress for the death-sentence ceremony. Anton and Basson exchanged brief words relating to the procedure of the morning. Then Basson nodded to Kenneth Khumalo, Accused No 1 and the court interpreter invited Kenneth to say a few words to the court before sentence. Most of the accused were wearing their maroon tracksuits, sent by the South African Council of Churches. Kenneth, forever dapper, always with a sense of occasion, wore a dark suit and tie. 'I know that I am not guilty. The evidence produced in this court does not justify my conviction and sentence. Lies were told, fabricated lies, and the court was misled.' Kenneth looked away from the judge. He was silent and still for a few seconds, hesitant, and then he delivered his last words: 'My lord, this trial will act as a scale which will measure justice in the legal system of South Africa.'

It was strange to watch the accused rise to address the court. They had been so resolute that they would not give evidence that I imagined they might refuse the judge's invitation to talk before sentence. But one by one, they spoke to Basson with passion and dignity and no hint of preparation. Many of the condemned simply wanted to restate their innocence or express their fears of losing their families or their dreams, like Xolile Yona, Accused No 20: 'I beg the court to have mercy because I have young children. I was an orphan and would not like my own children to grow up without a father. I would like to be a good boxer. I ask the court for a last chance.' When Accused No 10, Justice Bekebeke, rose to speak, all the condemned turned to watch him. He spoke slowly and softly and I think Basson listened to every word. 'I, as a black man, thought I would get justice in this court. I have found none. This whole case was based on racial prejudice. People have deliberately made examples out of us. In a country like South Africa, I wonder how justice can really be applied. I certainly haven't found it. But, my lord, I would like to ask: Let's forget our racial hatred. Let us see justice for all humanity. We are striving for each and every racial group to live in harmony. But is it possible, in the name of the Lord? Is it possible in such a country?...I would like the Lord to give you many years so that one day you can see me, a black man, walking on the streets of a free South Africa. May the Lord bless you, my lord.'

'The man died,' said Accused No 11, Zonga Mokhatle, 'that is correct, but I did not kill him.' Evelina de Bruin, Accused No 18, her maroon tracksuit top pulled down over a floral skirt, went further: 'This court is the guilty party in this case. I am an elderly woman and have been found guilty for something I have not done. I feel very sad for my children and my home. I've been taken away from them for something I didn't do.' Her husband, Accused No 19, Gideon Madlongolwane, assured the judge that his conscience was clean. 'If I am hanged,' he said, 'I will surely go to heaven. As I am standing here today, I have not done anything wrong. I did not give evidence on my own behalf because I knew I would be branded a liar.' In some detail, Gideon began to criticise the judge's approach to his failure to testify. Basson interrupted Gideon's critique insisting that the merits of the case were for argument by his counsel on appeal. This was not the time for such analysis. The last to speak, Accused No 21, Albert Tywilli, had no desire to hide his contempt: 'I am not glad that I have been found guilty. A more clever judge would not have found me guilty at all. You have robbed me of my children. Congratulations.'

Justice Basson hardly waited for a period of grace. He was perhaps keen to do the deed and leave. He called out the numbers of the accused. 'Accused numbers 1, 2, 4, 5, 6, 8, 10, 11, 13, 15, 18, 19, 20, 21,' and added, as a matter of course, 'you are sentenced to death.' Some of the condemned clapped their hands in mock celebration and uttered: '*Dankie*' ('Thank you'). The judge pushed back his chair and slid out of court. It was a sweeping achievement. Fourteen people sentenced to death in less than a few minutes. Sentenced to death for a single murder in which the court had found most of them had played no physical part. I turned to look at the fourteen. They stood, motionless, not knowing where to go next or what to do. One of the policemen started to herd them out of the dock and their families began to push forward, reaching out to touch them. I called out to the man in control, the big policeman at the front of the court who had watched the proceedings impassively and ordered his men about. '*Meneer*, can the accused have a few minutes with their families before they leave court?' I had little idea what would happen once we all left. We would be back on the following Thursday to present the case on mitigation of sentence for the remaining eleven accused. But what happened now to the fourteen? Would they be taken back to the Upington Prison, were they to be driven straight to Pretoria? The policeman agreed to my request and announced the favour, as if he was a good guy. He even developed a work plan which he spelt out in detail. The accused were allowed to see their families, four at a time. All those who were not relatives were to leave the court. The first four accused were to take up their positions in different corners of the courtroom, as if manning stalls at a market. Their families were then allowed to approach, until all fourteen had taken succour.

The accused milled about, waiting their turns, then embraced their families and wrote down messages for those unable to be present. It would be the last chance for many months, perhaps even years, to hug, kiss, to weep into open arms. At Pretoria Central visits would be behind thick panels of glass. Even in these last intimate moments, the South African Police Video Unit felt the need to intrude and filmed the pockets of distress. Outside the court building, families and friends of all the accused had gathered to await the emergence of those whose loved ones had been condemned. As the relatives came out of the court, they wept and comforted one another. The crowd began to sing and sway and the media mingled with their cameras and microphones. We stood at the entrance to the court and I said a few muddled words to an impromptu press conference and returned to the courtroom to go down to the cells. The accused were waiting to climb into the yellow vans parked at the back of the courthouse. They were to travel through the night straight to Pretoria. An early morning arrival was scheduled.

Police and dogs stood at the entrance to the under-court cells. They gave the all clear and the accused started to move towards the trucks. Two for the men and one for Evelina. I held their hands as they passed, and once they were inside the vans, Anton and Andre and Colin moved from truck to truck, talking to the accused through small holes in the wire. From the outside, you could barely see their features. They were dark figures, truck loads of condemned. I pushed my hands against the wire and tried to touch their fingers and promised to visit soon. I spoke to Evelina in her solitary van but there was silence from the inside, not even the usual 'Ja, Andy', which signalled she felt a little comfort. As word got out that the accused were about to leave, the crowd moved to the side of the court building. The singing grew full and each word left its mark. '*Senzeni Na? Senzeni Na?*' ('What is our sin?...it is our black skins. They have caught us, now they are trying to murder us. What is our sin? What have we done?') The engines started and the vans pulled away from the court and drove around the corner into the main street. We followed shouting, waving and singing '*Nkosi Sikelel' i-Afrika*' and the accused answered, shouting back '*Amandla*'.

We turned into Schröderstraat and people lined the pavements, crying and cheering. The crowd, waiting for the vans to pass, surged forward onto the street and the police, with their snarling dogs straining on their leashes, beat the people back. A group of young men, protected by a circle of supporters, broke into a *toyi-toyi* as the yellow vans, escorted by police vehicles with sirens wailing, sped away by a different route. Suddenly a gathering of women outside the court burst into whoops of laughter and applause when an unmarked police car, confused by the detour, smashed into the side of another police vehicle parked outside the court. Still singing, the crowd moved along the streets of Upington, accompanied by a trail of television cameras and a strong police contingent. The police thrust out their batons and one of them gave the order to leave the area. 'We are going to take action against these people. Turn back.' Emergency regulations prohibited the press from reporting on any 'unrest incidents'. The government's rationale for the prohibition was that press coverage of such 'action' provoked unrest. The media, not the police, were the *agents provocateurs*. On a generous reading of the police instruction, preventing coverage meant that the media was not tempted to breach the prohibition. In reality, it meant that police action against individuals went undetected and uncorroborated.

•

In the afternoon we drove to Upington Prison to collect the bundles of clothes and books and belongings of the fourteen which were forbidden on death row. We had agreed to deliver them to their families before we left Upington for the weekend. We first visited the remaining eleven accused to report on the morning and to reassure them that we would travel to Pretoria to see the fourteen after their sentencing the following week. Like us, they were worried about Evelina—suddenly separated from Gideon, the other accused, and all friends and family—but we feigned a confidence that she would be well cared for and that after the appeal she would be free. The bundles lay on the floor of the Captain's office. There were piles of books tied with string. Brown paper packets with names and addresses. I looked at the motley collection of possessions and the short-sighted, ironic words of Judge Basson came to mind: 'This is a court case, not a burial.'

For many of the families, the fourteen had gone for good. The sheer distance between Upington and Pretoria made future contact difficult, for some impossible. The parcels at the prison were the remains of their lives. As we packed them into our car, it felt like 'this courtcase' had become a mass burial and that the funeral rites had just begun. Maybe it was our imagination, but as we drove into Paballelo there was a sadness and a quietness, as if the town had turned inward to mourn. There were sombre words exchanged as we drove from house to house delivering the packages. Later, as we drove to the airport for our Friday evening flight out, I felt a strange lightness, a sense of resolution. The grim deed, anticipated for many cruel months, had been executed. In Upington we had become stuck, waiting for the worst. We were about to enter a very different phase of the trial, to move forward, beyond Basson and the fetters on his world.

On the flight home, Colin and I read and swapped newspapers. David Beresford's report in *The Guardian* on the fourteen sentences of death carried a contrasting footnote: 'In Cape Town, Parliament yesterday rejected a motion by anti-apartheid legislator, Mrs Helen Suzman, to censure a judge for imposing only a fine on a white farmer who beat a black worker to death over a two-day period. The Justice Minister, Mr Kobie Coetzee, opposing the motion, said that censure of Judge JJ Strydom would amount to "intimidation of the judiciary".' John Carlin in the *Independent* ran a similar line: 'South Africa's cavalier imposition of the death sentence highlights the inevitable skewed apartheid morality which the authorities lay down as the social norm. Between 1985 and mid-1988, according to Amnesty International, South Africa carried out 537 legal executions, placing it third in the world rankings after Iran and Iraq. The most recent figures available to illustrate the racial disparity in the hangings were in the period June 1982 to June 1983: of 81 blacks convicted of murdering whites, 38 were executed; of the 52 whites convicted of murdering whites, one was hanged; while none of the 21 whites convicted of murdering blacks was executed.'

During the period 1979 to 1988, 1423 people were executed at Pretoria Central. The Upington 14 had the potential to improve our world ranking in hangings.

I arrived home to telephone messages and telegrams of condolence. Ian was back from his term as acting judge. He had heard the news. We arranged to meet midweek with our witness on mitigation, Dirk van Zyl Smit, and to review the reports of a National Institute for Crime Rehabilitation and Prevention (NICRO) panel commissioned by the court to assess the suitability of our remaining eleven clients for rendering community service. Saturday, my usual day of rest from the week in Upington, was filled with visits from friends and acquaintances. With flowers and chocolates, they came to pay their respects. It was hard to be sociable and I shied away from their expressions of horror and grief. Disorientated and weary, I sat as witness to these feelings, barely able to respond. My delayed reaction came later that night. At a movie with friends, I cried in the dark.

17

•

A measure of mercy

It was a day of celebration. Ian was back to lead the team for the final few days of the Upington trial. The first of June marked the thousandth day of the case and the birthdays of Accused No 1, Kenneth Khumalo and Innocentia, Xoliswa Dube's daughter, who was to turn two. We had arrived on the early morning flight and court had started slightly late. Once again the gallery was packed, although the dock was considerably depleted without the fourteen condemned to death, now ensconced in Pretoria Central.

Ian began the day with a request to hand in as evidence, an 80-page report of a survey conducted by the University of Cape Town's Institute of Criminology. The report clearly favoured a sentence of community service for the remaining eleven accused as an alternative to imprisonment. Ian read from the introduction to the report: 'It is a penological truism that the attitude of the community to sentence is a factor to be taken into account when deciding on the sentence to be imposed. It is difficult, however, for a court to assess the attitude of "the community". This is particularly true in a divided society like South Africa where communities are frequently isolated from one another.' The Director of the Institute of Criminology, Professor Dirk van Zyl Smit and two of the institute's key workers on the survey, Desiree

Hansson and Derrick Fine, sat near the front of the gallery, watching Basson, waiting his response to their offering.

The judge looked stern and unimpressed, and Ian soldiered on. 'In summary, the report will show that 57 per cent of residents in the township of Paballelo felt that the policeman, Lucas Sethwala, had been killed for his "improper and violent treatment of people".' This statement met with a low chorus of 'ja, ja' from the gallery. 'Not convinced of their guilt,' Ian continued, 'the majority of the residents interviewed did not support any punishment for any of the accused.' These were strong words and Ian was adamant that they should get out. If dismissed by Basson, they might at least attract media coverage. I began to feel edgy, that we were on antagonistic ground. 'What will also emerge from this report is that even among the minority who supported punishment, the largest proportion favoured leniency. In addition, there was overwhelming opposition to the death penalty and clear majority support (69 per cent) for release of the accused back into the community. Given these views and in particular the community's accepting attitude towards release, the report will recommend that community service be given serious consideration in the sentencing of the accused. My lord, I call Professor Dirk van Zyl Smit, Director of the Institute of Criminology, to speak further to the report.'

Dirk stood up to move towards the witness box. 'There will be no need to hear from you, Professor. Thank you.' Basson smiled at Dirk, a polite, dark smile. 'I have read the report and I have listened to what Mr Farlam has to say. There is no reason why I should not be able to determine the real interests of these people, why I am any less qualified than a bunch of faceless uninformed people (*'n klomp gesiglose oningeligte mense*). I rule that the survey and report are inadmissible but I will allow them in as an exhibit.' The judge turned his gaze to Dirk. 'Professor, you may be excused.' We adjourned for the morning tea-break. It was a puzzling decision by the judge, a strange compromise. The report was ruled inadmissible as evidence but permitted to form part of the record. Perhaps this was a demonstration of fair-mindedness, a striving for balance. Downhearted, Dirk, Derrick and Desiree made the late morning flight back to Cape Town and we handed out shavings of cake and sang 'Happy Birthday' to Kenneth and Innocentia.

Social worker and probation officer Mrs Nelmie Barnard was due to present the NICRO panel reports after lunch. Before the break, Eben Boshoff stood to address the court on mitigation for his client, Accused No 7, Enoch Nompondwana, the only accused not guilty of murder. We thought Enoch, convicted of attempted murder, would be a strong contender for a suspended sentence. In his plea for suspension of sentence, Eben declared that his client was prepared to pay restitution to the Sethwala family. When his sentence was announced the following day we were thrown by the verdict: Enoch was sentenced to eight years in prison.

Mrs Barnard's reports were so meticulous in their detail and the state was so careful to detract from positive insights of the accused with matching reminders of the gravity of the crime, that court did not end until 7 o'clock that evening. To allow for time to review the evidence, Basson adjourned court to the following afternoon, requesting Ian to see him late morning to confirm the time of sentence. That night we had a quiet dinner at Le Must. It was to be our last for a long time, certainly our last as the legal team for the Upington 25. It was uneventful, unlike the night before the death sentences were handed down. I felt as if we had begun to lose steam, as if we had been battered once too often and every last spark of will had been punched out of us. It was hard to imagine how we would continue this fight, and whether we would all be in it to the end, whatever that might bring.

In the morning, Colin and I visited the accused at the prison and talked about the appeal. It felt better to deal with the sentencing as an inevitable step towards the appeal, rather than speculate about imprisonment or community service. Soon after 11 o'clock, lunchtime at the prison, we drove to Paballelo to visit some of the families. Reverend Benyani, Evelina de Bruin's brother, had motored down from Namibia and was staying with the de Bruin–Madlongolwane children for a few days. As we entered the house, he asked us to be seated and immediately launched into prayer, asking for forgiveness, asking for freedom and peace *'in ons land'* ('in our land'), beseeching the Lord to bring Evelina and Gideon back to *'hierdie huis, wat so leeg is, sonder 'n moeder, sonder 'n vader'* ('this house, which is so empty, without a mother, without a father').

The judge had set the time of sentence for 2pm. As we arrived at the court, Mr Abednego Matshoba, Elisha's father, present in court for the death sentences and now back again in the hope of a community service order for his son, came over to share his grief: 'This case weighs very heavily on me. They say Elisha did not kill the man but that he is also a murderer. I cannot eat or think because this whole thing constantly stands before me. I spend the whole time just looking at Elisha. My heart breaks every day, but being able to see my son keeps me going.'

The court was called to order. Basson began with a reference to a 'measure of mercy' which informed his sentencing. 'Mercy is an ingredient of justice itself,' he said, 'but, one cannot allow that people murder an innocent person if they have grievances against the state authority.' With mercy in mind, he handed down the sentences: 'Accused number 3, Abel Kutu, number 12, Ronnie Masiza, number 22, Jeffrey Sekiya, number 23, Sarel Jacobs.' They stood in the dock facing the judge. 'Six years imprisonment.' 'Accused number 7, Enoch Nompondwana and accused number 9, Elisha Matshoba.' They stood and joined the others. 'Eight years imprisonment.' I turned to look for Mr Matshoba in the gallery. He was struggling to stand. Those around him pulled him back and held his crumbling frame. He was weeping into his jacket.

The judge continued. 'Accused number 14, Barry Bekebeke, number 16, Xoliswa Dube, number 17, Elizabeth Bostaander and accused number 25, Neville Witbooi. You are each sentenced to a six-year jail term suspended for five years on condition you render community service and are not convicted of any offence involving violence...' Basson's voice was lost in the shuffle of surprise and joy, the tiny shouts and whispers, the sighs of relief. I scribbled down the terms of the community service order: 1200 hours completed within 40 months—a minimum of 30 hours per month at a coloured old age home, assisting with the physical care of the inhabitants, kitchen/garden work and the administration of the institution. Accused number 24, Roy Swartbooi and number 26, Ivan Kazi, the last to be sentenced, also received suspended six-year jail terms and were to render their community service under the care of a priest at the Upington Roman Catholic Church, performing allocated tasks, in particular cleaning and the beautification of the church grounds.

Ian stood to address the court. He was wasting no time in letting Basson and the prosecution know that the case was far from over. 'My lord, I should advise at this point that we are instructed to make application for leave to appeal.' 'Yes, Mr Farlam,' Basson was checking the court diary, flicking pages with a certain nonchalance. 'I will hear the application for leave in the Kimberley Supreme Court on Monday, 26 June. That gives you three weeks. How long will you require for the hearing, Mr Farlam, Mr van Rensburg?' We settled on two days and then Basson asked for silence and thanked his assessor, the defence and the prosecution, his staff, the court staff and the police for a job well done, for the hard work, a difficult task. We nodded and he left the courtroom and that was that. A short sharp end to the Upington trial.

Van Rensburg and Jaap Schreuder were packing up their books, folding their gowns, talking in low tones to the police. I went over and said goodbye. We shook hands and I agreed to send them a copy of our leave application a few days before the hearing. The dock was an unpleasant mix of emotions. Sadness, joy, envy, fear. It was a grim and disruptive end. All twenty-five accused were deemed murderers. Fourteen were sent to their deaths, five to prison and the others would sleep at home each night and beautify the grounds of the Upington Roman Catholic Church by day. I tried to believe that the measure of mercy was hidden in the cruel disparity of the sentences. Johanna, who served us tea each day, Xoliswa Dube's aunt, came rushing into court and took my hands in hers. '*Is dit waar, mevrou? Is dit waar dat Xoliswa kom huistoe?*' ('Is it true, is it true that Xoliswa's coming home?') As we walked out of the court, thronged by the six community servers and their jubilant friends and families, as I watched them welcomed back into the heart of the Paballelo community, a strong ambivalence of feeling took hold. At the back of the court, their fellow prisoners were climbing into vans to be taken to Kimberley Prison. There was no fanfare for them, only quiet weeping and the odd '*Amandla*'.

Back at the hotel, we started packing. Boxes and boxes of files and documents, books, reports, exhibits. Weeks of work. We filled six trolleys and arranged for couriers to freight our Upington office back to Cape Town. Between us, we had all the material necessary to draft the leave application. The rest could wait in boxes until we knew our chances of appeal. At 6 o'clock a meeting began in my room arranged by Reverend Beukes and the parents of the accused. We all squeezed into the room and then came a knock on my door, and the arrival of the six community servers. It was a shock to see them free, on new ground, at ease. Barry Bekebeke spoke on their behalf. 'Going home this afternoon was like waking from the most horrible of all nightmares. Thank you for all you have done. I believe heaven must be missing some angels. I am glad those angels are on our side, working for our rights and our beings. We believe in you, we respect your service and admire your energy and what you are capable of doing. God bless you all.' Reverend Beukes handed me a small box and a glass vase with one red rose. 'A small token of our appreciation. May you always remember us by this small gift as we will remember you.'

As we loaded up our hire cars in the hotel carpark, the hotel staff came to say goodbye and welcome us back at any time. Willie Burger, manager of the Protea Hotel, offered to take some of us to the airport. I ran across the road to say goodbye to Neil Stemmet and the young women who worked in the kitchen at Le Must. Walking back, I looked down Schröderstraat. It was Friday evening and workers were leaving town standing on the backs of trucks, silhouetted against the light of dusk. There was a slight chill in the air. It was time to go, to break the cord and leave Upington for another time.

18

•

Death row

A few days after sentence, more than 3000 people packed the Cape Town City Hall for the launch of the campaign to save the Upington 14 from the gallows. The following week, at a public meeting, the head of the Society for the Abolition of the Death Penalty in Cape Town, Dennis Davis, called for a moratorium on all executions until a judicial commission had been appointed to investigate and report on the death penalty regime.

Two weeks later, Mr Justice Basson, sitting in the Kimberley Supreme Court, listened to a day and a half of argument as to whether leave to appeal should be granted to the Upington 25. There was no automatic right of appeal, even when the sentence of death had been imposed. We first had to seek leave from the Supreme Court, in this case from Mr Justice Basson, to grant us our right to appeal against the twenty-five convictions and sentence. In seeking leave, we had to persuade the Kimberley Supreme Court that the highest court in the land, the Appeal Court in Bloemfontein, might find differently to the court of first instance in Upington. Ian Farlam, assisted by Andre Landman, detailed thirty different grounds on which the Court of Appeal might take a different approach. We contested all the convictions, arguing in particular that the Upington Supreme Court had erred in holding that those who threw stones at Sethwala's house were party to a common purpose to kill and that those who chased Sethwala intended to kill, rather than assault, him. In addition, we contested the rejection of extenuating circumstances in respect of the fourteen condemned and the failure by the Upington Supreme Court to impose community service orders for more of the accused.

It was an odd convention that the judge who convicted and sentenced be asked to rule that another court might take a contrary view to his own. Some might say it provided an opportunity for a judge to exemplify an adherence to objectivity, to admit doubt and allow for some margin of error, particularly when the application of the law resulted in people being sent to their death. The Honourable Mr Justice Jan Basson demonstrated an unwavering belief in the impeccability of his original findings and dismissed our application for leave to appeal in its entirety. His conclusion was brief: 'Due to the death penalty imposed on the fourteen appellants and the wide publicity the case enjoyed, including internationally, one would wish the Appeal Court could make a final decision on the matter. The crucial test was whether reasonable prospects existed for success on an appeal, and if such grounds were present then the application could be granted; in the absence of which the application should be rejected to prevent saddling the Appeal Court with appeals which have no grounds for success. All considered, it is my opinion that no such grounds and reasonable prospects for success in the application exist, and all the applications are therefore rejected.' All the sentences would stand; the condemned would stay on death row. We had one remaining avenue open to us in our attempt to save the Upington 25. We could petition the Chief Justice for leave to appeal.

We had a few hours in Kimberley before our flight home and we dabbled with the notion of playing 'tourist', to be without care for a while. But I was not sure a trip to the world famous Big Hole, the old Kimberley diamond mine would still my anger and loathing for the insular arrogance I had witnessed that morning.

So Colin and I agreed to meet Ian and Andre back at the hotel and decided on a visit to the Duggan-Cronin Bantu Gallery. Duggan-Cronin was an English photographer who had migrated to South Africa in the 1800s. The gallery was filled with an extraordinary collection of sepia photographs of the black people of Southern Africa. He had captured expressions still fresh from conversation, simple in line and telling tales of a hard-won life. It was in the gallery that I read a quote from a fellow English settler, John Blades Currey, which I would reread newly arrived in Australia some years later. For some reason, I felt compelled to write down his words and later found them by chance in the back of an old diary. He wrote: 'Why do people emigrate...The compulsion of the discontented fiery spirit that will face anything in a new country with possible openings rather than lead the peaceful but weary life in uncongenial surroundings to which so many are doomed at home.' If anything, it was the absence of a peace which kept me at home, bound to the land of my birth. It was this peace which I found, first despised and then cherished in Australia.

•

We were advised that we had three weeks to lodge our petition with His Lordship the Chief Justice and the Judges of Appeal of the Appellate Division. The Chief Justice would designate two Appeal Court judges to review the petition and our grounds of appeal. These judges would issue a decision that was final. If our petition failed, the legal options for rescue of the twenty-five would be exhausted. All that would be left were pleas for clemency to the head of state, our hard-headed State President. Armed with one last chance and a flimsy hold on hope, I prepared for my first visit to death row to see the Upington 14.

We compiled a folder filled with newspaper clippings and letters of support. The folder included a special envelope addressed to Xolile Yona. After the fourteen had been sentenced to death, various international newspapers ran profiles of each of the condemned. Xolile's appeal to Basson to spare him the gallows so he could pursue his boxing career had made an impact in Sweden. We received in the post a big box for Xolile containing a fine pair of black boxing gloves, a gift from the Swedish National Boxing Team. We would keep them for him, I told Xolile, until his release from death row. In the meantime, I gave him a photograph of Sandra Liebenberg, a young lawyer from our firm who visited the accused and a hot favourite with Xolile, standing with the gloves poised, ready to fight for Xolile's life.

Death row, in the maximum security wing of the prison, was an abundance of cement: hydraulic doors, airless rooms with high windows, barred slits in the walls and corridors of thick linoleum. The gardens of the prison were well kept and pretty. The natural life on the outside—the ducks and white rabbits, the streams and ponds decorating rich green lawns—stood in grotesque contrast to the unnatural on the inside. As did the sounds. Outside were the soft sounds of an ordinary day, inside was a dreadful, sharp noise. A din of singing and calling out from cells hidden from view, of banging on walls, of rhythmic clanging of cages being opened and shut. Warders shouted commands at one another and at prisoners in convoy. Bunches of oversized keys rattled around the warders' waists as they stamped their heavy boots into the floor, saluting their superiors. I sat on a hard wooden chair filling out thirteen forms in duplicate—name of prisoner, number, conviction, court, reason for visit—and then I was shown into a small consulting room, functional and cell-like. I was to see the men first.

At first, the sight of my clients being herded into the meeting room came as a terrible shock. With heads shorn and dressed in the green of prison uniforms, they looked unfamiliar, hard and sinister. But as we spoke and eased into old ways, I was filled with an overwhelming desire to giggle at the sheer incongruity of the scene. The thirteen men seemed unaccustomed to their new personae, awkward and comical as if dressed for the part, but lacking fervour for the role. These people did not deserve such drapery. As we began to talk, three warders moved amongst us, listening and watching. I asked them to wait outside and as they left, I noticed in the corner of the room a large scale with sliding weights across a bar and next to it, a neck-measuring device, pre-execution apparatus clearly on display for our benefit. These were cold-blooded reminders of the premeditated death by hanging confronting the men, which South African law maintained was death 'by natural causes'. At a later visit, Xolile and Zonga spoke of further encounters with accessories of death. Some of the longer term prisoners had access to various supplies through an established system of privilege. A hit of *dagga* every now and then brought sleep and a temporary relief from boredom. These prisoners offered my clients a *stop* of *dagga* in return for washing the soiled hoods of executed prisoners in preparation for a next round of hangings.

We covered much ground in the short hour we had. Loss of hope was a common element in the discussion and it was hard, even inappropriate, to cultivate optimism amidst such despair. Few believed the petition would succeed and it was not foremost in their minds. Rather, the plight of those left at home concerned them. They worried about the disintegration of family structure, the prospect of eviction, the absence of central familial figures and primary breadwinners, the struggle to make ends meet.

My visit had coincided with a trip to the prison by some of the families. They had arranged a special deal with a van driver. Each month, different family representatives, sharing costs and carrying messages from Paballelo, would travel the 850 kilometres to Pretoria, a ten or twelve-hour drive each way, for a forty-minute visit with the fourteen condemned. I met Noah Gubula, brother of Zonga Mokhatle on my way from the men's section to Evelina's jail. He looked tired and greeted me with weary words. 'Our visits are short and the time in between too long. They are killing us spiritually, those of us who wait outside knowing our loved ones are suffering on death row.' One of those outside could not bear to wait. Mrs Lekhanyane, mother of Andrew and David, both on death row, had died of a heart attack.

Permission for the brothers to attend their mother's funeral had been refused by prison authorities.

I had a new topic of conversation for my next visit and this one lifted spirits and turned attention outwards. I was going to London to put the case of the Upington 25 to European Community representatives and anti-apartheid groups. Throughout the trial, I had been in discussion with the Anti-Apartheid Movement (AAM) and Amnesty International in London. Their support and coverage of the trial had been consistent and strong and it was largely due to their efforts and the work of international journalists that the international community had become aware of and engaged in the fight for the Upington 25. If, ultimately, we were forced to rely on the political option to secure stays of execution, we had to be able to harness and trigger overseas leverage with little delay and to good effect. The news that leave to appeal had been rejected by Justice Basson gave added impetus to the mounting international pressure and calls on the South African judiciary to dispense justice were intensified. Despite the need to prepare for attack should our petition fail, I was concerned that strenuous campaign pressure should not be seen as an attempt to undermine the judicial process still on foot and so prejudice our petition before the Chief Justice. I still believed that the Appellate Division, if given the chance to hear the case, would overturn most of the murder convictions and all the sentences of death. For the highest court in the land to make those findings would be a far greater victory than to achieve stays of execution by begging our State President for mercy.

It was hard to convey the sense of balance required to overseas lobby groups without appearing dismissive of their efforts. It was harder to communicate the nuances of this approach from afar and to leave full responsibility for transmission of the message to one man, Paul Brannen, who had more than enough on his plate as an AAM heavyweight. He was also convenor of Southern Africa the Imprisoned Society (SATIS), which initiated and co-ordinated campaigns in Britain and internationally for the release of political prisoners and detainees in Namibia and South Africa. There was an added complication to the conduit role assigned to Paul. Other anti-apartheid groups, not sympathetic to the line of the AAM, would resent direction from a competing source. And so, with Paul's careful planning, my trip to London to talk to government representatives, lobby groups, activists and lawyers began to take shape.

We lodged the petition on 17 July 1989. It was a document of some 3000 pages and we did not anticipate a rapid reply. It was Anton's last piece of work for the case. He announced with regret that given swift moves towards the Namibian elections and the return of thousands of exiles, he had no option but to withdraw from the team. He had to give undivided commitment to assisting SWAPO in preparation for independence. It was an inevitable choice but I still suffered pangs of deep sadness when he told me over dinner at a Cape Town restaurant. I was losing my friend and confidant, my fellow traveller on a most important journey. As we talked of his entry into a new world, his dream of a free Namibia soon to come true, I reminded him of the time his father, Wilfried, had travelled from Cape Town to Upington to attend the trial for a few days.

Wilfried told me that he had come to Upington because he knew how deeply Anton was affected by the case. He wanted to show his support and solidarity for the accused and for Anton's work. After Wilfried left, Anton told me of the pride his father felt in him, of how he had pleaded with Anton to stay with the practice of law and walk away from political life. Now, as we spoke of his decision to leave the case, I detected a wistfulness in Anton, a yearning to stay with us and escape the turmoil of politics. He shook his head and banged the table with his fist, as if to bring himself back to the present and then he ordered more wine. 'I must be optimistic about this future of mine,' he lectured himself. 'There is no real choice. I must go with it, and believe I took the right turn. You know that don't you?' He looked at me and I nodded, a most ambivalent nod.

19

———————— • ————————

A slight shift in hope

Jill was my 'best friend'. We'd met at age twelve when such anoint-
ment was how we told the world of true friendship. She was born
one day before me and we thought that was the central reason for
our instant compatibility. We'd grown together through our
teenage and university years, times of secrets, change and separation. We had taken very different paths, but despite geographical
separation, whenever we met or talked from afar, we would click
into one another with ease, as if never parted. Jill had lived in
London for some years, working as a freelance photographer. She
had come to stay with me the previous year during a visit to South
Africa. I had been deep in preparation for the Upington case and
Jill soon came under its hold. She watched us work at night and
on weekends and she was excited by Anton's invitation to visit and
photograph a free Namibia the following year. It was only a few
weeks before Namibian independence that I arrived in London to
speak to members of the European community about the lives of
the Upington 14. Jill met me at Heathrow Airport and we drove
to her home in Kentish Town on a warm August night, less than
a week before our birthdays.

Paul Brannen was on the phone soon after my arrival. He had
devised a tough itinerary. I had the weekend to play, he said, and

then work would begin at a solid pace. We met at AAM head-quarters in Camden Town on the Monday morning. I felt strangely defiant asking the cab driver to take me to 13 Mandela Street, but walking in to the AAM offices, housed in a building clearly under surveillance, and meeting exiles and comrades left me feeling a slight unease. I had trouble adjusting to the freedom to trust. We talked over tea in an office filled with books and posters deemed illicit in my country. And then we left for the House of Commons for my first official appointment. The week was packed with meetings and interviews often with little time in between. Paul was my constant adviser and critic. He would read my audience and direct rehearsals in tubes and cabs, tinkering with my lines and emphasis to suit the interests and inclinations of those in attendance. Amnesty International; Gerald Kaufman, Labour Party MP; Lawyers against Apartheid; the Foreign Office; Commonwealth House; the British Council of Churches and the Church of England; Norman Willis, General-Secretary of the Trade Union Council (TUC); Lord Tony Gifford, the Office of the Republic of Ireland, representing the EEC; journalists from the print, radio and television media—the list was exhausting.

There was something immensely refreshing about the Irish approach to the case. Unlike representatives from the Conservative Party government and the British Foreign Office, who hedged their bets, never bringing themselves to outright condemnation of injustice, the Irish were open and forthright in their criticism of the South African state and its arms of government. There was no diplomatic caution in their expression of anger and they were keen to make their position heard, with passion and no ambivalence. It was then that I knew I would love Ireland and her people forever.

After our meeting with Norman Willis and Michael Walsh, the TUC's International Affairs Officer, Norman invited Paul and me to a party at Congress House to farewell hundreds of Namibian exiles who were flying home for independence. The hall was filled to capacity and there were representatives and bottles of wine from every country favouring the free world. From Cuba and Angola, from Nicaragua and Poland. Guests were dressed in magnificent clothes and turbans of contrasting colours and there was a spirit of great triumph and solidarity. I wanted to capture the scene and the mood and take it back for Anton, a gift of hope and celebration. As Norman Willis called on us to join in song and pray for peace and freedom, he asked the assembly to walk with 'Andrea Durbach, who celebrates with us tonight, in the fight for the Upington 25'. A man standing next to me turned and said: 'Who the hell did he say? Andrew who?' 'I haven't got a clue,' I replied, 'but let's drink to the twenty-five anyway.'

Three days before my return to South Africa I met Jill at the Hayward Gallery for lunch on the Thames and to see an Andy Warhol retrospective. It was part of our extended birthday festivities. En route to the gallery, Jill received a message on her bleeper. I was to call my office in Cape Town. I ran to a public phone and with no respect for gallery quiet, I shouted my joy across an exhibition wing to Jill. 'We can appeal. We've got leave to appeal.' The Chief Justice of the Appellate Division had announced that the twenty-five had been granted restricted leave to appeal. All those sentenced to death could appeal against their death sentences; twenty-three of the twenty-five could appeal their murder convictions (all except Justice Bekebeke and Elisha Matshoba). Of the twenty-three, sixteen would not be permitted to contest the Upington Supreme Court's finding that they were part of the crowd that had stoned Sethwala's house. This restriction was of little concern. To compound our delight, no restriction had been placed on the appeals of Boy Jafta, Xoliswa Dube, Elizabeth Bostaander, Jeffrey Sekiya, Roy Swartbooi, Neville Witbooi and Ivan Kazi.

The official letter of leave was being faxed to Birbeck Montagu's, the office of Bill Frankel, lawyer and administrator of core funding for the trial. We would now have to ask him to extend his clients' generosity and fund the last leg of the case. Bill met me at the door to his firm. He was thrilled with the news and gave me a hug. It was a great relief. The fax from the Court of Appeal was accompanied by another from Dennis Davis. It read:

'Dear Andy, Thank God there is still an Appellate Division in this country which if there is any legal sense left in South Africa will put a stop to the agony suffered by your clients and their families. I'm sure all the effort will still bear the fruits of justice.'

20

•

Too big for this world

The drive to Heathrow was filled with a madness. We hurtled through the London traffic in Jill's Mini Minor and laughed at our days together. There had been a furious passage of time, packed with dinners and theatre and old friends, and lots of after-midnight chatter when we wrestled with life's choices and creeping old age. The work was hard and fraught at times but there was an absence of urgency and I wanted it to last. As an assignment, the trip had been enormously successful. We had brought the case to life in the minds of those who could exert pressure on the South African government and we had demonstrated its simple horror to those who really fought the struggle from abroad. As I recalled the telephone call from South Africa announcing leave to appeal, the excitement bubbled up into my throat and I rolled down the window and screamed at freeway fences while Jill sounded the horn with the boldness of a winner. But beneath the glow, there was something that worried me that night, maybe a sadness or a pulling back and I couldn't quite locate its source.

It was strange but good to be back. At my parent's home, there were flowers and messages of support and the smell of baking bread and cake. They had planned a welcome-home dinner which wasn't really what I had in mind. I wasn't in the mood for fuss.

I was tired and weary and felt disorientated. I felt a sudden need to call Anton in Windhoek, to reconnect. I wanted to tell him everything about the trip and especially to share the excitement I had felt at the TUC's Congress House party to farewell some of his exiled Namibian colleagues returning to their country. And, of course, to share delight at news of the appeal. A few months earlier, Anton had been appointed deputy director of SWAPO's election campaign and he had been working endlessly managing the return of thousands of exiles and the arrival of the President, Sam Nujoma. Not surprisingly, being the eve of the President's return home and the beginning of celebrations for an independent Namibia, Anton was in meetings, on the phone and channelling the media. So I left a message of much love and good luck and promised to call him the following day.

Soon after my arrival home, John Carlin called from Johannesburg for news of London. Almost within days after my return from our first trip to Upington, some sixteen months earlier, John Carlin had tracked me down from his base in Johannesburg for an interview about the case. He had spent six years in Central America before taking up a post in South Africa. John had been in South Africa barely five months when we met for lunch in Cape Town. He was intrigued with the case and fascinated by the strength and humility of the twenty-five. Throughout the trial, he visited Upington several times and he wrote about the case with great care and compassion, direct and uncompromising in his views. John and I became close friends fairly quickly. Despite his English reserve, he found the madness in the Upington trial and with him, Anton and I could laugh and abandon fears and burdens. John was coming to Cape Town the next day and asked if I would join him for lunch and explain the terms of the appeal for a piece he was writing for the *Independent*. I chose the restaurant Rosenfontein, our old favourite, and we agreed to meet at one o'clock. Much later that night, John called again. I teased him, getting in first: 'I know, you've got some big scoop. Can we cancel lunch?' There was a long, uneasy silence. And very slowly, very quietly he said: 'Andy, I'm not sure if this is true. But something's just come up on the wires. I think I must tell you. Anton's been shot, nine times. Assassinated.'

I think I shouted out something like 'Oh, no. It can't be, it's not'. My father, hearing my call, came rushing into the study. I was shaking and gasping and begging him to take the phone. 'Please say he's not...' I couldn't say the word because it meant describing Anton in a way I could never imagine him. Dead. I was trembling and a cry began to climb up from within. By now my mother was with us and grabbed a whisky bottle from a cupboard which she gave to my father, saying, 'Try to make her drink a little'. He held it to my mouth and I had a sip, and then some more. Later, when we could look back, we laughed at the scene of my parents forcing whisky down my throat. They told me that I seemed to descend into shock and they feared some harm would come to me. In retrospect, it was a wise move and it did slow the banging of my heart.

I called John back. I had to know more. Anton had arrived at his Windhoek home late for a dinner. He had begun to walk from his car to the front of his house. There were shots fired at close range from a red car parked nearby.

A neighbour recognised the sound of automatic gunfire. Anton was slumped against the security gates to his home. He had been shot in the head and the back. I called everyone, far into the night—my partners at the firm, Colin, Ian, Andre, the Gubulas, close friends. I couldn't bear to face the night holding the news until morning. I rang Jill in London and we wept at the cruel unpredictability of it all, at the swift enormity of change.

I lay awake all that night, listening, waiting, frozen. I traced the sound of cars, voices in the street, dogs barking, straining to hear until I felt secure that the sounds had moved to silence. I pictured Anton over and over. His strong, imposing frame, his dark curls and big embracing hands, now lifeless, cut down. And I remembered the night we talked about death, and with a sense of inevitability, his own. It was in his room at the Protea Hotel. He was flippant, almost brazen and he spoke with a sense of resignation. He showed me a large crumpled piece of graph paper he had received in the post. On it was a computer drawing of Anton's face. And through the paper there were bullet holes. An explanatory note said the paper had been used as a target in shooting practice.

Morning came with grim relief. Anton was on the front page of the paper. The photograph was of a policeman at the scene of the crime, loading Anton's body into a plastic body bag. It was an undignified image, almost ridiculous in its lack of homage. I turned away unable to read the words. I wanted to stay with my version, untainted by the common, transient daily news. I was exhausted but the idea of staying at home was unbearable. I needed to be in my office, to be with those who might have understood. I wanted to be close to the trial, to the files and the boxes which lined the walls of my office. In some way, they held our times together, they carried a short and precious history, and they offered a fragile link with Anton. I emptied boxes, searching for documents with his writing, for faxes with his signature, for handwritten afterthoughts. And with the late-morning light came a flood of calls of consolation. From Upington, London, New York, Johannesburg, Windhoek, Bonn, Sydney. From friends and colleagues, from our funders, from churches and embassies, journalists and politicians. In his short life of thirty-seven years, Anton's reach had been boundless.

'It is a terrible thing. Almost as if a dark cloud hovers over Paballelo. We feel bitter, almost more about Anton than about our own people in Pretoria on death row. There are few like Advocate Lubowski, believing in mankind.' Mr Alfred Gubula called back later in the day and read out these words. He wanted me to tell Anton's family that Paballelo was in mourning. My lunch engagement with John Carlin had been moved to dinner and we were joined by lawyer and friend Halton Cheadle, down from Johannesburg for a few days. We all had tales of Anton, memories of his powerful eagerness for life. We drank too much and tears of laughter turned to grief. We stayed at the restaurant until the owner dimmed the lights. We were loath to leave and face our loss in isolation. I would see John a few days later on my first trip to Namibia, to Windhoek for Anton's funeral.

I boarded the Saturday morning plane to Windhoek. The memorial service at the Lutheran Church in the township of Katatura was scheduled for 3pm. I was relieved to find that I would be travelling with friends, including labour lawyer Clive Thompson and Anton's sister-in-law, Connie, and her husband, Julian, a childhood friend. Also on the flight were the British Ambassador, foreign diplomats, journalists and a sprinkling of South African parliamentarians. Within minutes of boarding, we were asked to disembark and identify our luggage which had been removed from the hold. On the tarmac, police had arrived with sniffer dogs and, one by one, we claimed responsibility for our bags. Despite a lack of explanation, intelligence seeped through with reports of a bomb threat. Anton's law colleague and close associate, David Smuts, met us at Windhoek Airport. The air was hot and dry and the city, with its small-town desert feel seemed insular, hemmed in by a heavy German heritage. Colonial architecture mingled uneasily with pre-independence, prefabricated structures, gifts from nation states and investors in the new South West Africa/Namibia. The city was host to United Nations Transition Assistance Group (UNTAG) personnel, peacekeepers for the UN-supervised elections set for 15 November, less than a month after Anton's funeral. Their presence did nothing to lift the layers of fear and foreboding which informed our every move. The fear of snipers, of parked cars, of hidden harm.

We drove to Katatura early in the afternoon as part of a motor procession through the township. More than a thousand people, some in traditional dress, others draped in SWAPO colours and carrying flags and banners of blue, green and red, filed into the Lutheran Church. We sat near the front of the church, watching Anton's family arrive. His father and mother, Wilfried and Molly, his sisters Joleen and Anneliese and his former wife Gaby and their children, Nadia and Almo. Almo, Anton's young son, had the warrior air of his father. He walked into the church, his head held high, proudly wearing a SWAPO T-shirt.

When I first met Anton, he and Gaby had recently separated and she had moved to Cape Town with Nadia and Almo. Anton missed them all terribly and when in Upington would call his children most nights and try to share in the news of their day: the ballet classes, school fights, homework, their new friends. He adored them and worried that the tenets by which he chose to live his life would make their own engagement with life more difficult. He feared they would have to carry the burden of his beliefs. As the mourners packed the aisles and crowded around the doors of the church, Theo-Ben Gurirab, in line to become independent Namibia's Minister of Foreign Affairs, began the service, speaking with great fervour about Anton's inspirational contribution to the struggle for an independent Namibia. He ended his lament, looking at Almo and Nadia who sat in the front row of the assembly: 'Anton's memory will continue to live on in our hearts and in a special way find resurrection in the lives of his beautiful children.' The air filled with clenched fists as we stood to sing '*Nkosi Sikelel' i-Afrika*' and then I walked up to the coffin to lay a wreath from the Upington 25.

I was staying with Herman Raath and he had arranged to take me on a brief tour of Windhoek and then to dinner at the Centraal Cafe. As we drove into the city centre, Herman pointed out a well-known German restaurant, the Kaiserkrone. 'I had thought we might go to the Kaiserkrone tonight. Anton liked to dine there but often, when he entered the restaurant, many of the diners would get up and walk out. They felt such intense contempt for him. So we'll eat at the Centraal Cafe instead, in solidarity with our friend.' I hated this stuffy city and its mean spirit. I felt out of place and ill at ease in Windhoek. Not even the veal and dumplings and the beer at the Centraal Cafe could win me over. I was deeply unhappy. There was something about the city that made me feel sluggish and I wanted to leave and avoid a night of unsettled anxious sleep. Perhaps I was being unfair, blaming Windhoek. It was Anton's town and perhaps I hated the fact that I had come to visit and he had taken leave, abandoning me to face this alien city alone.

A few days after the service, I drove from Johannesburg Airport to Pretoria Central to see the fourteen condemned. I was worried that I had not been able to make contact with them after Anton's death except via a message of bare comfort taken to them by Johannesburg-based Sheila Weinberg and John Wills of Halton Cheadle's firm. Given the distance between Cape Town and Pretoria, it was hard for me to see the fourteen more than once a month. Sheila and John had offered to visit death row each week and act as liaison officers between the fourteen and Colin and me. The fourteen had first heard the news over the radio in an early-morning report from Radio Highveld, a constant presence channelled into their cells, beyond their control. The men had sat in silence for a few minutes, heads bowed. It was my first visit to death row since my return from London. It should have been a visit of triumph, excitedly discussing the granting of leave to appeal. Four days after the Chief Justice had allowed the petition, Anton, who believed so completely in that inevitability, had been killed. The fourteen had worshipped Anton. He was their pop star, he made them feel better and he gave them hope. He was their comrade from SWAPO, their link to a democratic, non-racial future in Southern Africa.

I began to tell the accused about my journey to Windhoek. I wanted to grieve with them, to bring them closer to Anton's death. I spoke of the ceremony, of the wreath that I had laid for Anton from us all, of his children and his Namibia. There was little I could say to lift their sorrow and, in some way, I think they read Anton's death as meaning their own was drawing closer. They told me that they had requested permission to send a message to me to be read out at the memorial service in Windhoek. Major Cronje, big on prison regulations, had refused. The following night, a further memorial service was to be held at the St George's Cathedral in the centre of Cape Town. I promised that their message for Anton would be read out there. A warder knocked on the door. My time was up and I was due at the women's prison to see Evelina. 'Tell his family,' Justice Bekebeke called out as I walked down the corridor, 'that our hearts are bleeding with theirs.'

21

•

At odds with life

I could not begin to touch my hurt at Anton's death. I neither had the skills nor the inclination and besides, there were competing needs to which I would rather turn and bury my grief. And so, for many years, I would keep a crust around my heart until it was time to reveal the wound and let it heal. My immediate task was to prepare bail applications for some of the twenty-five pending the hearing of their appeals. It was important for the accused that we sustain the momentum of challenge, to keep on fighting standing orders. And for me, the energy of the work provided a welcome diversion, a postponement of pain.

Bringing a bail application for a convicted murderer awaiting probable execution on death row was viewed with a scepticism that even I felt was justified. In deciding whether or not to grant bail, a fundamental consideration is whether an applicant for bail is likely to abscond and so evade justice. If an accused was charged with murder and awaiting trial, bail might be granted if the prospect of absconding could be negated by the imposition of certain conditions. If, however, bail was sought for a convicted murderer who had been sentenced to death and was awaiting appeal proceedings (which in the eyes of the Upington condemned would have appeared bleak), the temptation to abscond would be viewed as irresistible by those deciding the question of bail. The longer Evelina de Bruin remained in isolation on death row, the more a bail application became imperative. We had no alternative but to weather an anticipated austere response from the bench. At the very least, we believed the application might serve to draw attention to Evelina's tenuous survival on death row.

Somehow, my visits with the thirteen men at Pretoria Central were never as bad. They had each other, most of them were literate, physically strong and robust. Despite adversity and long days of boredom, they continued to develop their capacity for innovation and stoicism. In June 1989, Evelina de Bruin, prisoner number V4203, Women's Prison, Pretoria Central, was the only woman on death row. Within days after Evelina's arrival from Upington, Sandra Smith, a convicted murderer awaiting execution, was hanged. The rumour that succeeded Sandra Smith's hanging was that the execution was finally ordered to make room for Evelina. Evelina de Bruin, aged 57 years, mother of ten and wife of co-condemned, Gideon Madlongolwane, sick in her heart and numb with fear, sat in a chair, waiting.

Our first visit (and often our subsequent talks) was filled with her confusion, her quest for explanation. Evelina's face was without expression, draped in a shroud of deep despair. She had no recollection of how she had come to Pretoria Central, how long she had been there. It was as if the shock and disbelief of the death sentence had combined to protect her from her memory. Some initial guidance from a prison psychologist and the chaplain may have made things worse. They had thought it best to introduce Evelina to hard fact, to reinforce reality and tell her that she was a prisoner facing possible execution. I hugged her heavy body and brought her news from Upington. She was withdrawn and could hardly offer a response and in the silence she would cry and rock, back and forth, cradling her pain.

I checked the standard provisions. Evelina had a Bible. She had received a letter and a card, so mail was getting through. These privileges were of little comfort to an illiterate woman. I asked Evelina if she had seen Gideon. '*Ja,* Andy, *ja*' ('Yes, Andy, yes'), she sighed, looking down at the floor and wiping a handkerchief across her face. Once a month for thirty minutes they sat, separated from one another by a glass pane, and talked via a microphone. She was offered thirty minutes exercise each day but creeping arthritis in both legs made walking difficult and painful. So a warder sat with her on a bench in a prison courtyard and they would talk in the sun. Sometimes, *Sersant* (Sergeant) Zwane would read to Evelina or teach her *hekelwerk* (crochet). Although permitted to crochet—unlike pointed knitting needles, crochet needles were regarded as safe for use by prisoners—Evelina was not allowed to keep wool in her cell and could only crochet during exercise time. The explanation came when I offered to send wool from Cape Town. 'We have to be very careful. There is always the threat of suicide.' Major Botma, head of the Women's Prison, declined my offer.

•

Evelina de Bruin was born on Christmas Day in 1933 or thereabouts, she could not quite remember. She grew up in Postmasburg, a small town in the Northern Cape, during the great drought of the late 1930s and early 1940s. Her father was a farm labourer when the drought permitted work and her mother, a domestic servant. Evelina's early life was bound by the rituals of poverty. As a young child, she would crouch behind bushes watching people eat *mielies* (corn), waiting to collect discarded cobs which her mother boiled for soup. She spoke of the Northern Cape winter and of days so cold that her mother would lay Evelina and her seven siblings in the sun to stop the trembling of their bodies. Evelina's parents could not afford to send her to school and she learnt the skills of cooking and keeping house from her mother in preparation for her working life. In her late teens, her family of ten moved to Upington to a one-bedroom house with no toilet, electricity or running water. Evelina worked as a domestic worker for white families in the Upington area, her primary role as nanny to their children. Most of her working life centred around the Steenkamp family for whom Evelina was servant for thirty years. She was in their employ, earning R100-00 per month, when arrested for the murder of Lucas Sethwala.

With her first husband, Wellington Dandiso, Evelina had seven children. After her marriage to Gideon Madlongolwane, who had two children, Shadrack and Welcome, from a previous marriage, she and Gideon had two more children, '*my laat lammetjies*' ('my lambs, late arrivals'), a daughter Adelaide (Tutu) and a son, Mbulelo. They were ten and eight years of age when their parents were arrested on charges of murder, and not much older when Evelina and Gideon were convicted and sentenced to death.

I visited Tutu and Mbulelo at their Paballelo home soon after their mother and father had been driven to death row in the back of police trucks. On the wall of the small King Street house hung a plaque with the inscription: '*Wat is 'n huis sonder 'n moeder?*' ('What is a home without a mother?'). Shadrack Madlongolwane, working as a labourer to bring in the family income, had come home early to supervise homework and cook the evening meal. 'It is very hard to be in a home without parents. Life begins with parents. We were made orphans because our parents have been withdrawn from us. It would have been much easier if they had been taken away by God. Now we have to play the role of a mother and a father. And the question is, will we be able to satisfy them?' Shadrack looked over at Tutu and Mbulelo. They sat together upright on a couch, studying our conversation. He turned to face me. 'Is it possible that you've never been in jail, never had a crime, and then, at the age of fifty-three, a mother to two young children, you would kill another woman's child?' Shadrack breathed out an angry leaden sigh. 'How do we explain to Tutu and Mbulelo that they may not visit their parents because they are too young to be taken to death row? How do you answer to a child who fears her mother may die before she sees her again? But I know one thing. If Evelina has to die, then be sure that she will be in heaven, next to God.'

•

'*Vlerke. Andy, ek het vlerke.*' ('Wings. Andy, I had wings.') Evelina and I had begun a visit. She leaned forward to tell me about a dream, unusually animated. '*Met my vlerke, vlieg ek vanaf hier Upington toe. Ek bly in die lug en sweef, skaars vir 'n oomblik. Ek wil net Tutu en Mbulelo sien. Toe sien ek hulle. Hulle stap huis toe vanaf skool. Ek vlieg terug na Pretoria.*' ('With my wings, I flew from here to Upington. I hovered in the sky, for a moment, waiting to see Tutu and Mbulelo. Then I saw them. They were walking home from school. I flew back to Pretoria.') It was a short burst of happiness, followed by the weeping of loss as reality shot down her dream. Tutu and Mbulelo, she said, were too young to be separated from her, without their mother's love, to be without her guidance and encouragement. She felt that she had abandoned her most precious gifts and she was besieged by guilt and hopelessness, dragged towards a debilitating depression. It was clear that my one visit to Evelina each month was entirely inadequate and that her emotional and physical needs had to be sustained by additional and regular interaction with someone she could trust. I worried about her obvious deterioration and the flagging of her will to live and I was immensely relieved when friend and colleague Joan Cameron agreed to visit and counsel Evelina each week. For many years, Joan, who lived in Johannesburg and worked as a researcher at the Centre for Applied Legal Studies at the University of Witwatersrand, had counselled the friends and families of political trialists and condemned prisoners. She had a gentle warmth and a unique understanding of the distress they suffered.

With each visit, Joan reported Evelina's further decline. She continued to lose weight, showing little interest in food despite being prescribed appetite stimulants by the prison doctor. And there were more props: sleeping pills, painkillers for her arthritis, medication for her heart condition, pills for high blood pressure. No matter how determined she was to stay with life, I feared that Evelina de Bruin would die of a broken heart. Visit notes from Joan Cameron had a repetitive and disturbing quality.

Today, Evelina appeared withdrawn and unhappy, down and defeated and it was again difficult to coax her into communicating. There is nothing for her to do all day, every day, except think about the trial and implore her God to help her. None of the other women in the prison face the death sentence, so she can not share her thoughts and fears with them; in any event they all seem to be out and at work of some kind. Evelina spends all her time alone, thinking, waiting and praying...She tells me that often during the night she wakes with a jolt, heart pounding, and it sometimes takes her ten minutes to sit up in bed, from the stiffness and arthritis. '*Dan sit ek op my bed en kyk vir hierdie ou liggaam van my, die wat so hard gewerk het en so veel kinders gemaak het, en ek pas nie met hierdie prentjie van 'n moordenaar nie.*' ('I sit up on my bed and look at this old body of mine, this body which has worked so hard and borne so many children, and it does not fit the image of a murderer.')

•

On 23 October 1989, we launched six bail applications before the Kimberley Supreme Court, presided over by none other than Mr Justice Jan Basson. The application was brought on behalf of Abel Kutu, Ronnie Masiza, Jeffrey Sekiya and Sarel Jacobs, convicted of murder and sentenced to six years; Elisha Matshoba, convicted of murder and sentenced to eight years; and Evelina de Bruin, convicted of murder and sentenced to death. Abel, Ronnie, Jeffrey and Sarel, young energetic men in their twenties, were released on bail of R500-00 each, on condition that they report to the Paballelo police station every day. Elisha Matshoba's application was refused. The findings against him by the trial court—that he had participated in the attack on Lucas Sethwala, attracting the classification of principal offender—diminished his chances of release on bail.

Senior counsel for Evelina de Bruin, Henry Viljoen SC, conceded at the outset that the granting of bail to a condemned murderer, a death-row prisoner was unusual. Evelina's circumstances, he suggested, were unique and extraordinary and warranted her release. Evidence in support of Evelina's application was provided by two clinical psychologists: Dr Herman Raath, one of our key witnesses in the trial on extenuation, who had interviewed Evelina both prior and subsequent to her removal to death row and Lloyd Vogelman of the Psychology Department, University of Witwatersrand, whose recent research had dealt with the psychological lives of death-row prisoners. Herman Raath testified that the absence of 'group cohesion' at Pretoria Central, developed amongst the accused over the three-year period of the trial in Upington, had accelerated Evelina's physical and emotional deterioration. Each day of the trial, the accused had sat together in the Upington Supreme Court—Evelina next to Gideon—and returned to jail each night. In Upington prison, Evelina had enjoyed the comfort and companionship of two fellow women accused, Xoliswa Dube and Elizabeth Bostaander. Evelina's loss of the group and her sudden isolation as the only woman on death row compounded by her inability to read or write, precipitated a tendency to depression.

Lloyd Vogelman's testimony centred on Evelina's 'psychological functioning' on death row and the potential for her further impairment over time were her conditions of confinement to remain unchanged. 'She indicates feelings of extreme sadness and distress and habitual crying; poor appetite and resultant weight loss; insomnia and multiple awakenings at night, feelings of guilt and worthlessness and lack of self-confidence; agitation, restlessness and loss of energy; fears, anxiety and anticipation of misfortune; slowed thinking and attention difficulties.' At the core of her depression, Lloyd told the court, was her separation from her two youngest children, Tutu, aged 14, and Mbulelo, aged 12, and the stress of awaiting possible execution. 'The fact that she cannot read or write or exercise means she cannot communicate by letter with her family or structure each day and dampen her depression through activity. The intensity of her depression and loneliness, together with the lack of structure in her day, has led Evelina to believe that she has been on death row "for years".' Under cross-examination, State Advocate Terence van Rensburg suggested to Lloyd that therapy might alleviate Evelina's condition. 'It may be possible for her to undergo therapy while on death row, it may even have some short-term benefits. But therapy is of little use,' Lloyd was clearly irritated by the question, 'if it takes place in surroundings which undermine its value. Death row is hardly the environment from which Evelina could draw the social support and love needed to reinforce the therapeutic treatment.'

Earlier, van Rensburg had reminded Herman Raath that 'the [trial] court had found the offence to be politically motivated. Surely this means that there is a substantial danger of Evelina de Bruin absconding.' Clearly van Rensburg believed Evelina had the makings of a freedom fighter. Herman shook his head and stared at the punter for the state. 'Your Honour, Evelina de Bruin has no history of political activity. Her apparent involvement in the murder was a one-off incident where she had been trapped in a crowd situation. Evelina is 57, she has a husband on death row to whom she is devoted and she longs to live with her children. Prior to the trial, her simple existence in Upington rarely took her beyond the boundaries of the town. She is illiterate, she has advanced rheumatoid arthritis and a heart condition. I think these are factors which make her escape from the country more than doubtful.' Van Rensburg decided on a different tack. He turned to the judge and declared his trump card. '*U Edele, dit moet herinner word dat Evelina de Bruin is ter dood veroordeel. Sy is 'n moordenares. Sy is nie op vakansie in Pretoria nie.*' ('Your Honour, it must be remembered that Evelina de Bruin has been sentenced to death. She is a murderer. She is not on holiday in Pretoria.')

In his closing address, Henry Viljoen SC said the evidence painted a picture of a woman who 'was busy disintegrating. Evelina poses no threat to the community. She is a woman with high moral and ethical values, a committed Christian, attending church each Sunday for almost all of her life and doing voluntary church work on weekday evenings. The prison authorities, and particularly some of the warders, have treated her well. Her quarrel is not with them but with the harsh circumstances unique to her confinement, her isolation as one of the "living dead". Evelina de Bruin's personal circumstances suggest that she is the least likely person to break her bond if released on bail. I ask this court to release her on bail on whatever conditions it sees fit to impose.'

Mr Justice Basson had listened to the evidence closely. At times, he seemed moved by Evelina's predicament. We knew him, however, to be a man capable of resisting compassion. His judgment started slowly: '*Ek glo, ek verstaan dat Evelina de Bruin regtig ly.*' ('I believe, I understand that Evelina de Bruin is indeed suffering.') We were momentarily fed by hope. '*Maar, dit is te wagte dat enigiemand wat wag om tereggestel te word, sal ly.*' ('But, it is to be expected that anyone awaiting execution, will suffer.') Basson concluded that Evelina's circumstances were not sufficient to make her case so unusual as to justify granting bail. In any event, he said, '*Ek is nie oortuig dat sy nie sal probeer ontsnap nie.*' ('I am not convinced that she will not try to abscond.')

Back at our hotel, I telephoned Joan Cameron and asked her to hurry to Pretoria Central to tell Evelina the outcome. I was concerned that she would hear the news over her cell radio, alone and without proper explanation or support. Later, Joan sent me her notes from the visit.

I explained what you told me: how Judge Basson had been very different, that he had not interrupted but had listened attentively; how he had so nearly granted bail, but in the end he did not have the courage to do so. I told her that you were hopeful for an early appeal date; that if it had not been for Evelina's own application, the other four would never have been granted bail. Evelina took it all in, nodding and murmuring about understanding, saying that it was a difficult thing for a judge to do, to let someone who was supposed to have committed a murder out on bail. She was trying hard to be nice about it. She said: 'Andy should not feel bad, Joan should not feel bad, Advocate Viljoen should not feel bad, it was to be expected.' She was trying to make it easy for me to tell her. Then the shock wore off and the tears came. No noise, no hiccups or sobbing, just an enormous resigned sort of hopelessness. Perhaps there was a touch of fear in her weeping, but mostly there was an overwhelming sense of defeat.

We talked quietly and *Sersant* Zwane held her arm and by the time I left, Evelina was smiling shakily, reassuring me and herself that '*Ek moet net hierso sit en wag. Die Here sal op 'n einde die storie verander. Ek moet net moed hou en bid dat die appèl gou sal gebeur. Ek het mos Sersant Zwane hier by my, ek sal maar net moed hou.*' ('I must just sit here and wait. The Lord will change the story in the end. I must keep courage and pray that the appeal will happen soon. I have Sergeant Zwane at my side, I will just keep faith.') But I wonder how long Evelina will be able to keep her courage up, keep her sanity, with every day ahead of her devoted to nothing but waiting and hoping and praying, with no end in sight, and dying just a little more each day.

The news of Evelina's failed bail application spread quickly. Newspapers in South Africa and abroad ran feature articles on Evelina, with large colour photographs of Tutu and Mbulelo. Editors of women's magazines filled their editorials with pleas for action. Jane Raphaely, well-known South African editor of a series of women's magazines, introduced Evelina to her readers through impassioned editorials: 'Evelina's greatest wish is to see her children. If any of you are asking yourselves what can be done, the answer lies in appeals to the state president himself: appeal for hospitalisation and a reunion with her children in normal circumstances. At the very least, ask him to arrange for her isolation to be alleviated by the right to work, sew or knit. And say that you are praying. FW de Klerk is a religious man.'

From November 1989, the Evelina de Bruin lobby had become substantial and vociferous. Women's organisations like the Black Sash and Soroptimist International held meetings, initiated letter campaigns and sent petitions to State President de Klerk. We met with Opposition politicians who raised Evelina's case in parliament. We stepped up our communications with anti-apartheid organisations in England, Europe and America which continued to press their governments to intervene and nudge the South African government towards a show of clemency.

In early December, we had our first hint of reaction from the state. The prison authorities granted Evelina permission to see Gideon once a week, instead of monthly. As pressure mounted and the campaign around Evelina had the potential to embarrass the de Klerk administration, there were further signs of a slow bending of the rules. In May the following year, Evelina was allowed to have wool in her cell and began crocheting full-time. More importantly, the prison authorities permitted a visit from Tutu and Mbulelo. In July, they travelled to Johannesburg to spend three weeks with Joan Cameron and accompanied her on visits to Evelina. And finally, in late August, Justice Minister Kobie Coetzee announced that he would agree to moving Evelina de Bruin back to Upington Prison to await the appeal. Evelina, strangely comforted by a familiar prison and its staff, was overjoyed to be close to her family and friends. A few months after Evelina's transfer, Marion Upton, my firm's office manager and administrator of the needs of the Upington prisoners, wrote me a note: 'Evelina is very happy and is being treated like royalty. She has a visitor's list that is in need of alphabetical listing.'

•

The days after the bail application were long, with sudden gaps of inactivity. The preparation for the application had been an intense period of focus and the appeal proceedings were some months away. I now had time to pause and that made me feel restless. What returned to fill this time were the images and sensations surrounding the trial, the sentences of death and the assassination of Anton. The cycle of triumph and disappointment, the heavy burden of feigning strength when surrender was so inviting. My reluctance to entertain these feelings came from my fear of their content and my lack of knowledge about how to achieve and retain the stillness required for their admission. My response was to dismiss them, which translated into an unhappy anger with the world, a grim irritability and an incapacity to ask for help which might bring me some relief. I may have been unaware of my external manifestations of this need to retain control, to keep my emotional world in check, but those close to me felt the tremors and one of them was bold enough to suggest I seek help.

Soon after Evelina's bail application was refused, senior partner and firm friend, Allan Potash, called me into his office and told me that he was worried about me, that I did not appear to be giving myself time to deal with the grief and horror of the past few months. 'You may see this as presumptuous and intrusive,' he gave me an out, 'but through some of my cases, I have come to know the work of a psychologist who is extremely talented. I think you would like his manner and he might help you move through the pain quite quickly. I have managed to get you an appointment. Here are his details.' Allan handed me a small white card. 'Feel free to cancel the booking.'

My first response was shame. Obviously, I was not holding up and Allan had noticed. I felt my chest tighten and then came a lightness and I was suddenly at ease. With delicate, understated caring, Allan had shown a generous understanding. But even when I drove up the avenue to an old Victorian house of quiet corridors and consulting rooms, somewhere in Tamboerskloof, I was not convinced that I wanted to talk to some Jungian about my own peculiar and private world. I was scared to start to talk, scared of where it might lead me. And then it felt indulgent. That was my opening line. 'I am embarrassed to be here, it feels unnecessary and extravagant, very middle class. There is nothing wrong with me, nothing that I can't sort out myself. Talking to friends. I'm not sure why I've come, quite honestly.'

David was unmoved by my introduction and he said there was no obligation for me to stay. 'I'm here now.' I knew I was being defensive. 'I may as well stay. I'm vaguely curious.' He asked me what I had been doing in the past few months, what it was that I thought had brought me to him. I had no feel for detail. I darted from one event to another, a rushed, self-conscious description. After about five minutes, I stopped and no words came. We sat with the silence and then I cried and cried, a deep and longed-for cry.

David said very little but I remembered the analogy he drew. He explained that when people live through and share a close, intense and painful experience, they begin to exist in a world which they create for themselves, with its own language and codes. In isolation. They find it hard to express the nuances of this world to those who do not inhabit it. And, as in a wartime experience, when they move away from their world, they feel alienated, aimless and frightened. 'It seems to me,' he was coming to the end, 'that you are emerging from such an experience. What makes it so hard for you is that one of your most important links to that time, a link which sustained you through it all, has been severed.' He was referring to Anton. Years later, after the appeal and when I was coming to terms with the finality of the Upington trial, I realised a wider implication of Anton's death. He had bolstered me and I had kept up an impeccable appearance. Anton had made me feel brave in action.

When my time was up, David, without making it sound like a suggestion, asked if I had ever thought of going away from South Africa for a while. To think about my own needs, to try and connect with what it was that I was feeling, away from the pressures of my country. The relief which had come from the hour with him was replaced, perhaps suppressed, by a burst of anger. 'I will never leave this country,' I growled, 'It has shaped me, it's who I am.' I was shaking and holding back some wilful tears. I got up to go and thanked him for his time. A few weeks later, I left South Africa to visit my brother, Neil, and his wife and my friend, Margaret, in Sydney, Australia. I was taking an end of year break, a few months respite before the Upington appeal. We would lodge the appeal record of over 20 000 pages with the Appellate Division by the end of November and anticipate a hearing in September 1990—the following year. I packed the blue Upington files, the essentials—the media kit, the summary of appeal papers and the judgments on conviction and extenuation. In between the paperwork were some crushed clothes and my diary, which carried the beginnings of a written dialogue with myself. I told the Upington prisoners and their families that I would be away only for a short time and I argued fiercely with friends and colleagues who questioned whether I would return. As I flew over Cape Town and then across the Indian Ocean, I was filled with a sweeping sense of release and I did toy with the fantasy of never coming back.

22

•

An unknown home

I arrived in Sydney, Australia, in November 1989, a stranger in a distinctly familiar paradise. I had planned a three-month trip, some time away to be still, to grieve, perhaps even to consider the prospects of living a while in a new country. Within days of my arrival, however, I developed an uncomfortable reluctance to give Australia a chance, a jealous irritation with its easy spirit, and I made up my mind I would never live in this place with no obvious fire in its belly. The people were straightforward and unaffected and their city sparkled with the lazy confidence of a land waiting to be discovered. We sat in beachside cafes drinking pineapple juice with mint and then slowly turned our minds to ordering a 'short black' or 'flat white'. It took some time before I stopped feeling a stupid discomfort with these descriptions of the city's favourite beverage; it took a little longer to let go of my irritation with a people so seemingly free of the white man's burden, so untouched by his harm. When the burning sun had left for the day, the Sydney sky sometimes filled with fireworks and I discovered the sweet smell of citronella and the night cicada song which filled the air while we lay back and planned more holidays. Having lived in Sydney for almost eight years, Neil found my observations somewhat ungracious and refused to take me on, welcoming me instead to the land of the long weekend. To make matters worse, in early February 1990, just as I had begun to settle down and fathom this new environment, the South African government released Nelson Mandela into my mother city.

I called my office in Cape Town. They held the phone to the window of our office building so I could hear the echo of celebration, the shouts and cheers of 60 000 people who lined the streets to welcome *Madiba*. I longed to be in the thick of it all, to be part of a history which I never imagined occuring in my lifetime.

The release of Mandela followed President de Klerk's dramatic opening of parliament a few days earlier. De Klerk had declared that the time for negotiation had arrived and lifted bans on the African National Congress (ANC), the Pan-Africanist Congress (PAC) and the South African Communist Party. His reform measures bore direct application to the fourteen Upington condemned. He announced a review of the death penalty and suspended all executions pending its outcome. Not long after this announcement, my office advised me that the appeal of the Upington 25, which we had hoped would be heard in September or November that year, had been postponed. The appeal judges, we were told, would not be able to digest the 20 000-page record before the year's end. The appeal looked set for April 1991, in a little over a year's time. A whole year more on death row, a whole year, though, for South Africa to leap into change and never look back.

Despite de Klerk's bold rejection of the underpinnings of apartheid, those responsible for its upkeep held on to its cruel legacy and its dirty tactics, and I remained obsessed with the place, hankering for news and keen for contact with friends and colleagues. At the beginning of 1990, Justice Minister Kobie Coetzee announced a one-man commission of inquiry into the activities of hit squads. As the inquiry unfolded, evidence emerged of the existence of the defence force death squad, the cynically named Civil Cooperation Bureau (CCB) and its links to Anton's murder. Defence Minister, Magnus Malan, denied any knowledge of the CCB. But he went one step further and adopted an old plan of attack, sowing the seeds of doubt with a strong dose of misinformation. Before parliament, neatly protected by the cloak of parliamentary privilege, Malan announced that Anton had been an agent of the state. 'I wish to reveal today,' said Malan, 'that Mr Lubowski was a paid agent of military intelligence. I am assured that he did good work for the South African Army. General Witkop Badenhorst, Chief of Security Forces, would, therefore, not have authorised any action against Mr Lubowski.'

John Carlin called me at midnight and read out Malan's desperate claim. I was far away and powerless to dispute it. I hurt for Anton's family whose pain eventually forced them to withdraw from any further participation in the commission proceedings. In the early hours of the morning I wrote the final lines of a piece for the *Independent*, a tiny cry against those who damaged the truth: 'Anton was clearly too big for this world—he was larger than life in every way. He had no time for petty, malicious tasks which he believed should be serviced by the small-minded and those lacking in vision. There are hundreds of people around the world who knew Anton as a great human being, compassionate and dedicated. It is only those who detest such qualities who will seek to portray him differently.'

With the delay of the appeal came disappointment and anxiety. Anxiety, because it meant going against my word to the twenty-five. Before I left for Australia, I told them I would be away for a few months, a short break; that I would be back in no time, with new energy to continue battle. Three months seemed too long for some, particularly those on death row. They felt insecure, fearing I might walk away from them when I tasted life outside Upington. I wrote the twenty-five a letter of explanation and tried to make a year sound short and fast. The delay of the appeal presented a series of unpredictable events of some benefit to the twenty-five. And for me, the extra time brought the opportunity that would edge me into Australian society. With the immediate pressure of the case now lifted, I had time to stop and I slowly gave in to fate and to the offerings of a new world. But it was not without some struggle, a drawn-out tussle between the pull of my native earth and the draw of an unknown home. I would stay and work in Sydney and return to South Africa the following year for the appeal. In that time I would learn more about myself than I had ever planned, and with that knowledge came my gradual acceptance of my other country.

Throughout this period, I never depicted myself as a potential emigrant. Rather, I would explain that I was simply having some time away. Any gesture towards emigration was too final and I feared would be judged an admission of failure, an immoral commitment to letting South Africa go. I spoke always of my inevitable return to South Africa, but, unwittingly, my conviction waned with my extended sojourn in Australia. In Australia I began to feel absence of my need to be a woman in action. Australia made no demands and it offered no promises. It simply extended an understated invitation to be.

•

Although temporarily separated from the action of the Upington trial, the just resolution of the case was very much at the centre of my journey in a new land. It was a complicated attachment given that I was geographically removed from the day-to-day involvement in the case. I wanted to see it through and although some part of me yearned for a different focus, I was determined to stay with the twenty-five until we had achieved the grace to which they were entitled.

It added to the complication that I had started work for a large Sydney commercial law firm early in March 1990. To their credit, they gave me a job and it was here that I learnt about the practice of Australian law and made friends for life. I was no commercial lawyer, and my new firm was not an environment that easily embraced nor understood the practice of law within the confines of a cruel and inhuman state. To be fair, there would not have been many big commercial law firms in Australia with such familiarity. But my involvement in the Upington case introduced me to an Australia that was not at first evident.

I was invited to present briefings and talks to lawyers' organisations and human rights bodies about the Upington case and through these invitations I began to meet an extraordinary array of people who divulged a society that was passionate and strident and openly linked to a universal rights culture.

•

I was in weekly contact with my Cape Town office, with Stefan Raubenheimer and Sandra (Sandy) Liebenberg who had carriage of the Upington case in my absence. They were hard at work with Ian Farlam and our two new Cape Town counsel, old friends and political soul mates, John Whitehead and Les Rose-Innes. Andre Landman had returned to his Johannesburg practice and remained our consultant. In addition to preparation of the appeal papers, Stefan and Sandy were hard-pressed to assume an expanded caretaker role as the extended time on death row precipitated despair and anger amongst the condemned and their families. Resources and compassion were stretched. The visits to Pretoria Central were costly and took people away from work and their own families. The condemned began to lose hope and their patience withered with debilitating speed. Mistrust and division set in amongst the prisoners and then wedged their way into the Upington community. With the resultant anger and confusion came a request from the men that they be managed separately, a development which, given the accumulated tension of some five years, seemed inevitable.

The crux of disagreement stemmed from the impossible juggling of demands from the inside and outside worlds. The rift that had evolved within the Upington community, essentially around the distribution of scarce resources for visiting the condemned in Pretoria and the selection process of who was entitled to visit, had seeped through to Pretoria Central. Conflict between the condemned had flared to such a degree that one group had refused to see their visitors, while the other broke rank and ignored the boycott. Stefan wrote of the force carried by particular figures, such as Kenneth Khumalo, and the effect of his approach on those less articulate and forthright in his group. He described a meeting with the group during which Xolile Yona had lost his temper, precipitating a scuffle with the warders in attendance. Blood had been spilt and Xolile emerged from the prison hospital with six stitches in his head.

Our assessment that the prospect of success on appeal was certain to increase as the political climate changed in line with de Klerk's reform program offered little comfort. It was probably true that the movement of time might bring about an appeal bench sympathetic, or at least receptive to our clients, and that their increased time on death row was bound to influence the sentences handed down on appeal. Knowing their discomfort, it was hard to write letters of encouragement to the fourteen, praising their resilience and courage. So acrimonious was the battle and so erosive of a united front that Stefan persuaded the two factions to attempt to contain the damage. They agreed to participate in a formal mediation in the prison under the auspices of trained mediators skilled in community dispute resolution. A mediation agreement, reflecting a consensus, was drafted and signed by the contesting groups in Pretoria Central and the divided sectors within the Paballelo community. But the conflict obviously ran deep and the two groups still insisted that Stefan meet them separately on his visits to death row.

Outside prison, political developments emerged which had implications for the future lives of the fourteen. In May 1990, the Criminal Law Amendment Bill was tabled in the South African parliament. In essence, it proposed that judges should not be bound to impose the death penalty in the absence of extenuating circumstances. Rather, they would have a discretion to order a sentence other than death if so persuaded by the presence of mitigating factors. The bill also proposed an automatic right of appeal when the death penalty was imposed. Given the changes envisaged, it was suggested that a panel of legal experts and appeal court judges be appointed to review the cases of the more than 300 people on death row who may have exhibited mitigating circumstances justifying a sentence less than death. It was too early to know exactly how this development might impact on the lives of the fourteen Upington condemned. In any event, it gave us hope that their appeal might be treated with some flexibility.

With signs of political and legislative change, we were caught between the opportunities presented by the new emerging South Africa and an unsteady belief in the ways of the old. This conflict took the form of two opposing strategies: responding to an invitation to apply for the indemnity and release of the twenty-five under the Pretoria Minute or adhering to a commitment to participate in the judicial process and submit to the conservative wisdom of the highest court in the land. In December 1990, we received notification from the appeal court registry in Bloemfontein that the appeal had been set down from 6–10 May the following year. It was also in December that we lodged a memorandum with the Legal Office of the African National Congress in terms of Government Notice R2625, known as the Pretoria Minute.

The Pretoria Minute, negotiated between the ANC and the South African government earlier in the year, included an agreement by the ANC to suspend the armed struggle. It also allowed for submissions to be made for the indemnity or release of prisoners convicted of a political offence. The Minute defined a 'political offence' as one 'committed for political not personal motive, in the course of and as part of a political uprising or disturbance'. The political nature of the offence could be inferred from the fact that it advanced the ANC's objective of rendering the country ungovernable and was committed with ANC tacit approval. Ostensibly, the case of the Upington 25 offered a prime example. The offence was directed against a municipal policeman, a perceived symbol of authority. The state had convinced Justice Basson that the murder of Sethwala had not been a 'spontaneous isolated outburst' but rather an orchestrated incident linked to a national political plan aimed at rendering the country ungovernable. His judgment on extenuation concluded that the murder was a 'semi-organised revolt' and that had the accused testified as to their feelings on the day of this pre-determined revolt, Basson had reason to believe that their 'apparently irrational behaviour' might have washed up as perfectly rational. In addition, it was arguable that implicit in the court's reasoning and the evidence of state witness Dr de Kock was the inference that the murder had been committed with the tacit approval of the ANC.

While these findings suggested a clear case for an indemnity application, the temptation to apply was eroded by our belief in a different version, one that we had presented at trial to no effect and would subsequently ask the appeal court to uphold: that the accused suffered a history of deprivation and political oppression; that these factors combined with provocative conduct by the police on the day of Sethwala's murder caused the accused to exhibit unusual and irrational behaviour. The evidence, we would submit, demonstrated that the accused had acted in a deindividuated state rather than with calculation. Primarily, we would ask the appeal court to dismiss convictions of murder. Perhaps more importantly, we would seek to convince the appeal judges that the accused were deindividuated and had acted out of character, that on a balance of probabilities, extenuation had been proved and that the penalties of death could not be upheld. These submissions, however, would be in stark contrast to those we would proffer in support of our clients' application for indemnity in accordance with the guidelines contained in the Pretoria Minute.

Despite the apparent conflict, we had to confront our dilemma head on and act with some degree of speed. To deny the accused a possible release through political channels by invoking the Pretoria Minute and rather rely solely on a potential judicial victory was not a risk we could take. But neither could we afford to prejudice our chances on appeal by adopting a contrary argument in support of the indemnity application. To avoid a compromise of either approach, we would lodge the indemnity application relying primarily upon the state's assessment of the case and the congruent findings of the Upington Supreme Court: that the purposeful murder of a municipal policeman, perceived to be a symbol of authority, was the result of a concerted political uprising against the state. The political motive underlying the murder, required by the Pretoria minute, was part of the ANC plan to render the country ungovernable.

The targeted deadline for the completion of the indemnity process and the possible release of political prisoners was scheduled for 30 April 1991, one week before the appeal of the twenty-five was to begin. Although outwardly in favour of the indemnity application, deep down I feared that the proximity of the appeal date might mean that consideration of the indemnity application would be delayed and dealt with only were the appeal unsuccessful. However, it gave the accused a new focus of hope and secured them a place in a process which might serve their needs in later years.

•

I was booked to leave Australia and return to South Africa for the appeal on 20 April 1991. It had been a strained few months of preparation, not so much as a consequence of the actual planning of the appeal, but more due to my exhausting and at times schizophrenic attempts to keep my involvement in the case separate from the demands of my new job. Working for a commercial law firm by day, I drafted applications for bankruptcy and tried to fathom how to trace funds owing to a client that had been invested offshore. At night, when time differences between nations allowed for interaction, I slid back into the world of criminal law and kept up with the progress of twenty-five clients on death row awaiting their appeal in another country, in another home.

I communicated with various journalists and lawyers around the world, with the International Commission of Jurists, the Anti-Apartheid Movement and with Amnesty International, requesting their attendance at the appeal as international rapporteurs and observers. 'With optimism accompanying so many apparent changes in our country,' I wrote in introductory lines of entreatment, 'there is great concern amongst the accused and their families that the international community will lose sight of some of the cases such as that of the Upington 25, the continued existence of the death penalty, detention without trial and deficiencies in the application of justice in South Africa. Our clients believe it is essential that the international community continue to monitor developments in our land in the belief that participation as observers and critics will facilitate the emergence of a truly just and democratic South Africa.' We had an impressive response and I was relieved to find that the dedication and commitment of the international community was still solid and that they were cautious about change.

Within Australia, support from the judiciary, the Bar, academics, the Department of Foreign Affairs, the media and particularly from Amnesty International was extraordinary. The Australian public sent petitions to the South African government and lawyers in Sydney established a committee on the common purpose doctrine and its application, drafting a detailed memorandum of cases to assist in the presentation of our appeal. Amnesty International arranged a tight schedule of speaking engagements and interviews with the press, radio and television, my favourite being a spot on the 'Midday' show with TV host and institution, Ray Martin, whose recounting of the case reduced me and the studio audience to tears.

The night before I left Sydney for South Africa, friends gathered in the kitchen of the Paddington terrace where I was living. It was important to have them with me. They gave me memories of a place to which I felt I could return. They packed my bags with notes and poetry, with trinkets of support and we ate dinner and talked into the night about fate and the turns we take through life. I was apprehensive about going home. In the year away I had developed a liking for Sydney, not necessarily a passion, which I still reserved for South Africa, but a comfort with the place and an easy familiarity with its people.

As I flew to Perth in the morning, I read the copy of an article that the *Sydney Morning Herald* was to run the following week, days before the appeal. 'The trauma Durbach experienced in fighting the Upington case,' wrote *Herald* journalist Tony Kleu, 'was largely responsible for her decision to leave. The same force is now drawing her back. There are memories to be exorcised before Durbach can settle peacefully in Sydney.' Strong words, strange words when I read them captured in print. Perhaps I did go back to find an ending, to draw a line.

But I had no firm intention. Rather, I fell in with plans already made. I was determined to bring the case to an end, no matter how long it took. However, I did not have an equivalent resolve about where I might live. At least, not consciously. Undoubtedly, my year in Australia had beckoned me to a different life and I was drawn to the possibilities of change and an escape from the raw recent memories of the sentences of death, and of Anton's murder. In the year, I had found a stillness for myself, a space unencumbered by the fierce demands of the outside world. Ultimately, my inclination about where to live would be informed by my desire either to explore that space or turn away from the self that it had begun to reveal and cling to my identity so embedded in the psyche of South Africa.

23

•

The new South Africa

The sprawl of Johannesburg lay below us. Grids of townships and smoke from uneven chimney stacks. The Highveld sun lit the tips of golden mine dumps and lines of blue swimming pools that marked dry suburban streets. In my memory, I could smell the air, the mix of paraffin fumes and wood fires and industry. Despite the heralded loosening of the regime, I still felt anxious about this arrival. Change had been rife and history had moved on without me. Would it feel like home, would everyone remember and welcome me despite my leaving them, would I feel needed, would I know what to do and where to begin? The uniform and glare of the airport police were unchanged, and the fear they induced came back with queasy familiarity. The man at customs was pleasant enough and asked if I had any firearms. A stock question asked with stock lack of interest. He checked my entry card and with pen poised in reproach, queried my failure to complete all the details. 'You haven't ticked box E. Are you a citizen returning?' he asked. 'No, not really,' was the best I could muster.

Not returning, not staying, neither in South Africa nor Australia. Just sliding hopelessly between the two, without taking sides, without offending either. This was my way of shifting the pain of making a choice. I knew, however, that at some point I was going to have to drop this ambivalence and come to terms with the loss of an identity so precisely defined by my past.

Stefan and one of our new counsel, Les Rose-Innes, were waiting for me. We had all been at law school together, tied up in friendships and falling-outs, confidences and aspirations. As they came forward to meet me in dark suits and ties, they seemed so grown-up, reserved and sweet. I felt like a young sister returning from summer camp, slightly overwhelmed by the time apart and the changes in us all. Over stale white scones and stainless-steel pots of Five Roses tea in the airport cafeteria, we loosened up and spoke of friends and colleagues who had left South Africa and the confounding pull of the place. As we walked from the airport building to the car, police hovered around a fence of yellow tape, taking samples from the debris of a recent bomb blast. The scene drew no comment from my comrades so I bit my nervous tongue and remembered how this country had a knack for moving on.

Stefan had arranged a consultation with our clients at Pretoria Central. The thirteen men knew I would be at the appeal but this morning's visit was a surprise. In the midmorning heat, Stefan drove us out of Johannesburg on the road to Pretoria. I felt slightly detached, like a tourist, and silently thrilled that I could remember the road signs and buildings, the numberplates, the curve of the freeway. As we entered the city of Pretoria, the Voortrekker monument stood high on the hill to the left. To the right was the concrete vault that housed the University of South Africa, correspondence university to many prisoners and death-row inmates. The city reeked of a legacy of order and control and was filled with bureaucrats in polyester short-sleeved shirts and soft brown shoes, servants of the state. Yet despite its status as the hard-nosed centre of apartheid rule and home to army generals and high-ranking police, the city felt different, less rigid and self-assured. Change had begun to seep into even the seemingly inpenetrable foundations of white rule.

The boom at the entrance to Pretoria Central lifted, and we were greeted with curt recognition. As old hands, we were ushered in to maximum security without the need for identification.

A voice from a wall asked us to report our arrival and we spoke into a cemented slot, announcing our visit to invisible prison officials who sat behind opaque glass. A large steel door slid back and in a passageway we completed the standard thirteen forms and then followed the *kolonel* across a well-maintained garden of ponds and coloured flowerbeds to the prison building. We stepped inside to a familiar scene. A wide staircase rose to the cells, sweeping upwards in a grand and majestic gesture. The prison staff were busy fumbling with their keys, bunches hanging from leather belts. Messages were relayed via the prison intercom, mumbled in some sort of self-important prison code. The rubber soles of prison shoes squeaked on linoleum floors and the smell of cleaning fluid and disinfectant reminded me that this was a proud prison with very high standards.

Stefan had warned me that the two factions that had developed amongst the men were still entrenched. We decided to see the small group first—Justice Bekebeke, Myner Bovu and Boy Jafta. Initially, there was great excitement and laughter and a closeness. We talked about the indemnity application and our doubts that it would be dealt with before the appeal had been decided. The men suddenly seemed worn down and disappointed. Even so, I read their subdued spirits as shyness. But as conversation began to falter, I saw them as trampled, tired and despondent. For some inane reason I had thought they would be the same men I had visited almost two years ago—inquiring, boisterous, relentless in their fight. Justice, always strong on enthusiasm, tried to lift the others and distract me. 'I recognise that briefcase,' he said pointing at my black bag which had carried various trial documents over the years. 'It's travelled far. It must have many stories, many secrets.' We all stared at the case for some minutes and then it was time to end the visit. Les reassured us that the appeal was looking very good and that Ian was hard at work and confident. I got up and shook our clients' hands. 'Until Bloemfontein. Ten days to go.'

Les had to return to Cape Town to settle the final details of the appeal argument and so Stefan and I planned a meeting with the bigger group the following day. We drove Les back to Jan Smuts Airport under a rose and purple sky, an exquisite combination of evening light and Johannesburg smog. I stayed overnight in Johannesburg with an old friend, Melinda. We had shared a house in Cape Town some years earlier when my involvement in the case had just begun. Melinda was an architect and had come to Cape Town to design a 'struggle building' as she called it, a vast complex that was to house various political and labour organisations. It was built, decorated with grand murals depicting freedom, and then blown up by 'unknown forces'. In keeping with old Cape Town rituals, we ended the day's work with a whisky on the rocks and Melinda cooked a perfect homecoming dinner of her celebrated marmalade chicken. She said I had changed a little, that I seemed less 'wired' and she saw evidence of a softening of will. I was happy to hold Australia responsible for both progressions and we took bets to see how long the Australian influence could last out against the draw of my past.

The next day Stefan and I returned to Pretoria to lunch with Tim Yeend, Second Secretary at the Australian Embassy, whom I had met in Canberra shortly before he took up his posting in South Africa. It was refreshing and comforting to talk about things Australian, to move, for a short hour, away from the ANC and rival Zulu-based organisation Inkatha, and de Klerk, away from violence and record crime rates, from the almost monotonous chant of the changing South Africa.

Back at Pretoria Central for our meeting with the 'big group', the surprise of my visit was short-lived when Gideon spotted my hair rising above Stefan as I walked behind him into the consultation room. Gideon chuckled and gave me his hand and said I'd 'gone smaller'. After an exchange of greetings, the men were keen to unload their anger and confusion. They wanted to talk about the split with the others, to justify their position. There was something distressing about the slow splintering of the group. As we spoke, it became clear that the division was more the consequence of the relentless trial and its continuing lack of resolution rather than the overt design of strong personalities over weak. The cruel reality was that the division played into the hands of those whom the group had always opposed and, as inmates of the prison and in dire need of relief, they now tried to please. The separation exacerbated dissent as distrust and rumours had begun to weave between the two groups. As I tentatively suggested a rapprochement, Xolile Yona stood up and cried out: 'I'm sorry for losing Lubowski and I'm sorry for losing you. Can't you see?' Xolile looked at me with wild eyes. 'None of this would have happened if you had stayed.'

We drove to the airport in silence. Stefan tried to talk but it made things worse. I felt culpable and disorientated. The visits had not gone as I had imagined and I was worried about the rest of the twenty-five. I still had to see Evelina in Upington Prison the remaining men at the Kimberley Prison and those released on bail. I was exhausted and now lacking in energy and motivation. I would put all my trust in my mother city, Cape Town, to revive my spirit and supply me with a new slant on my world. As the boundaries of the Cape peninsula came into sight, with its backbone of mountain graded to the Cape of Good Hope, I was gripped with an excitement of the city's exasperating beauty. 'Ja,' came the voice of the pilot, as he swooped down to sea level and passengers leant into the turn, 'welcome to the new South Africa'.

Stefan had organised lunch at the Kaapse Tafel (the Cape Table) in Queen Victoria Street with the appeal team, Ian, John Whitehead, Les and Colin. We went straight into appeal talk and it took me a while to feel a comfort with the group and get a grip on my role. Despite the warmth of our reunion, I felt estranged from the circle, from the case, and I missed Anton. After lunch, we walked back to the firm, across Greenmarket Square with its stalls and street musicians and I smelt the sea in the air of the afternoon breeze that blew in from the docks. The firm was slightly changed, some new faces and more offices. The files and boxes of the Upington case still held their place and I was pleased to be back amidst case history and familiar tools of the trial. I had a drink with the old guard in the boardroom at the end of the day and as I drove home with my friend and colleague, Liz, we spoke of different times and changed sentiments and I think I knew then that I could not go back.

Two days later, Sandy Liebenberg and I caught the Sunday-evening flight to Upington. I broke with tradition and had a gin and tonic instead of my customary tomato cocktail and packet of salted peanuts. It was almost three years to the day that I had landed at the Pierre van Reyneveld Airport to meet the twenty-five for the first time. The afternoon air felt just as heavy and the town was quiet and moved slowly with the heat. We drove past the prison to Schröderstraat and had tea on the lawn of the Protea Hotel. One by one the hotel staff came out to welcome us back—the manager, Willie Burger, and his wife, Kathy, and the waiters, Phineas and Simeon, in maroon jackets with gold buttons and matching felt fezzes. Bonnie and Regina, in starched white aprons, brought us news from Paballelo and reported that the accuseds' families were gathering at Mr Gubula's house in preparation for our visit that evening. We arrived in Paballelo at dusk, my favourite time, when the light was softer on the arid earth and women stoked cooking fires and young girls and boys stood at street corners talking and swaying to music from portable cassette players.

As we drove past the Take Over Cafe and turned into the centre of the township, Paballelo seemed different. In my brief absence it had become an urbanised village. It had been built up, with more streetlights, paved roads and a real soccer field with goal-posts and stands for supporters. We parked outside Mr Gubula's house in King Street and entered the yard. The families and friends of the twenty-five, holding candles and oil lamps, rose to their feet and sang a hymn. We took each other's hands in greeting and one by one they sat down on wooden boxes and chairs to form a semicircle. At the back sat Barry Bekebeke, Xoliswa Dube, Elizabeth Bostaander, Neville Witbooi, Roy Swartbooi and Ivan Kazi, convicted murderers but fortuitous recipients of suspended sentences. With them sat Ronnie Masiza, Jeffrey Sekiya, Abel Kutu and Sarel Jacobs, sentenced to jail terms for Sethwala's murder but released on bail pending their appeals. They had an air of ease about them and remained detached from the main discussion, talking and joking amongst themselves, perhaps fearing any reassociation with the horror of times past.

Sandy and I were invited to sit in two chairs at the front of the setting and Mr Gubula welcomed us and thanked God for our arrival. There were whispers of 'Amen' and Mr Gubula asked me how far it was to Australia. We talked for some three hours about my visit to Pretoria Central, the indemnity application and the appeal. Mrs Kutu moved her chair. She raised her hand to speak and gently asked who was replacing Anton. Final arrangements were made about the trip to Bloemfontein and the list of names of those attending the appeal hearing was confirmed. Despite the difficulties that had precipitated the split between the thirteen men on death row, the meeting displayed no apparent division, but rather a shared concern about the appeal and the fate of the fourteen condemned in particular. We drove Mrs Dube and Xoliswa home so I could see Innocentia and give her a toy koala. She was round and lovely and shy at first, staring at the koala and then at me. Our next stop was the de Bruin–Madlongolwane home. With Evelina's transfer to Upington Prison, the whole family seemed slightly at ease, and Tutu and Mbulelo had become more confident. They showed me paintings and craft they had made at school and stored in a special place for when Gideon and Evelina came back from prison.

There was no other way to end the night except with dinner at Le Must. Neil, still the bubbling maître d' shrieked and lifted me into the air. He decided we should dine on steak and green pepper sauce and a throaty bottle of red and we battled to leave at a reasonable hour, reminiscing about meals at Le Must and the hard periods in between. I woke early the next morning and from my window watched the sunrise change the colour of the Orange River, and after breakfast at our old corner table in the hotel dining room, we drove to the Upington Prison. Women prisoners, cleaning and dusting, beckoned us close to ask our advice. Sergeant Lyons, blonde and buxom in her uniform of green, extended her hand. '*Aangename kennis. Ek is bly om u te ontmoet,*

Juffrou. Evelina praat altyd van Andy.' ('How do you do? I am pleased to meet you. Evelina often talks about Andy.') She asked us to sit in a waiting room and minutes later led Evelina towards us instructing her to keep her eyes closed. I got up quietly and moved towards Evelina and she opened her eyes and hugged me and sobbed into my chest. I held her heaving body until the sergeant issued her next command, as if talking to a child or a dog. *'Kom, Evelina, sit.'* ('Come, Evelina, sit.')

Evelina looked well. She walked upright, no longer with a stoop. She was thinner and said the food was better in Upington Prison and that she was taking fewer pills. She crocheted a little each day and her arthritis had improved and best of all, she said, she was close to Tutu and Mbulelo. The sergeant stepped forward with pride. *'Ja, sy het haarself reggeruk. Maar ons sorg vir haar.'* ('Yes, she has pulled herself together. But we look after her.') And then in a moment of insight, she turned her back to Evelina and added: *'Dit is vreeslik dat iemand soos Evelina—so oud—in hierdie toestand beland het.'* ('It is terrible that someone like Evelina—so old—has landed in this situation.') Evelina, excluded from the sergeant's conversation, continued her dialogue with me. She had planned a party for her release and talked of the dress she would wear. She would be cooking all day, chickens and beans and potatoes, so people would have to come and visit her. She would not have the time to go to them. For our next visit after the appeal hearing, Evelina was to prepare her guest list for the party. *'Miskien kan Anton's se ouers kom?'* ('Perhaps Anton's parents will come?') I said they would be thrilled to receive an invitation and Sergeant Lyons nodded her own RSVP and showed us to the door.

24

•

On appeal

Telephones were ringing at reception at the Landdrost Hotel, Bloemfontein. It was Sunday, 5 May, the eve of the Upington appeal and we all seemed to arrive simultaneously. Judges, lawyers, the media, observers. The Landdrost was obviously where appeal court guests were housed. There was a hint of chaos in the air as introductions and old connections were made. Guests stood on their toes pointing out their luggage to porters and shook hands and arranged to meet one another for a drink before dinner. A journalist came over and asked Ian Farlam for his views on an article in a morning newspaper. Evidently, our pre-appeal briefing to the media had gone too far. News of the indemnity application had appeared along with editorial comment speculating as to whether the outcome of the appeal would be influenced by the lodging of the indemnity application. Ian read the article and shook with anger at the foolishness of our trust in the press. The appeal court might be reminded that the indemnity application still stood and that the case could therefore be resolved in other quarters. The timing of this link in print was regrettable and Stefan and I went up to our rooms in disgrace.

We set the time for a group dinner. I was thrilled to meet up again with journalists who had covered the trial years earlier and with London-based lawyer, Geoffrey Bindman, who was representing the International Commission of Jurists (IJC) at the appeal. I had first met Geoffrey when he visited South Africa in 1987 as part of an ICJ mission to examine the extent of non-compliance in South Africa with international human rights law and principles. Representing Amnesty International were Geoffrey Robertson QC and Rosy Parsons. Their visit neatly coincided with the international release of an Amnesty publication focusing on the death penalty in Africa and the press were delighted with the synergy of events. Geoffrey Robertson's involvement in landmark human rights cases around the world was well known as was his energetic television program 'Hypothetical', which I'd watched religiously each week as a new television recruit in Australia. Geoffrey had been born in Sydney and visited Australia from his London home each year. We talked of his old haunts and he described Australia as a country of layers, slowly revealed. I should go back, he said, and give it time. Conversation at our dinner table steered clear of the appeal. Lawyers spoke of clients and cases and the journalists prompted comment 'off the record' and made notes on the backs of cigarette packets. I waived dessert and I went up to my room and read the heads of argument for the appeal one last time. I ran a bath and asked room service for tea and a pot of honey. And just before I dropped into a restless sleep, I said a prayer to life for Evelina and the thirteen men.

At breakfast I recognised some of the appeal court judges dining at nearby tables and wondered whether we had drawn any of them for our hearing. We had arranged to meet Bloemfontein attorney Jim Newdigate soon after 8am at court to set up the dozens of files of court record in a system accessible to our advocates. Jim's firm, Webbers, had organised all the appeal arrangements for us and Jim was familiar with court staff and etiquette. It was my first appellate division case, and Jim's presence and ease with the occasion made it a little less daunting. As we approached the court, a grand old stone building set back in green lawns, a queue of people in bright clothing and scarves and hats began to wave. The accuseds' families had driven from Upington overnight and had been waiting outside since 6am. They had driven straight to court to make sure they were in line to secure a seat at the appeal. They had been refused entry, told to wait outside until half an hour before the proceedings began.

I walked into the entrance of the building and spoke to a white man with a grey moustache and a security badge on his jacket. 'The people outside are the families of my clients,' I said in my best Bloemfontein accent. 'They've driven from Upington through the night. Would you allow them into the court a little early to sit quietly before the appeal begins? They've been standing outside for hours.' He looked down at the floor and shook his head. This was clearly a big ask, entailing a shift from procedure. After a respectable mull-over period, he raised his head. 'Is this that case of the twenty-five blacks who killed a policeman?' He was keen to establish the credentials of the families. 'Ja,' I responded with a contrived lightness of tone. I gave him the bare bones of the case. He cocked his head and sought further confirmation: 'So, those blacks killed a black policeman?' I nodded. 'Hell man,' he looked me in the eye, 'I'd never kill a white man.' He was proud of his stance, a man of some discernment when it came to killing, and having got that off his chest, he let the families in.

Towards the centre of the bar table, from which the advocates would address the court, a wooden stand was perched. Face downwards on the lectern was a white piece of paper which indicated the judges assigned to hear the appeal. We were reluctant to know who they were, but temptation won out. Stefan and Jim stood next to me as I turned the paper over: Smalberger, EM Grosskopf, Nienaber.

It was a good call. A strong, conservative bench not known for liberal tendencies. If they were to differ from their brother Basson and overturn his findings, it would be seen as a rejection by the highest court in the land which was sound in law. Had the bench been more progressive in its constitution, findings contrary to those of Basson might be dismissed as a soft inclination towards justice. We walked to the back of the court to tell the families. As we talked, a low hiss came from their mouths and they slowly shook their heads from side to side. State attorneys Terence van Rensburg and Jaap Schreuder had arrived. We kept up appearances and greeted one another like old friends, colleagues with a shared history. Ian and John and Les entered the court with our observers and received a very different welcome. The families stood to greet them and reached out to the international contingent. A court orderly called for order and the appellate division was declared in session, Justices Smalberger, Grosskopf and Nienaber presiding.

Ian's initial delivery lacked cohesion. He was awkward, wavering and without a clear focus. He was finding his way with the judges and fashioning his pitch and he took a little time to get into his stride. He dealt first with the alibi defences of the accused and their wholesale rejection by the Upington Supreme Court. He reminded the court that seven of the accused had been convicted of murder on the evidence of a single witness only. He argued that the circumstances surrounding their identification—a moving, agitated crowd, dust and tear-gas in the air, shouting and the sound of gunshots ringing out—would have made conclusive identification extremely difficult, not to say unreliable, and that corroboration by at least one other witness should have been required. As he moved on to the disingenuous application of the common purpose doctrine to twenty-five individuals, he began to argue with conviction and vigour and I eased back into my chair and watched the judges listen. By lunchtime the court was filled with more families and media, diplomats, the clergy and our Johannesburg visitors to the fourteen on death row: Joan Cameron, John Wills and Sheila Weinberg. As people squeezed onto benches and chairs the public gallery exuded strength and solidarity, and I thought then that we might win. But the experience of the trial and its cruel twists and disappointments meant that I had come to expect the worst, and towards the end of the day, my euphoria had been replaced by a familiar despondency.

The second day of the appeal restored my early confidence. As Ian unfastened the judgment of Basson and stripped it of reason, the bench cautiously shared his irritation with findings lacking in substance and clear errors of law. Ian was on a roll and we were loving every wicked moment of revenge. At the lunchbreak, we gathered outside the court with the accuseds' families who broke into a joyous *toyi-toyi* and then asked us to bow our heads in silence and pray for our overseas visitors, for Ian, and for the judges.

Ian concluded his argument by midafternoon and van Rensburg began the state's case with a show of force. He portrayed the crowd on the soccer field as antagonistic towards the police and so set the scene for the emergence of a murderous group of people intent on killing Sethwala. He felt little need to draw on facts to substantiate the bare conclusions he presented to the court. By the third morning, as van Rensburg stuck to his technique of bald assertion, the bench intervened. 'Mr van Rensburg,' Justice Grosskopf leant forward, 'it is our task to decide whether the trial court was correct. Yours is to give us the basis for the conclusion.' Van Rensburg, realising the need to change tack, moved swiftly from his argument on conviction to sentence. Perhaps in an attempt to save face, the state reduced its claim for fourteen death sentences to four: a definite change of heart since Upington. The damage, however, to those van Rensburg would now excuse from death had already taken hold.

The appeal ended shortly after 6pm, with judgment reserved. We packed the files into boxes and said goodbye to the families and the orderlies and the women in room 9, who typed and photocopied and quietly wished us everything of the best. Back at the Landdrost Hotel, we ordered champagne for the first time in the history of the case and Ian divulged a confidential communication. After court, as we packed up the case, Ian had gone to say goodbye to Justice Smalberger, before whom he had previously appeared. They had talked a little and the judge disclosed that he had been born in Upington. He told Ian that we could expect a joint judgment, divided into three sections. Given the nature of the case, the judges would endeavour to have it written by the end of the current term and hand it down before June. Ian swore us all to secrecy. I called South African Airways and changed the date of my return to Australia. I would stay a week longer, until the beginning of June and hope that Justice Smalberger's secret would be out by then.

•

My friend Jill was visiting from London. I spent a few days post-appeal on holiday in my home town before my next round of meetings. I had planned to fly to Kimberley to visit two of the accused and report on the appeal and then drive to Upington to see Evelina and the families. I had regretted the fact that we had not taken any photographs during the trial, none of the fourteen before they were sentenced to death, none of Anton before he was killed. Jill was a portrait photographer and agreed to travel with me and photograph my visits with the families, those accused out on bail and the six on community service.

•

There had been no time to see Accused No 9, Elisha Matshoba, before the appeal. The artist and apple of his father's eye, Elisha had been sentenced to eight years' imprisonment as had Enoch Nompondwana, Accused No 7, who had been convicted of attempted murder and was separately represented. Elisha had been granted leave to appeal against his jail sentence only; his conviction of murder would stand. Lieutenant Clapton led me to the male section of the Kimberley Prison. I had asked to see Elisha first and then have a short visit with Enoch just to say hello. Enoch had not been granted leave to appeal either his conviction or sentence. Elisha was the star pupil of the prison, according to the lieutenant. He was studying art and history, and was drawing and painting. He made excellent use of his time. Elisha, looking much younger than his twenty-five years, did not agree with the lieutenant's analysis. He was bored and anxious and eight years in jail for being part of a crowd was not what he had planned for his life. Of all the appeals, I was worried most about Elisha's. His conviction of murder had not been open to appeal given his apparent participation in the crowd attack on Lucas Sethwala. He was, however, permitted to appeal his prison sentence of eight years. A jail sentence of eight years for murder was fairly standard, and in Elisha's case, it was unlikely that the appeal court would commute the sentence to community service. He felt isolated, especially from those on death row, on whom most of the attention was turned. Of the twenty-five who had been sentenced to jail terms, all except Elisha had been released on bail.

The road from Kimberley to Upington took us across the edges of blue ground where diamonds had been mined, to flat country of lone farmsteads and smallholdings. As we crossed the Orange River, the sun-baked earth turned to green and we arrived in the *dorp* of Groblershoop, stopping at the Grootrivier Hotel for lunch of thick cheddar cheese and tomato on pure white bread. In the foyer was an old wind-up telephone for public use and a wooden board displaying hotel tariffs. It was 1991 and these were not items of memorabilia. Accommodation was reasonable, although slightly more expensive for 'Europeans'. 'Non-Europeans and drivers' were offered a lower rate in rooms at the back. Underneath the tariff for 'non-Europeans and drivers' and typed in brackets were the words: 'supply own bedding'. Jill and I played with the receptionist and said we were lucky that we had a booking at the Upington Protea Hotel for the night, otherwise I, being 'driver', might have had to sleep on a bare bed in a back room at the Grootrivier Hotel.

The excitement of the appeal hearing had spread through Paballelo. For nights after the families had returned from Bloemfontein, people met in yards and talked about their trip to the judicial capital of the country and their three days in the highest court of the land. Even Evelina had been thoroughly briefed. '*O Meneer Farlam. Nou het hy daardie Vis gewys.*' ('Oh, Mr Farlam. He has now shown that Fish [van Rensburg].') It was hard to dampen high spirits, to lower expectations and so I adopted the line that even if we did not make it on appeal, there was still the indemnity application. From Upington, I flew to Johannesburg and met up with Andre Landman. I had asked him to accompany me on my penultimate visit to death row. Andre looked remarkable: younger and open and it was wonderful to see him. We drove to Pretoria and talked about his life and mine since late 1989 and how we had dealt with our hard separation from the hold of the case. The thirteen were delighted to see Andre. We were at a strange time of the case, an ending of one sort or another. We had no plans to discuss, no signposts to aim towards and all that was left was to wait for judgment from the court of final say.

•

During the morning of Tuesday, 28 May 1991, I received the call from Jim Newdigate. The appellate division would be handing down its judgment in the case of Khumalo and others at 9am the following morning. We decided that Stefan and I would go to Pretoria and wait there for news from the appeal court. Les would travel to Bloemfontein to receive the judgment and call us with the results, and Sandy Liebenberg would field calls in Cape Town. Bloemfontein was 500 kilometres away and it would be impossible to receive the judgment and then fly to Pretoria to be with the thirteen before the court's findings had seeped out on the wires. It was important that they hear the news from us. If the judgment was against them, I wanted to be able to explain it in detail to the accused, to answer their questions and try and find some comfort for them. We called the families in Upington, Namibia and De Aar, and the Upington and Kimberley prisons. We sent out a press alert and notified diplomats and parliamentarians, interest groups both locally and overseas, our funders and all our expert witnesses. Herman Raath and Joan Cameron were on standby to counsel the accused if necessary. 'If necessary.' I was not sure what I meant by that. In retrospect, it seemed a stupid qualification to make. Even if the appeal was to provide some softening of the Basson approach, not every accused would feel that justice had been done. Not everyone was in with an equal chance. When one's clients had endured such harsh times, it was difficult to keep in mind that Lucas Sethwala had been killed and those found to be responsible for his death would not avoid liability.

25

•

A short walk from death

It was just after 8am and the offices of Lawyers for Human Rights (LHR) in downtown Pretoria were filled with clients and families. We had asked LHR Director, Brian Currin, if we could use his office as our base for the day. Much of the organisation's work - centred on filing last-minute petitions for stays of execution of death-row prisoners. We were in good hands should the appeal court confirm any sentences of death. The minutes between 9.00am and 9.20am were filled with my own false alarms. I was convinced every telephone rang for me and when Jim Newdigate finally called from Bloemfontein, I took the receiver with faint hope. I could hardly hear him with the chattering of fear in my head and I asked him to start again.

'The appeals of accuseds 16, 24 and 26 against their convictions are upheld.' He was translating from the Afrikaans. He continued: 'Each of their convictions and sentences are accordingly set aside.' Numbers 16, 24 and 26—Xoliswa Dube, Roy Swartbooi and Ivan Kazi acquitted and free. Absolutely free. Jim was reading from the end of the judgment at page 210. 'The appeals of accused 11 and 20 against their conviction of murder are dismissed. The appeals of accuseds 10, 11 and 20 against the death sentence are upheld. The death sentences are set aside and substituted with ten year's imprisonment in respect of accuseds 10 and 20, and twelve years in respect of accused 11.' The death sentences imposed on the worst offenders had been overturned. Justice Bekebeke (who, with Elisha Matshoba, Accused No 9, had not been granted leave to appeal against his murder conviction), Zonga Mokhatle and Xolile Yona had been classified as principal offenders by Mr Justice Basson. That their death sentences had been set aside signalled great prospects for the other eleven on death row.

I repeated Jim's words and Stefan scrawled them down in shorthand. The appeal in respect of accuseds 1, 2, 3, 4, 5, 6, 8, 12, 13, 14, 15, 17, 18, 19, 21, 22, 23 and 25 against their convictions of murder had been successful. The murder convictions had been replaced by convictions of public violence and carried suspended jail sentences varying between one and two years. We were surrounded by most of the LHR staff who stood silently, watching Stefan write. Someone had done the numbers and shouted out: 'Twenty-one out of 25 murder convictions overturned. Three of them quashed. All death sentences overturned. So far, three will serve jail terms. It's unbelievable.' I was shouting with excitement and relief. 'Wait', I said looking at the faces around me, 'what about number 9, Elisha Matshoba?' We had appealed his sentence of eight years. Jim read the last line of the judgment. 'The appeal of accused 9 against his sentence is dismissed.' I adjusted the final figures in my head: four to serve jail terms.

We telephoned Mr Gubula in Upington and then the prisons and Andre. Sandy called from Cape Town. She had received a fax with the details from Jim and had telephoned Ian and John with the good news. She said the office was ecstatic and cake and champagne were being served for morning tea. We made a few more calls: to Bill Frankel and the funders in London, to Amnesty and the Anti-Apartheid Movement, to Herman Raath and Martin West and Joan Cameron and Sheila Weinberg. The press began to ring and ask for explanations, but we had to leave and tell the news to the most important players. Stefan and I ran to our car and drove through the streets of Pretoria at a dangerously high speed.

As we badgered our way through to the men's prison, subverting entrance requirements, the warder told us that the thirteen were playing soccer. It was their exercise time. Perhaps we could come back later. I said it was impossible. We had urgent and important news to convey. We had to see our clients right away. Could he call them off the field? The warder, slow and irritated in his manner, turned to Stefan, as if he would understand, and said, 'They are not going to be very pleased. They're winning the game'.

While we waited, Major Cronje arrived to greet us. He had heard that judgment had been handed down and asked if he might attend our meeting. More warders filled the corridor and our meeting room. Perhaps the major thought reinforcements would be required. The accused arrived, dishevelled and grumpy. They crowded into the room and the soccer professionals among them stood surly against the wall with arms folded. I tried hard to be even-handed. Although all their death sentences had been set aside, three of the thirteen had been sentenced instead to relatively brief terms of jail. Despite my intentions, I could not hold back my joy. 'The appeal court this morning overturned twenty-one of the twenty-five murder convictions and all the death sentences have been dismissed. You will be leaving here today.' There was a roar of delight and the men jumped up and down, hugging us and then one another. They were laughing and singing and slapping open hands. The warders softened, their stern faces turning to smiles and they shook the hands of the accused. The Major, in unexpected fine spirits, wished us all well. 'I will arrange for their transfer to the release section. You can come back at about 2pm and take them home.'

I moved between the echoes from the shouting in the small consultation room and just to make sure he realised what had happened, took the old man's hand and whispered in his ear: 'Gideon, Evelina will also be released today. She will be waiting for you at home in Upington.' I walked away and turned back to see Justice Bekebeke warmly embrace the old man. We caught each other's eye. Justice knew he was not bound for home but he was thrilled with the outcome of the appeal and his grace gave me the confidence to ask for silence. 'There is some sad news. For Justice, Xolile, Zonga and Elisha. The court did not dismiss their convictions and they must spend more time in jail. You have not done too badly.' I was looking at Justice and he nodded his head. With a shaky voice of little volume, I read out their jail terms. 'Elisha still has eight years. Justice and Xolile have ten. Zonga, you have twelve.' Xolile turned to face the wall to sob and beat his fist against the stone. 'Know that we are here and our fight is not yet over,' I mustered all my enthusiasm and said, 'Remember, there is still the indemnity.' Zonga, red-eyed from too much *dagga*, angrily shouted down my optimism and moved away from the group and sat, head down, in the corner of the room.

Back at LHR, we booked ten men on the 6 o'clock flight to Kimberley. They would stay there overnight and the Reverend Aubrey Beukes promised us two South African Council of Churches kombi-vans in the morning. 'There will be a royal procession back to Upington from Kimberley. What a glorious day.' Aubrey paused and then whispered into the phone, 'Thanks be to God'. We drove back to Pretoria Central in a LHR minibus, arriving at 2pm sharp. A crowd had formed in the parking lot in front of the prison. A guard approached us and announced that the prisoners would be driven from inside the prison grounds and 'off-loaded', as he put it, in the visitors' parking area. The area filled with more press, supporters and friends, diplomats and priests. Andre Landman arrived from Johannesburg, followed by Joan Cameron and Sheila Weinberg. Photographers and television crews were setting up tripods and checking sound bites. Rob Rushke, South African correspondent for the ABC in Australia, asked if I ever imagined this day would come. Then he made it hard for me and asked how I felt to be going back to Australia.

Across from where we had gathered stood a vast face-brick building. Prisoners having served their term or succeeded on appeal were moved to the block before their release. The windows of this fortress were covered with horizontal steel slats and from inside we could hear the voices of the ten men to be released. My friend, John Carlin, journalist from the *Independent*, who was standing in the road beneath the building, called me over and pointed to the top of the block. As I looked up, I could see clenched black fists pushed through the slats into the air outside. I was not sure if they could see us and I shouted, 'Upington 25'. In return came a call: '*Amandla*, Andy, our mother of the nation.' We laughed and some minutes later I heard engines starting up not too far away. A young sergeant in khaki uniform and canvas hat asked us to make way. The boom at the entrance to Pretoria Central lifted and two white minibuses drove out from the prison grounds.

The crowd started cheering and clapping and formed a circle around the vans as they drove into the parking area. The drivers got out and opened the doors and one by one, the ten stepped into the sun. They were dressed in grey-green pants and olive shirts with open necks, topped off with navy jackets. And on their feet, they wore their old faithfuls, blue-and-white soccer shoes, gifts from the South African Council of Churches. They carried cardboard boxes and books and paper bags, small belongings from time behind bars.

As the crowd moved in to hold them and take their hands, the men talked in quiet tones, almost shy, bewildered by this sudden transition to a world without boundaries or purpose. Andrew Lekhanyane leapt forward and lifted me into the air. His movement broke the reserve of the group and there was an explosion of chatter. In every corner, the accused were in conversation with the press. 'It's unbelievable.' Andrew Lekhanyane was talking to John Carlin. 'I didn't dream this would happen. That place death row is not suitable for a person. I was thinking every day I would be hanged.' Behind us, Myner Bovu uttered words of sad relief to Drew Forrest from the *Weekly Mail*. 'It was terrifying to hear the men being taken to be hanged. In the morning they would shout: "Stay well, boys, we are going." Now I am free.' He was calm in anger. 'Judge Basson was very, very unfair. But I am at peace with myself. I will not forget him, but I will forgive him. I just hope that in the new South Africa, there is no room for such judges. They are bad for the country's image.'

We drove the ten back into town, a joy-ride through the streets of Pretoria with Radio Highveld turned way up. At LHR, a press conference had been organised around tables filled with paper plates of doughnuts and jugs of coloured cooldrink. The accused spoke with quiet confidence and strong emotion. Telegrams and messages kept coming in from all over the world and Ian Farlam telephoned from Cape Town to ask after his clients. I told him how the thirteen had to be called away from a soccer game to be told the news of freedom. Ian was clearly moved but reverted to the dry and rational in his response. 'After all,' he spoke slowly, 'there is a kind of symmetry to the case: it started and ended on a soccer field.'

The afternoon sped by until it was time for Andre and Stefan to drive the men to Jan Smuts Airport in Johannesburg. Most of the accused had never travelled by aeroplane and as they approached the departure gate for their South African Airways flight to Kimberley, they began to fear the trip and were reluctant to board. After a brief period of paralysis and some negotiation, Andre was permitted to walk the men across the tarmac and onto the plane. They entered the plane clutching their meagre belongings, still dressed in prison uniform. As Andre consoled them and helped them find their rows and buckle their seatbelts, passengers stared and shifted in their seats. It was time for departure and Andre said goodbye to his longstanding clients and walked towards the front of the plane. A passenger reached his arm into the aisle to block Andre's path. 'What are *they* doing on our plane?' He was a passenger with rights of entitlement. *They*, according to his intonation, clearly were not. 'Don't worry about those men,' Andre raised his voice a little, 'they're just a bunch of murderers out from death row for the day.'

On our two-hour flight to Cape Town the next morning I had the first real opportunity to read the appeal court judgment in some detail. There was no doubt that Mr Justice Basson's reasoning had taken the doctrine of common purpose to an unwarranted extreme and the appeal court had corrected the imbalance. The appeal judges had viewed the accused as individuals, capable of individual intent. Before any of them could be found guilty of murder beyond a reasonable doubt, each had to demonstrate their own particular intention to kill. In direct contrast to the approach adopted by the Upington Supreme Court, the appeal court declared that a crowd could not have such an intention, only the individuals who comprised it. Justice Basson, wrote the appeal judges, was therefore wrong to rule that the whole group had the intention to kill. Nothing more had been proved against most of the accused other than that they had stoned the young constable's house. That they threw stones at him did not mean that they wanted or intended to kill Lucas Sethwala. It was a clear rejection of Basson's thinking and a vindication of our claim.

As I read the judgment and the press reports, I remembered the words of Dennis Davis in a letter he had sent me when the fourteen were sentenced to death: 'Thank God there is still an appellate division in this country which, if there is any legal sense left in South Africa, will put a stop to the agony suffered by your clients and their families.' The appeal court judgment, John Carlin wrote in the *Independent*, was 'at once an indictment and an endorsement of the South African judicial system'. It was significant that we could still boast an appeal court which, unlike many of the lower courts in the country, clearly distanced itself from a discredited political system. The black newspaper, the *Sowetan*, honed in on the fickle turns of South African justice: 'Many people will no doubt be shocked that one judge can sentence people to death while another, with the same evidence before him, can set them free on suspended sentences. Men of the law will be able to produce many arguments explaining this astonishing phenomenon.'

Perhaps one aspect of the trial that could not be dignified with explanation was the fact that many of the accused had spent a considerable time in jail before the appeal court dismissed or substantially reduced their sentences. Some had spent more than five years in prison during the trial and the case on extenuation when bail was refused, and then on death row in anticipation of the appeal. With the drawn-out reversal of fate, many of the accused had ended up serving time in jail that more than exceeded the sentences imposed by the appellate division. Under South African law, compensation for such forfeiture of life was not countenanced.

26

•

A reluctant departure

The following morning, close to noon, a convoy of heroes in prison garb drove along the main road into Paballelo. People lined the dry dust streets of the township, jostling and twisting, some dancing with their fists in the air. Women stood arm in arm, talking in excited tones, tilting forward as cars drove past to catch a glimpse of those inside. Among circles of dust at the far end of King Street, a crowd of young men *toyi-toyied* behind the minibus carrying the ten death-row prisoners and directed it to the home of Mrs Gerelina Gubula. As the van stopped, the procession waited for the first of the prisoners, Tros Gubula, to climb down onto home ground. They sang a few lines of a protest song, and as Tros emerged they called out '*Amandla*'. He turned to greet them, clasping their hands one by one. Tros Gubula, Accused No 2, pushed open a wire garden gate and tentatively stepped onto coloured blankets laid out in a path leading to the front door of his house. As he walked up the path, friends and family threw water from bowls, splashing his head and shoulders. At the front door of his small home stood his elderly mother, Gerelina, and sister, Francis, watching him approach, motionless except for their weeping.

'It has been the greatest day ever for Paballelo,' said Mr Alfred Gubula when I called him in the late afternoon. He described the homecoming of his nephew, Tros, and the water ceremony that greeted each man on arrival, a ritual symbolising cleansing and protection from the harm they had suffered. 'We followed the van from house to house as each man was brought home. They are still dancing outside.' Mr Gubula paused. 'You can hear them, I am sure. Tonight we will feast. There will be no time for sleep.'

I wished I could have been there to wallow in the joy. But my travels were almost over and I had little time left to prepare for my own return to Australia. I telephoned the de Bruin–Madlongolwane household next. Evelina had been released from Upington Prison the afternoon before. She had heard her name mentioned on the lunchtime news while listening to the prison radio. At first she was not sure what the report meant. Then, minutes later, Major Mans arrived at her cell and told her to pack. She was going home. At the entrance to Paballelo, people gathered to cheer as Evelina was driven into her township. There were more people waiting for her at her home. Close to midnight, in a state of deep weariness, Evelina climbed into her own bed, Tutu and Mbulelo curled up beside her. '*Deur die nag het die kinders my vasgehou. Hulle wil nie hê dat ek hulle verlaat. Vanmôre was ek nog in my nagrokkie wanneer die pers gekom het, wanneer Gideon huistoe kom.*' ('Through the night, the children held tightly onto me. They would not let me leave them. This morning I was still in my nightgown when the press arrived, when Gideon came home.')

It was hard to know how they must have felt, separated from the group, returned to a life that would have to be different, each to their own. Lloyd Vogelman, the psychologist who had given evidence during Evelina's bail application, spoke of this return to life. 'For those condemned prisoners who are reprieved—the living dead—it takes years to recover. With gratitude comes exhaustion, resentment and anger at having endured the experience.' For me, gratitude and exhaustion came as well and so did confusion and a sense of emptiness. We had done what we had to do and it was time for us all to move on. That, I reminded myself, was what endings were for. But I hated endings and although a great proponent of change when it came to the outside world, I was an ambivalent recipient of the new.

The evening before my flight to Sydney, the firm held a party to celebrate the appeal. The corridors and offices overflowed with all those who had been part of the Upington 25 history. A few days after my arrival in Cape Town, I had spent an afternoon with Anton's parents, Molly and Wilfried. Wilfried looked strained, the consequence of his daily work dedicated to uncovering the true details of Anton's death. Molly had begun to lose her sight from the strain, but despite their grief they were as warm as always and keen to talk at length about the appeal. I told them that Evelina had included them on the guest list for her release party and Molly said she would not miss it for the world. Molly and Wilfried came to our party and so did Sue van der Merwe, whose husband Tiaan, a progressive Afrikaner and member of parliament, our friend and a fighter for the twenty-five, had been killed in a car accident only a few weeks earlier.

It was a party reminiscent of many others I had attended over the years in different parts of South Africa. One which brought us together to celebrate great joy and mourn immeasurable loss. I looked around and saw the extraordinary mix of people with whom I had worked, whose friendship and care had carried me on a journey I had never imagined I might take, and I began my speech with words of thanks. 'Sometimes, the fullness of the past three years makes it difficult for me to express any one aspect or to talk of a particular individual with the distinction they deserve. But one coincidental meeting and one man will always merit mention. Anton Lubowski brought me to the case and to the lives of the Upington 25. I have learnt about the law, and through it, I have discovered the resilience of the human spirit. I have met the most remarkable people—many of you are here tonight—and I have shared times of great intensity. It has been a period of enduring discovery. Who knows what comes next?

•

About two months after my return to Sydney, I received a letter from Stefan. He had appeared before the Indemnity Committee to address the representations made in the indemnity application on behalf of the five remaining prisoners, Elisha Matshoba, Justice Bekebeke, Zonga Mokhatle, Xolile Yona and Enoch Nompondwana, all of whom had been held at Kimberley Prison to serve their post-appeal jail terms. The committee had granted an amnesty for four of the five. Elisha and Enoch were to be released in February the following year, serving only eight months of their eight-year sentences. Justice Bekebeke and Xolile Yona were to serve only ten months of their ten-year sentences. The amnesty did not affect Zonga as he was not a first offender. He did, however, receive a remission of four years off his twelve-year sentence, less any parole period which might apply.

•

A few years later, a cruel irony was played out in two countries still ill at ease with change. With the contrived failure of the Harms Commission of Inquiry into Anton's assassination and the withdrawal of criminal proceedings against his alleged assassin, the High Court of Namibia was finally asked, in April 1994, to conduct an inquest into Anton's death. There was evidence that eight men from the South African Defence Force Civil Cooperation Bureau (CCB) had targeted Anton for elimination. They tracked his moves and plotted his murder and the inquest judge was asked to find that these men had associated themselves in a common purpose to kill Anton Lubowski. The very doctrine we had fought to undermine in the appeal of the Upington 25 had found appropriate application in the case of Anton's murder.

And in June 1995, just over a year after the inauguration of President Nelson Mandela and almost four years to the day that the Upington 14 were released from death row, the new South African Constitutional Court declared capital punishment inconsistent with the Constitution and abolished the death penalty. I woke to the news in my Sydney apartment, a bland report on

ABC Radio. I felt at once angry and elated, then immensely lonely and removed, frozen in isolation from such an enormous twist of fate. I imagined everyone on the bus to work would be talking about it, that there would be calls of congratulation and heated debate at work. But I was away from the world that fixated on such things and had to be content with a small-scale celebration.

With the pursuit for Anton's killers almost put to rest and the death penalty abolished, my life in a new land was free to begin. I had reached a truce with my restless soul that had paced back and forth between the exhausted land of my birth and the gentler plains of Australia. I hoped that given time, I would not feel compelled to measure each country against the other, continually testing my allegiance. Rather, what I had in mind was to attempt an accommodation of both countries and let them nudge one another in some comfortable coexistence.

27

•

Full circle

A cycle held me captive for the first few years of my separation from South Africa. In my need to maintain links with my past and so avoid the shock of its retreat, I would recreate experience from memory, drawing familiarity from both people and place. In doing so, I tried to build my present upon my history but in a time and place removed from my foundations. And I became lodged in a relentless dialogue of comparisons between the physicality of the landscapes and the temperament of the people. I held in view the compact beauty of the tip of Africa and set it against the sprawling grandeur of Sydney. Within that frame I saw an intense impatient people grasping the inevitability of change and alongside, on another continent, the easy open nature of a people seemingly content with the surface of life.

To a large degree, my process of comparison masked a discomfort fuelled by shame. To be a white South African in South Africa meant that we drew the lines of life fairly early on. We aligned ourselves with one side or the other and our political choice informed our personal decisions. Our lifestyle and friendships were almost always clear manifestations of where we stood politically and we went out into that world with an overt display of conviction. But a white South African outside this peculiar reserve, was not always afforded the luxury of home-grown gradations. Once outside South Africa, we were seen as unequivocal carriers of and apologists for the ruling view. There were times when I would fabricate my origins simply to avoid explaining myself and my political partiality in some hopeless attempt to resist a judgement on sight. In retrospect, I think the cycle of comparison was a way of vindicating my homeland, which I loved despite its dark, dark side. And it came from a clumsy desire to demonstrate its worth and believe in its capacity to mend.

In contrast to the south of Africa, the Australia I first encountered seemed able to hide the legacy of its own history. To a large degree, its dominant culture mirrored that of my place of birth. But, over months, as I rummaged beneath the coverings, I detected a nation and its leadership determined to turn their backs on white insularity and pledge us to the acknowledgment of an indigenous past and the embrace of a multicultural future. It seemed to me that I had arrived in Australia at a time of great shifts in confidence, when the country had begun to come to terms with itself, to like itself enough to tear its future from obsolete ties. Paul Keating, my new Prime Minister, led with this boldness of spirit. The words of his Redfern speech in late December 1992, cut out and pasted in my diary of keepsakes, were responsible in part for the easing up of my contest of comparison between my two countries. They brought home a commonality of history and the corresponding will to turn the past inside out.

'It begins, I think,' Keating said, 'with the act of recognition. Recognition that it was we who did the dispossessing. We took the traditional lands and smashed the traditional way of life. We brought the diseases. The alcohol. We committed the murders. We took the children from their mothers. We practised discrimination and exclusion. It was our ignorance and our prejudice. And our failure to imagine these things being done to us. With some noble exceptions, we failed to make the most basic human response and enter into their hearts and minds. We failed to ask— how would I feel if this were done to me? As a consequence, we failed to see that what we were doing degraded all of us.'

A few years later that act of recognition began to surface simultaneously in my two lands. In 1995, the new South African government passed the Promotion of National Unity and Reconciliation Act and the Minister of Justice, Dullah Omar, declared the establishment of the Truth and Reconciliation Commission, necessary 'to enable South Africans to come to terms with their past'. In the same year, the then Australian Attorney-General, Michael Lavarch, announced the National Inquiry into the Separation of Aboriginal and Torres Strait Islander Children from their Families. As the inquiry heard evidence of the harm caused by removing indigenous children from their parents, the Governor-General, Sir William Deane, reminded Australians that asserting 'our identity as a nation' entailed recognition that 'national shame, as well as national pride, can and should exist in relation to past acts and omissions'. The Australian National Inquiry into the Stolen Generation commenced hearings at the end of 1995. A few months later, the first witness took the stand before the South African Truth and Reconciliation Commission. Almost simultaneously, both countries, both of my countries, were embarking on the difficult process of looking back. To recreate the past, to shake off its rigidity, to uproot fear and look into pain. And so it was for me. A journey of looking back before feeling a comfort with stepping forward. Reduced to scale, those were the lessons I had in store.

•

'My friend, my husband, Gideon Madlongolwane, is not here next to me. He died last month. He was buried last week. He is dead today for the way he was treated in jail. But I knew inside that I should come here and tell the truth. The truth that there is a Judge Basson who will never see the heavens. They are shut, totally closed to him.' It was Wednesday, 2nd October 1996, five years after Evelina de Bruin had been released from death row. It was Day One of the South African Truth and Reconciliation Commission's Event Hearing in Upington that was to focus primarily on the Upington case. Evelina de Bruin was giving evidence. 'Since I was born, I have never seen the doors of prison. I was in the court and heard Basson saying he would sentence us. I did not understand what he was talking about. I saw people crying. People were throwing themselves onto the floor, people were fainting. In Pretoria, when I got there at sunset, I heard the truth of my sentence. I was taken to the women's prison and given a glass of water. I refused. I was not thirsty for water but I was thirsty for the truth.

'The evidence that was given in court was deceptive but our new President, talking about the Bible, says we must forgive each other. He says that we must throw these previous burdens into the Red Sea. I hold no grudge but I have pain. In Pretoria, they brought a rope, about a metre long, and put it around my neck. I think they wanted to know whether this rope was going to fit. They measured my neck and they recorded. I want to declare that both my husband and I were sentenced to death whilst innocent. Do they, do they think that we are mad? Do they think that we are going to kill somebody else's son? That is all I have to say.'

Evelina de Bruin's words were broadcast to millions of South Africans that night. On national television news, on local and national radio and in newspapers, she spoke so that her nation might hear. With thousands of others, her experience was brought into the centre of national life as the country was drawn together by exposure to the facts and memories of events, many previously unknown, which had been crammed into the years of apartheid rule. And across the Indian Ocean, that same courage and strength were being demonstrated as members of the Stolen Generation bore witness to their experiences of forcible removal before the National Inquiry into the Separation of Aboriginal and Torres Strait Islander Children from their Families. In April 1997, the National Inquiry, conducted by the Human Rights and Equal Opportunity Commission, submitted its report, *Bringing Them Home*, to the new federal Attorney-General. The Liberal–National Party Coalition government, in power for just under a year, chose silence as its initial response to the report. As the country waited for its leadership to take the report forward and show respect for its aims and findings, the careless quiet from the federal government gave rise to fears that the report would be ignored or dismissed. It was as if the openness and conviction that had heralded the commencement of the Separation Inquiry under the hand of the previous Labor government were replaced with a closed, defensive demeanour and a pitiable absence of grace.

In anticipation of the tabling of the report in parliament and its complex breadth of content and recommendations, the Human Rights and Equal Opportunity Commission held various briefings in major cities around the country. For the past five years, I had been working at the Public Interest Advocacy Centre, a community legal centre in Sydney. We had undertaken a project on behalf of members of the Stolen Generation and we were invited to one of the briefings in early May. The annexe at Saint Andrews Cathedral in central Sydney filled with a sadness as one of the speakers, a stolen child, pleaded with the federal government to listen to experience. 'You can heal that pain if you try to comprehend and acknowledge its depth. Let us talk and feel you understand us or want to understand us. Do not talk about this experience as being of the past. It is with us now and will be with us for the rest of our lives.'

As the speaker bent her tired body back into a chair, a young Aboriginal woman sitting behind me rose. 'As you spoke,' she stared straight ahead, 'a fear crept into my bones. I am frightened for myself and for my country. This feeling of being ignored and dismissed is overwhelming. It is as if I am drowning.' She turned her head towards the door. 'How do we make them take notice? I am beginning to think that we do so by looking outside. That is what is so sad.' She paused and then, with a sudden change of speed, she spoke each word with haste and emphasis. 'We need to look at what is happening in South Africa. Ask them to guide us as they revise their past. To rescue us from this silence.'

'Look what is happening in South Africa.' I felt a pull between my ribs. The tightness of a familiar tug of guilt and an instinctive desire to hang my head. For years, I had heard and read the words, 'Look what is happening in South Africa.' A pointing out, an undesirable example to the world of how it ought never to be.

I loathed how the words made me feel. A despair, an angry humiliation and a longing to disown my country and its many parts. But as I sat with the words now uttered by this woman, I let go of my breath and pride began to heat the inside of my skin. What I was hearing was South Africa being held up as some beacon of hope and respectability and a great relief fell upon me.

This feeling of sweet relief was quickly replaced as Aboriginal people talked to us of their twofold dispossession, of cultures lost and land taken. Of how, in the words of Aboriginal and Torres Strait Islander Social Justice Commissioner, Mick Dodson, himself a stolen child, they had had their Aboriginality 'belted out of them'. Some years ago, in the lead-up to the drafting of the new South African Constitution and laws that created rights and democratic institutions, I had proudly dispatched copies of Australian legislation on race discrimination and land rights and models of government structures to colleagues in South Africa involved in shaping the future conditions for their nation. I was thrilled that my new country could boast such fine samples of the fabric of a society that was evidently evolving with clear reference to tolerance and compassion. And the South Africans were surprised and envious and asked for more. But at that moment in the cathedral annexe, perhaps more explicitly than I had cared to see in the months that had gone before, it was as if all that had been nurtured and built over the years and then consolidated and carefully extended during my short residence, all the treasure that I had sent across the world in the hope that it might be replicated in some form to good effect, was being discarded and pulled to the ground. The great gains from daring to grow were being wound back. It was with great disappointment that I would have to concede that the country of my new life was letting me down.

•

Later in the month, the city of Melbourne was to host the Australian Reconciliation Convention to mark the 30th anniversary of the 1967 constitutional referendum. The referendum gave the federal government the power to make laws for indigenous people and provided for their inclusion in the census; first important steps towards a recognised citizenship in their own country. Alex Boraine, the Deputy Chairperson of the South African Truth and Reconciliation Commission had been invited to speak. I had known Alex and his family in Cape Town and I was thrilled to have been invited to have dinner with him in Sydney a few days before he left for the Convention in Melbourne. We sat at a restaurant overlooking sparkling city lights reflected in the harbour, beneath the majesty of the Sydney Opera House. 'The real backdrop to your visit,' Mick Dodson, outgoing Aboriginal and Torres Strait Islander Social Justice Commissioner, reminded Alex, 'is sadly one of a nation in retreat.' He spoke of wholesale cuts to government funding of the Human Rights Commission, of a deep racism edging forward with minimal prime ministerial check, of government condemnation of the Stolen Generation Report before its tabling in parliament, of a federal plan to undermine hard-won indigenous land rights. Mick reached across the table and told Alex that South Africa had to get it right. 'The whole world is looking to South Africa. We want it to work. Make sure it does because we want to be able to point to you and say, "You see, it did work and it can" and we want to celebrate that achievement.'

The shift away from the rights and values that had informed Australia's progress had been swift and Alex was keen to warn us of the consequences. 'South Africa owes Australia and the rest of the world an enormous debt—the people who stood in protest outside South African embassies, the sanction promoters, the churches and trade unions, the letters to the President. So when we get asked to speak, we must speak out as you did for us.'

That opportunity came soon after Prime Minister John Howard opened the Australian Reconciliation Convention six days later and turned his back on his role as statesman. 'Personally,' he was speaking from his distant heart, 'I feel deep sorrow for those of my fellow Australians who suffered injustices under the practices of past generations towards indigenous people.' He watered-down his sorrow. 'Australians of this generation should not be required to accept guilt and blame for past actions and policies over which they had no control. The public don't believe in intergenerational guilt but they do believe that this country has a proud history.'

In his keynote address to the convention, Alex Boraine spoke words of great deliberation, clearly informed by experience. 'It is wrong to simply say, "Turn the page". It is right to turn the page but first you have to read it, understand it and acknowledge it. Then you can turn the page.' He departed from his written speech and spoke to our Prime Minister. 'There has to be a time of repentance, not of parading national shame, but of establishing a coming together to corporately acknowledge the failures and sins of the past. I find it breathtaking that a government can refuse to acknowledge the damage that was done, the damage that continues.'

Alex's visit was unsettling. Not only for the warmth of the memories he brought but for the reminders about the nonchalant passage of time, and the inevitable cycle of change. His visit and all that it entailed threw up old conflicts between the here and the there, an ambivalent attachment to my past and present.

The day Alex flew back to South Africa, the biggest magnolia tree in the world, which stood below my apartment, tore in half. It had been raining for three days. The rain had fallen hard and the grass at Rushcutters Bay park reflected the sky. The magnolia tree was steeped in history, steeped in the soil of Rushcutters Bay, solid and present. On warm summer nights the perfume from its gigantic white flowers, tiny Sydney Opera Houses turned upside down, would creep in through my windows. When autumn came and her leaves began to fall, I could see the bay between her branches. But with the rain, my magnolia tree stood with drenched arms stretched against a steady slab of grey. Close to midnight, still writing at my desk, still raining, I heard the sound of tearing. A dragging, grumbling bellow and then the ground shook as a weight fell to earth. The magnolia tree had torn apart. In the morning, one half stood in waiting, dripping tears of after-rain. The other half lay at rest, flat to the ground. The tree doctor wrapped her grieving trunk with cloth. With tendering, he said, she could live for many years. Her half, her past, had let go to make room for the new. Days later workers came with electric saws to cut dead wood and stack it on a truck for removal.

That spring, I saw the first white magnolia flower open on the tree. That spring, in late September, my father, Max Allenby Durbach, died. Solid and present, he left us to grow where he had made tracks. Four years earlier, Max and my mother, Renee, had come to live in Australia. He had embraced this land with no hesitation and he loved its spirit of opportunity. I think the loss of my father in our immigrant land forever changed my relationship to Australia. Some months after he died, we planted a tree in Chiswick Gardens where Max had sat in the sun and talked each week to Terry Darcy, the resident gardener, about plans for planting. Terry had prepared the ground and we gathered in the gardens at 9am on a Monday in early January 1998 to plant a young *Alloxylon flammeum*, a tree waratah from Queensland. It was Max's tree with the promise of blazing red-orange flowers for years to come. As Terry kneaded the soil, I fixed my feet in Australian earth and said a prayer for life never forgotten and for life still unknown.

Glossary

actus reus: (in the criminal law) conduct prohibited by common or statute law; in the case of murder, the *actus reus* is the unlawful act of killing another human being

afropik: a hair comb

Amandla: power (usually followed by *ngawethu*, 'power to the people'); a populist slogan

bakkie: small light truck or van with open back

baaskap: white domination over black people

bantustan: an area set aside by the National Party government for the occupation of black people with limited self-government

berg wind: a hot dry wind that blows down from the mountains to the coast

The Black Sash: an organisation of predominantly English-speaking middle-class white South African women known for wearing black sashes at silent public protests against apartheid laws

boere: farmers; slang word for Afrikaners or police, often used disparagingly

casspir: a large police truck that could carry many armed policemen hidden from view; casspirs became associated with police action during times of unrest, particularly in black townships

common purpose doctrine: a legal doctrine that apportions equal liability to individuals participating in a criminal act, irrespective of whether they all contribute equally to its execution

263

cooldrink: a soft drink

dagga: cannabis or marijuana

deindividuation: a psychological theory utilised to explain individual criminal behaviour in a crowd situation

doek: headscarf

dominee: religious minister (usually to denote Dutch Reformed Church minister)

dorp: small South African village or town

dolus directus: describes intention (see *mens rea*), namely that the accused intended to perform an unlawful act and in so doing, achieved a criminal consequence

extenuating circumstances: (in the criminal law) factors taken into account by a court of law, which, on a balance of probabilities, serve to reduce the moral blameworthiness (as opposed to the legal guilt) of an accused, for example, youth, emotional factors, exposure to external forces

in camera: refers to legal proceedings from which members of the public are excluded

Inkatha: Zulu national and cultural movement led by Chief Mangosuthu Gatsha Buthelezi who also leads the Inkatha Freedom Party

inwoner: inhabitant or resident; often used to illustrate someone having a strong association with an area or a community

kaffir: derogatory term for black South African

kantore: offices

klipgooi: stone-throwing; usually descriptive of the action of black schoolchildren and students against armed police

laager: a camp often defended by a circular formation of wagons; the inner circle

laat'lammetjie: afterthought, late arrival (child), youngest child

landdroshof: magistrate's court

Madiba: Nelson Mandela's clan name, dating from the eighteenth century; used as a term of respect and affection by South Africans when referring to Nelson Mandela

melktert: milk tart; traditional Afrikaans dessert or tart

meneer: sir, mister

mens rea: (in the criminal law) an unlawful mental condition or state of mind; in the case of murder, the *mens rea* is the intention to kill. In general, every crime involves an unlawful physical act (*actus reus*) and an unlawful intention (*mens rea*) exercised contemporaneously

mevrou: madam, mistress

mielie: corn

mitigating circumstances: (in the criminal law) factors taken into account by a court of law which serve to diminish the possible sentence or penalty arising from a criminal conviction

necklacing: a brutal ritual where a rubber tyre (necklace) is placed around a person's neck and set alight; often used on political informers

pro deo counsel: legal advocates appointed and paid by the state to represent accused unable to afford their own legal representation; generally appointed only in cases of a serious nature, for example, murder

rand: the South African monetary unit; R1-00 is equal to 100 cents; a rand buys a half loaf of bread; a cup of coffee costs R4-50; a paperback book costs R70-00 to R100-00

Resolution 435: A 1978 resolution by the UN General Assembly calling for the withdrawal of South African forces from Namibia and the holding of UN-supervised elections

rondavel: a round hut, traditionally made of mud with a mud floor and thatched roof

rooibos: redbush; a South African grown tea

sersant: sergeant

sjambok: a short baton with leather straps attached to one end generally used by police during riots or to break-up gatherings or meetings

stoep: a verandah or patio

stompie: cigarette butt

stop: a pipe-fill, usually to describe an amount of *dagga*

TATZ: a psychological technique or test developed to evaluate the conscious awareness of an act; how an individual perceives and interprets the test material suggests aspects of his psychological functioning

toyi-toyi: the soldiers' dance of the military wing of the African National Congress, *Umkonto we Siswe* (Spear of the Nation); performed in mass demonstrations

tsotsi: township hoodlum, gangster

zol: hand-rolled cigarette usually filled with a mix of tobacco and *dagga*

Abbreviations

AAM   Anti-Apartheid Movement
ANC   African National Congress
AWB   *Afrikaner Weerstandsbeweging* (Afrikaner Resistance Movement)
CCB   Civil Cooperation Bureau
CNA   Central News Agency
HSRC   Human Sciences Research Council
ICJ   International Commission of Jurists
IDAF   International Defence and Aid Fund
LHR   Lawyers for Human Rights
NICRO   National Institute for the Rehabilitation of Offenders
NYA   National Youth Action
PAC   Pan-Africanist Congress
SACHED   South African Council for Higher Education
SATIS   South Africa The Imprisoned Society
SWAPO   South West African People's Organisation (Namibian liberation party)
TUC   Trade Union Congress
UNTAG   United Nations Transition Assistance Group
USAID   United States Aid for International Development
UYO   Upington Youth Organisation